The Wood Carvers of Córdova, New Mexico

D1332324

The Wood Carvers
of Córdova, New Mexico

Social Dimensions of an Artistic "Revival"

Charles L. Briggs

The University of New Mexico Press : Albuquerque

Copyright © 1980 by The University of Tennessee Press / Knoxville
All rights reserved.
1989 paperbound edition published by the University
of New Mexico Press by arrangement with the author.

Library of Congress Cataloging-in-Publication Data

Briggs, Charles L., 1953–
    The wood carvers of Córdova, New Mexico.

    Reprint. Originally published: Knoxville :
University of Tennessee Press, c1980.
    Bibliography: p.
    Includes index.
    1. Hispanic American wood-carving—New Mexico—
Córdova.   2. Hispanic American wood-carvers—New Mexico—
Córdova.   3. Santos (Art)—New Mexico—Córdova.
4. Art and society—New Mexico—Córdova.   I.   Title.
[NK9712.B73   1989]   730'.8968078952   88-27637
ISBN 0-8263-1125-3

To E. Boyd
　　who inspired this work,
to Helen Edith Diodati
　and Felicia Anne Diodati-Briggs
　　who shared the experiences that informed it,
and to the people of Córdova, New Mexico
　　who imbued it with meaning

Contents

Illustrations

Tables

Preface

Córdova, New Mexico boasts a thriving small-scale industry involved in the production of images of the saints and other figures from native woods. The community is situated in the foothills of the Sangre de Cristo range and lies approximately thirty-five miles north-northeast of Santa Fe, New Mexico. The carvers identify themselves as being of Hispano or Hispano-American descent. The Hispanos, as they will be termed throughout, are the descendants of primarily Spanish and Mexican citizens who settled in what is now New Mexico during the seventeenth, eighteenth, and nineteenth centuries. The ancestry of most contemporary residents includes a significant Native American element, but the Hispanos recognize themselves as culturally Hispanic.

The production of images of Catholic saints in Córdova stretches back at least to the previous century. Although this book briefly describes the "traditional period" of the carving art, it focuses on descendants of the earlier carvers who continue to fashion images in the twentieth century. Specifically, the innovator of the modern style of image carving, José Dolores López (1868–1937), and his son George receive the greatest attention. José Dolores was a carpenter and furniture-maker—common pursuits for members of his family. His repertoire was fairly standard until 1917. At that time he began embellishing his figures with elaborate designs carved into the surface.

The Santa Fe colony of artists and writers was gaining momentum at this time, and several of these individuals began making regular trips to Córdova in the 1920s. They enjoyed the atmosphere of this mountain community, and above all they enjoyed observing the public rituals of a local Catholic lay confraternity (the Brotherhood of Our Father Jesus the Nazarene). They soon "discovered" José Dolores López. These persons had initiated a "revival" of Hispanic arts and crafts in Santa Fe, and they persuaded López to present his wares for sale during the annual competition. Being gifted with a creative as well as an entrepreneurial spirit, López soon learned what types and styles of carvings would appeal to his predominantly Anglo-American clientele. José Dolores López thus generated a community enterprise that continues to provide income for many Córdovan families. His impetus also resulted in modifications in the appearance of Hispano images as well as the manner in which they are woven into the fabric of the society.

The rich historical and social context that surrounds this art prompts a broad approach to its description. The carvers, like other Hispanos, are proud of their heritage. Both ethnohistorical and ethnographic materials are therefore used in characterizing the images and their carvers. The bulk of my study deals with the manner in which the carvers relate socially, artistically, materially, and philosophically to their work. One of the primary goals of this account is to advance our understanding of the nature and significance of changes that have transpired in the production and utilization of images.

The proposed contribution of this book is twofold: First, it is intended to fill a substantial gap in the literature on the image-making art in New Mexico. Many accounts of the traditional art have appeared. With a few notable exceptions, however, these have attempted to discern stylistic, technical, and iconographic attributes of the images and the identity of the artists. Little substantive material has appeared on the relationship between the image producer and his audience. Similarly, many short and often superficial articles have emerged on the contemporary image makers. Intensive studies of particular artists and the meaning of contemporary images in cultural and historical perspective have, however, been lacking.

Second, studies of crafts in general have until recently tended to isolate the item and/or its producer from the cultural processes and specific contexts of production. Accordingly, the present work tackles the production and interpretation of wood carvings in a broader sociocultural context. This approach necessitates an expansion of the inquiry's scope to include not only a description of the craftsman and his or her workmanship but also information on the social situation of the person's community and ethnic group, the concerns of his or her patrons, and precedents for and subsequent developments from artistic innovations.

An expansion of the inquiry of course entails the examination of a broader range of source materials. Most of the data gathered in the course of the study were obtained during several periods of fieldwork in Córdova, which totaled about fifteen months from 1972 to 1977 and included both observation and intensive interviewing. Much time was spent with George and Silvianita López; nevertheless, the other carvers and many of their neighbors who were not carvers were interviewed as well. Some of this material was tape-recorded and transcribed, and the extensive quotations in the text were taken from the transcriptions. The fieldwork also involved a number of events that took place outside of Córdova, especially those connected with the marketing of wood carvings. An attempt was made to obtain information on the carvers' patrons partly through distribution by the artists of a questionnaire to the customers. The field materials were supplemented by research in specialized libraries and archives as well as by the examination of major collections of Córdovan wood carvings. It should be borne in mind that the following description of the industry is intended to reflect the changes observed up to and during the final period of fieldwork (1977). The responsiveness of the art to changing social conditions promises, however, to present those who visit the carvers, even in the near future, with many visible changes.

My motivation for undertaking the project was twofold. First, I had known George and Silvianita for many years and respected them highly. I was curious as to the manner in which their carving had forged such a lasting relationship with the world beyond Córdova. Second, my academic interest in the art of image carving had been frustrated by the dearth of available information about the relations of traditional and contemporary carvers to their society and to their art. My interest in the relationship between dominated groups and superordinate societies, along with my knowledge of Spanish, began with my upbringing in a multilingual/multicultural community in New Mexico. My approach to such problems was focused by academic training in anthropology. Research on this topic thus entailed the cultivation of a greater awareness of my own relationship to Hispano society as well as to my own (Anglo-American) background.

Part I is concerned largely with the development of the contemporary image-carving industry in Córdova and its historical context. Chapter I provides a general introduction to the production and veneration of images in traditional Hispano culture. Chapter 2 follows the work of one of the major artists of this period in Córdova and describes the emergence of José Dolores López from this tradition. Chapter 3 characterizes the influence of both carvers and patrons in the departure of the contemporary art from traditional precedents, and Chapter 4 traces the development of Córdovan carving from the death of López in 1937 to the present day.

Part II focuses on two major aspects of the contemporary carving industry: marketing and production. Chapter 5 details the differing conceptions of the economics of image production among the Hispano artists and their (predominantly) Anglo-American patrons. The importance of Hispano views of wood-carving technology is stressed in Chapter 6.

An attempt is made to synthesize the historical and ethnographic data on the meaning or symbolism of the images in Part III. Chapter 7 describes the dilemma of the contemporary carvers who sell to outsiders—and in many cases to nonbelievers—a type of object that holds great religious importance to their own society. The problems they encounter in justifying their enterprise to fellow Hispanos are analyzed in terms of the roles of the saints and their images as mediators in Hispano culture and society. Chapter 8 continues this discussion with an analysis of the manner in which images have become symbols of Hispano ethnicity in the last two decades. This movement is treated with regard to its effect on the art, its potential for overcoming carvers' ethical dilemma, and its implications for the future of Hispano image carving.

Verbal documentation has been supplemented by extensive photographic illustration. In addition to their role as documentary evidence, the photographs are intended to allow the reader to reach his or her own conclusions with regard to the art. (All photographs are by the author unless otherwise noted in the caption.)

In acknowledging the assistance I received in the course of this study, my first responsibility is to the residents of Córdova, New Mexico. This is really their book, and I can only hope that the accuracy of my description prompts them to concur in this assessment. George and Silvianita López deserve much appreciation. Besides sharing their time and daily fare with me, they patiently taught me the irrelevance of my initial questions and the limitations of my perceptions. Their niece and her family, the Ortizes, also extended friendship and trust. Other carvers who deserve special recognition are Ricardo López, his late wife, Benita, and their daugher Nora, as well as Eurgencio and Orlinda López and Herminio and Gloria Córdova. The late Federico Córdova included me in the long list of his students and shared with me the joy of discovery. Many other residents also took pride in teaching me what it means to be a Córdovan. I hope that the carvers' and their neighbors' investment in my work bears fruit both financially and in terms of increased sensitivity to their understanding of the image-carving art.

Two former residents of the community deserve mention. Lorin W. Brown claimed me as a colleague and allowed me to use the valuable contributions he made to the New Mexico Federal Writers' Project in the 1930s and to interview him in connection with his experience in Córdova. Eluid L. Martínez, a grandson of José Dolores López, generously assisted the project both materially and intellectually.

The encouragement of several individuals was crucial in the development of this work. E. Boyd, the late curator emeritus of Spanish colonial art in the Museum of International Folk Art, shared unstintingly of her knowledge of the image makers. She elucidated a number of the most fundamental problems in the field and helped me avoid some serious pitfalls; above all else, however, her faith in my ability to carry out the project convinced even me. Paul Kutsche provided perennial criticism and encouragement; his faith in the work of a young scholar will not be forgotten. Marianne Stoller assisted me in analyzing my materials with greater sophistication. Marta Weigle's friendship and willingness to exchange ideas and information were most helpful. Gilbert Benito and Juanita Córdova helped me through the *rite de passage* of initial fieldwork. Yvonne Lange placed many of the resources of the Museum of International Folk Art at my disposal, and she generously brought her knowledge of Christian iconography to bear on a number of challenging problems. William and Nancy Briggs, J. Donald Robb, and Edward H. Spicer extended support and encouragement. My photographic mentor John Kolar also deserves acknowledgment.

The following persons provided valuable criticism of earlier drafts of this work and of related papers: E. Boyd, Stephen Cox, Helen Diodati, Bernard Fontana, Douglas Freed, James Griffith, Jean Hess, Myra Ellen Jenkins, Paul Kutsche, Yvonne Lange, Christine Mather, Thomas Merlan, Nancy Munn, Marshall Sahlins, David Schneider, Heinrich Schultz, Andrew Smith, Marianne Stoller, Pauline Strong, Frances Swadesh, John and Chris Van Ness, Marta Weigle, and William Wroth. A number of institutions and their staffs generously provided assistance. I was aided in my examination of the various collections housed in the Museum of International Folk Art by E. Boyd, Charlene Cerny, Yvonne Lange, Christine Mather, Fred Vigil, and the museum's librarian, Judith Sellars. Kendra Bowers, Lisa Jucius, Martha Tilley, and William Wroth of the Taylor Museum of the Colorado Springs Fine Arts Center made my research there pleasant, while my work has benefited from conversations with William Wroth. Stephanie Eiger of the history library of the Museum of New Mexico assisted me in tracking down relevant papers from the files of the New Mexico Federal Writers' Project, and Arthur Olivas provided valuable prints from the museum's photographic archive. Richard Ahlborn of the National Museum of History and Technology, Smithsonian Institution was most helpful. Myra Ellen Jenkins, James Purdy, and J. Richard Salazar of the State Records Center and Archives provided assistance beyond the call of duty as well as guidance on archival matters. The following persons also assisted me in my research: William and Nancy Briggs, Rev. José Cubbels, S.F. of the Holy Cross Parish, Santa Cruz, New Mexico, Rev. Casimiro Roca, S. F., Rev. José María Blanch, S.F., and Josie Lujan of the Holy Family Parish, Chimayó, New Mexico, Ernie Knee, Benjamín López, Ernesto Roberto and Alicia Martínez, David Ortega, Leonora and George Paloheimo, John Donald and Harriet Robb, Ernestina Romero, Anita Thomas, and Sally Wagner.

Two sources of financial support freed me to devote myself to the project. My research in 1972–1973 was supported by Grant # 73/70.16 of the International Folk Art Foundation; their backing of the early stages of my work was crucial. Fellowship 1 F31 MH05928-02 of the National Institute of Mental Health (H.E.W.) allowed me to devote more time to writing up the materials.

Sondra Jones painstakingly typed the manuscript. Carol Hendrickson kindly redrew Figure 1 and the maps. The book benefited greatly from the staff of the University of Tennessee Press; the thorough editing of Marcia Brubeck is especially appreciated. Naturally, I alone am responsible for any shortcomings.

Charles L. Briggs

November 15, 1978
Chicago, Illinois

Part I

Beginnings

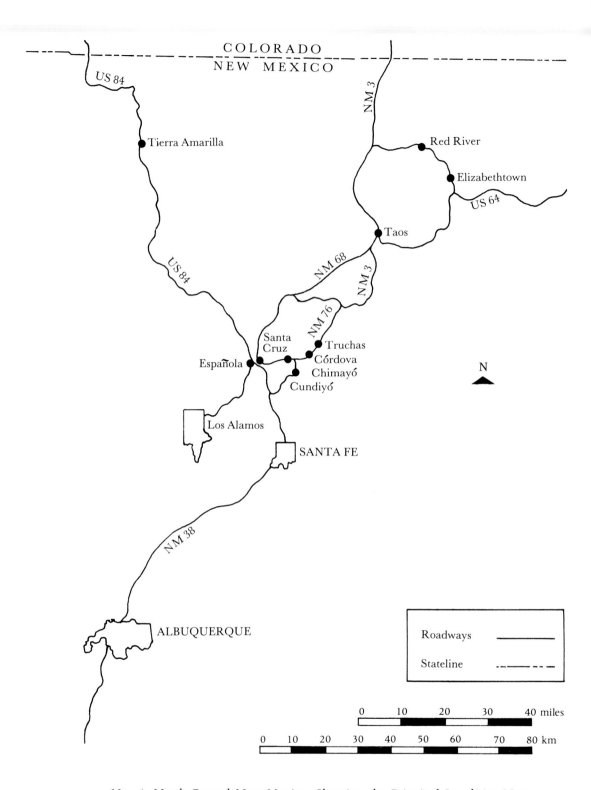

Map 1. North-Central New Mexico, Showing the Principal Localities Mentioned in the Text.

2   *Beginnings*

1.

Introduction: The Art of the Image Maker in New Mexico

New Mexico's Route 76 winds its way from the Río Grande Valley toward Taos, and it provides thousands of tourists each year with an ephemeral view of Hispano village culture. The community of Córdova (see Plate 1) is separated from the main road by a short spur, which *Plate 1* plunges into the Quemado Valley about four miles east-northeast of Chimayó. Even before one reaches the turnoff, however, a lone hand-painted sign marks Córdova as a center of the regional wood-carving industry.

Upon arrival in the valley, the visitor is greeted by further advertisements, each seeking to define the stranger's presence in terms of an economic interaction between carver and patron. The success of this mode of intercourse attests to the ability of the wood-carving enterprise to bridge the values and beliefs of culturally distinct individuals. The factors that have contributed to such an arrangement are many, and the beauty of their symmetry is enhanced by the sharp contrasts between the motivations carried into the workshop by each group.

The elucidation of the precedents to and products of the contemporary wood-carving trade will serve as a centripetal force throughout this book. Córdova provides the stage for exploring the processes involved in the evolution of the local wood-carving industry, while the actors are recruited from two distinct sides. On one side are found the nineteenth-century saint carvers of the community, along with their contemporary successors. Playing opposite this group are a number of artists and writers, including such figures as Frank Applegate and Mary Austin. Their role has been assumed during the last thirty years by a multiplicity of tourists and other visitors who continue to follow their predecessors' footsteps into Córdova. Images of the saints and other carved figures constitute the props, and they are visually represented in these pages. The script is largely provided by the set of symbols and meanings that each group has brought to the scene, but serendipity plays a major role in its dénouement.

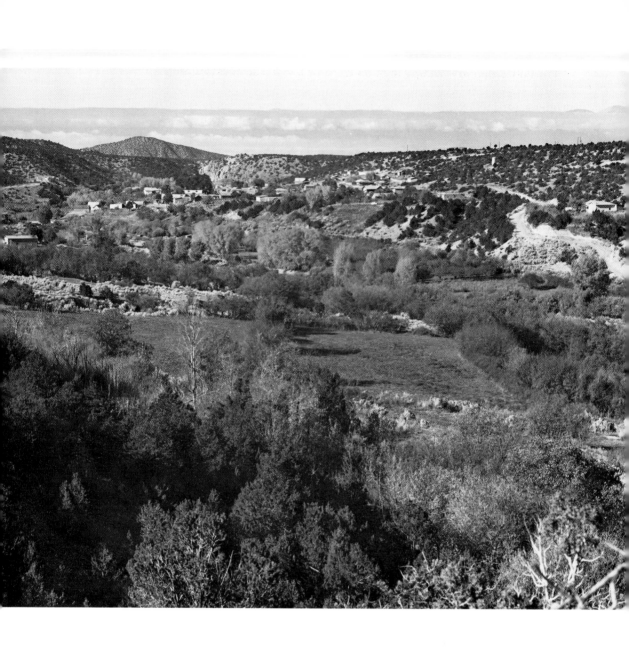

Plate 1. Córdova, New Mexico: A View of the Community from the South. The main plaza appears in the center, while the Lópezes' former house is on the right.

4   *Beginnings*

The contemporary leading man on the Córdovan side of this drama is George López. Mr. López is well known in his community, any native resident can tell you where he lives, and his contemporaries (he is seventy-eight) know early everything about him. The unusual thing about López is, however, that his reputation extends far beyond the confines of northern New Mexico and the cognizance of his own ethnic group. Quite simply, he is famous. George López's fame is based on publicity and long-standing relationships with visitors to his carving workshop. This situation, as any Córdovan will tell you, is symptomatic of increasing contact between Hispano villagers and the society beyond, which is dominated by Anglo-Americans.

As I mentioned above, this interaction has not been inconsequential for the community at large. There are at present about thirty-five full- and part-time wood carvers in Córdova, and there are five shops where carvings are sold. Beyond the immediate economic ramifications, the social effects of the industry have been many. Through the visits of strangers, Córdova has evolved a special relationship with the outside world. Just as visitors often define Córdova in terms of the wood carvings it produces, Córdovans have at times utilized contacts formed in this manner to obtain information about and access to the superordinate institutions that greatly influence their lives.

Still, George López is not responsible for initiating the present state of affairs. His father, José Dolores, was a creative genius. Steeped in the traditional Hispano cultural system, including its image-making vocation, he evolved a highly individual interpretation of the religious representations of his own society. The peculiarity of his vision was also shaped by the friendship and advice of a number of Santa Fe artists and writers. Being intimately acquainted with the aesthetic preferences of Anglo-American culture, they were in a particularly advantageous position to mesh José Dolores' artistic inclinations with the tastes of the nearby market. The annual reenactment of the passion of Christ by the local confraternity of Our Father Jesus the Nazarene provided a convenient opportunity for the initial meeting of these two groups of actors, thus setting the stage for the encouragement of a nascent handicraft industry.

Beyond a burning interest in the public rituals of the confraternity, the region's Anglo-American intelligentsia was fascinated with viewing and above all possessing the traditional polychromed images of the saints. Borrowing a bit of an alien tongue, they generally referred to these as *santos*. To their collectors, these objects held a fascination that did not emanate solely from their status as "primitives" or "antiques" but appears to have been enhanced by the animism that was supposedly associated with their veneration. Although José Dolores López's unpainted sculptures did not closely resemble the polychromed traditional images, the contiguity of the two artistic traditions certainly contributed to their popularity among Anglo-Americans.

It is becoming clear that both cultural groups frequently acted on the basis of dissimilar motives. In the case of the Anglo-American art lovers who "discovered" José Dolores, his works provided a means of obtaining images that drew upon the earlier tradition but was less constrained by its artistic conventions. The individuality of López's pieces drew them much closer to the canons of modern Western art than were the primarily anonymous works of his ancestors. For the Hispanos, however, the memory of the traditional image makers provided a basis for supplying new patrons and for satisfying a growing need for cash income. Indeed, such carvers as George López tell their customers that their work is in "the line of the old *santeros* (image makers)."

The fascination for both groups exerted by polychromed wooden images of the saints renders the images of central importance to the present study. For this reason, it might be wise to preface later discussion of specific carvers with a more general discussion of this religious art form and its artisans.

With regard to definitions, the use of the terms *santos* and *santeros* has become clouded by a troublesome ambiguity. Spanish usage in general reserves *santo* for holy personages (including the saints as well as the various advocations of Christ and the Virgin) and for blessed objects that represent or are otherwise associated with them. The term *santero* refers to a wide range of persons who care for a church or chapel and its furnishings or who make, repair, or repaint images. On the other hand, *santo* has become an "arty byword"[1] in the Southwest for polychromed folk images, especially for those produced in New Mexico. The use of the term *santero* seems to have become similarly restricted to just those persons who produce these images. In order to avoid the introduction of unnecessarily ambiguous and preconceived notions, I eschew the terms *santo* and *santero* in favor of the less fashionable "image" and "image carver."

As I have said, the term *santos* brings to the minds of most Southwesterners the brightly painted religious statues made in New Mexico in the eighteenth and nineteenth centuries. Nevertheless, images are used by Catholics throughout the world, and their popular production is quite widespread. Immigrants to Spain's colonies and Christianized natives, for example, frequently lacked an adequate supply of religious goods due to the difficulties involved in importation. Local industries arose in response to these needs, and although they have generally been displaced in these areas by the importation of mass-produced chromolithographs and lithographs during the last hundred years, such countries as Mexico still harbor folk image makers (cf. Giffords 1974; 1977).

The Philippines and Puerto Rico provide cases parallel to that of New Mexico. The native inhabitants of each of these areas were conquered by the Spanish, and the regions later fell into American hands. Images for both church and home were produced by Filipinos from the seventeenth through the nineteenth centuries. The artists, who remain primarily anonymous, worked in several types of wood and in ivory. Although the more formal Spanish and Philippine images served as prototypes, "vaguely oriental" techniques as well as canons of dress and appearance were highly influential (Zóbel de Ayala 1963:27). Three wooden Filipino images are illustrated in Plate 2.

Plate 2

The Puerto Rican production of images arose somewhat later, having become highly visible only after 1800 (Lange 1975:714). The artists either were self-taught or learned the trade from family or community members (1975:777). Images were carved from a number of types of wood, usually coated with gesso, and polychromed with oil, enamel, and other paints, creating an effect not entirely unlike that of traditional New Mexican statues. The comparison with the New Mexican devotion to images is strengthened by the shortage of priests in rural Puerto Rico and by the set of private devotions that surrounded the image makers' products (1975:766-73). Just as in New Mexico, the process of localization, the reinterpretation of local iconography according to local cultural canons, played a major role in the representation of holy personages. The Virgin of Hormigueros pictured in Plate 3 provides an apt example. The figure arose, according to Lange (1975: 277-92), through Puerto Rican reinterpretations of the legendary and iconographic attributes of Our Lady of Monserrat, the patroness of Catalonia. The local production of images in Puerto Rico has diminished greatly in the last forty years (1975:801-804).

Plate 3

When we turn to the production of Catholic images in New Mexico, three periods emerge from more than two centuries of the traditional era (i.e., pre–1900). The chronology of the image-carving art is closely related to that of Spanish colonization, however, and a rough sketch of the Spanish exploration and colonization of the province should be borne in mind. Cabeza de Vaca, who traversed the area in the 1530s, brought the viceroy tales of fabulous wealth in the "Seven Cities of Cibola" in the northern frontier country. Fray Marcos de Niza returned with a small party in 1539, and although it was unsuccessful, this expedition also spread the rumor of riches, prompting the governor of Nueva Galicia, Francisco Vasques de Coronado, to lead a substantial party northward in 1540. He soon learned that abundant wealth was not to be found in the region and returned to Mexico after two years of hardship and warfare. His journey nevertheless resulted in the exploration of vast stretches of this land.

The first attempt at colonizing the province was made in 1598 by Juan de Oñate, who of course operated under Spanish auspices. Images do not, however, appear to have been produced locally in New Mexico between this date and the Pueblo (Indian) Revolution of 1680 in which the Spaniards were expelled.[2] As trade with the Americans was outlawed under Spanish rule, all images were brought up by caravan during the colonial period (1598–1821). Both lay and clergy brought numerous articles of devotion with them, but these were never sufficient to satisfy Spanish needs, let alone to furnish newly founded mission chapels (Espinosa 1960 [1967]:12). In short, the early colonial period was characterized by a conspicuous shortage of Catholic religious images.

Soon after Don Diego de Vargas regained the province for Spain in 1692, however, a number of artists who were working in New Mexico executed

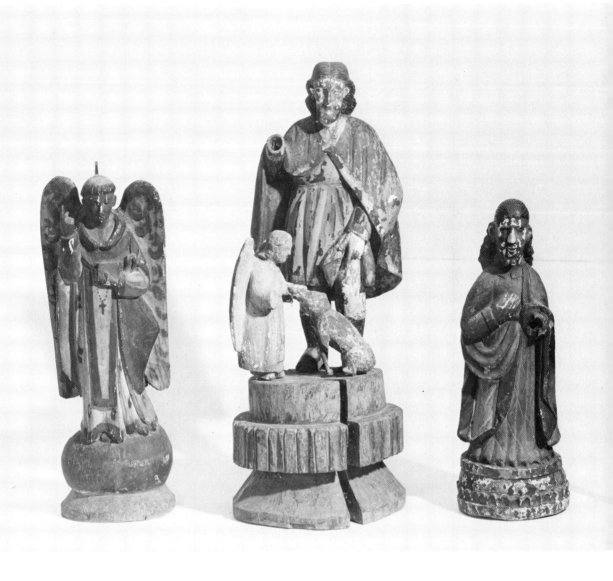

Plate 2. Images Executed in the Philippine Islands about 1900–1920. From left to right: St. Vincent (41 cm. or 16.4 in. in height), St. Roch with an angel and the dog that brought food (53 cm. or 21.2 in.), and a figure of a male saint, probably St. Joseph (36.5 cm. or 14.6 in. in height). Photograph courtesy of the National Museum of History and Technology, Smithsonian Institution, Washington.

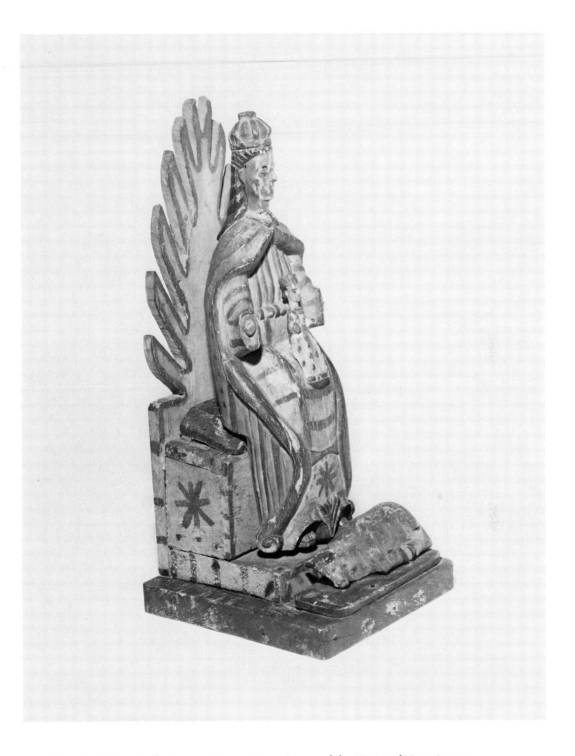

Plate 3. A Twentieth-Century Puerto Rican Image of the Virgin of Hormigueros (40 cm. or 16 in. in height). The identity of the artist is unknown. Photograph courtesy of the National Museum of History and Technology, Smithsonian Institution, Washington.

images on tanned buffalo, elk, and deer hides (Boyd 1974:118). Ecclesiastical disapproval began as early as the visitation of Don de Guevara in 1817–1820, and the production of painted tanned hides ended in New Mexico some 125 years after it had begun.[3] Two facts about this artistic phase are of importance.

First, although many of their materials were locally derived, extant examples demonstrate that none of the artists lacked at least rudimentary artistic training. Some authors have stated that these early artists were skilled in techniques for conveying perspective and the illusion of a third dimension on two-dimensional surfaces.[4] Second, they did not confine their efforts to the representation of the attributes of holy persons; their products were narrative and didactic. We presume this artistic goal to be related to the fact that the images served primarily in the conversion of the Indian "heathen" rather than in the devotion of the Spanish colonists (Boyd 1946:9-12). The images thus provided an important means for publicly articulating the relationship between Pueblo and Hispano societies.

The second period of the *santero* art took place during a brief interval in the eighteenth century. The work of two named artists has been identified: Fray Andrés García was a Franciscan born in la Puebla de los Angeles, Mexico; Captain Bernardo Miera y Pacheco was born near Burgos, Spain. Miera y Pacheco exhibited great versatility in New Mexico as a war captain and cartographer as well as in selling images to Indian converts for use in their chapels. The artists of this period used oil paints brought up from Mexico, and their intent was to reproduce the stylistic characteristics of the eighteenth-century Mexican Rococo. Whether or not their attempt was successful, they were well aware of its artistic conventions (Boyd 1974:96-102). Surviving works from this period consist of images carved in the round and paintings on wooden panels and on *Color Plate 1* canvas (see Color Plate 1).[5]

The final phase of the traditional image-carving art in New Mexico is frequently referred to as its golden age. Sometime after the middle of the eighteenth century a group of primarily native-born artists utilized both imported and native materials in an effort to fill the region's need for sacred images. Lacking academic training, many of these earlier artists began their work by copying from Mexican and European prototypes. Their lack of acquaintance with formal canons of perspective, anatomy, and architectural detail combined with local aesthetic preferences in the evolution of a distinctive style (see Boyd 1946:12, 29, 33).

Images were classified into two general types. The terms *bulto* or *santo de bulto*, which connoted solidity (Espinosa 1960 [1967]:52), referred to figures in the round of Christ, the Virgin Mary, and the saints (see Color *Color Plate 2*. During this period such pieces were carved from cottonwood, aspen, or pine, given a base coat of gesso and at times modeled with cloth soaked in gesso, and painted with water soluble pigments mainly derived from vegetal and mineral sources. *Retablos*, on the other hand, were originally hand-adzed and later milled panels that were similarly painted (see Color Plate 2). One particularly striking characteristic of their departure from Renaissance canons is a lack of the illusion of three-dimensionality (Steele 1974:7). The larger reredos or altar screens were also referred to as *retablos* (Espinosa 1960 [1967]:51). A rarer form intermediate between *bultos* and *retablos* and dating to the late eighteenth century was made by covering the surface of a board with gesso, carving out a design in bas-relief, and painting the surface (Boyd 1974:144-54; Mills [1967]:54).

Gettens' and Turner's (1951) analysis of the pigments revealed that the image makers' palette consisted primarily of imported vermillion and cochineal for red; yellow earth or ochre and occasionally vegetal yellow; a limited green spectrum derived from vegetal sources or mixed from other colors; imported indigo and Prussian blues; carbonaceous and iron ore browns; and strictly carbonaceous blacks. Tones and flesh areas were formed by allowing the gesso background (native gypsum in a base of homemade glue) to stand uncovered or by using imported white lead pigment. Panels were frequently sealed with a resinous outer layer.

The more specialized literature to date has emphasized stylistic and biographical evidence on individual artists and the attributes they utilized in portraying their subjects. In this regard it has been estimated that the polychromed images of eighteenth- and nineteenth-century New Mexico were fashioned by as few as a dozen individuals, excluding inferior examples, and that these persons derived most of their livelihood from their work (Boyd 1946:7).

Ethnographic characterization of the traditional image makers constitutes an arduous task for two reasons. First, surprisingly little is known about the actual working methods of these artists and of their relationship with their patrons. The data in hand are largely derived from scattered documentary evidence, published accounts of Hispano folklore and folklife, and from inquiries made of the image makers' descendants by writers and collectors in this century. Second, common generalizations concerning the homogeneity of traditional Hispano villages are contradicted by the wide range of differences exhibited between the various localities, and this variation is also apparent in the lives of the artists.

A case in point is provided by two roughly contemporary image makers, José Aragón and José Rafael Aragón. José Aragón was a Spaniard who is known to have lived in New Mexico and to have been producing images in the 1820s (Boyd 1974:366-74). In keeping with what one would presume to have been José Aragón's educational advantage, his vocabulary and calligraphy were much more sophisticated than those of most other New Mexican image makers. José Rafael Aragón lived in Córdova, New Mexico, where he left a number of descendants (see Color Plate 2). He was apparently not related to José Aragón. Similarly, Juan Miguel Herrera and José Gonzalez were two of the best artists in the latter half of the nineteenth century, but the former was a native New Mexican from Canjilón (Espinosa 1954:187) and the latter, who spent about ten years at las Trampas, was a native Sonoran of the traditional itinerant school of image makers (Boyd 1974:59, 343-44).

The Art of the Image Maker 11

Only the general nature of the production and marketing of images is known at this time. All available information indicates that individuals, groups, and the church itself placed orders with image makers. The fragile images may have been constructed in the patron's home rather than hauled from the artist's residence, although recent Mexican image carvers are known to have carried their inventory from hamlet to hamlet (Giffords 1977), and this practice may have been common in New Mexico as well. To quote one example, Juan Ramón Velásquez is said to have been given sufficient orders during the 1880s to warrant an annual three-to six-month trip, on which Velásquez took his family (Boyd 1954a:190–91). Payment frequently consisted of crops and livestock, although hard cash was not unknown (Boyd 1974:384–85). In the case of works commissioned by the church, inventories and other records indicate that images were produced both gratis, as acts of devotion, and for direct payment (cf. Boyd 1974:329, 384–85). Image makers were often commissioned by others to provide votive offerings for churches and chapels, and large pieces such as altar screens frequently bore inscriptions listing the name of the donor and the date (1974:167). The belief that it was blasphemous to place the artist's name prominently on sacred images contributed to the general anonymity of the image carvers' art (1974:329). Nevertheless, the wide distribution of the works of the more popular artists indicates that such persons were itinerant specialists.

Although the production of religious images in the region declined toward the end of the last century, these objects continued to be venerated by Hispano Catholics throughout New Mexico. Oral history and ethnographic accounts enable us to discern five levels in the use of religious images in worship.

First, individual households traditionally maintained a space for the display and veneration of images (see Plate 4). Both *bultos* and *retablos* were commonly housed there, and candles, rosaries, and other articles usually complemented the images. Espinosa (1960 [1967]:83–84) noted that the saint might be the patron of the head of the household or simply a past benefactor, but it was to this personage that the family frequently turned in times of need.

Plate 4

Second, more wealthy Hispanos often owned private chapels, and the provision of these structures was sometimes quite elaborate (see Plate 5). This level of image utilization is distinct from the preceding one due to the fact that these private chapels often served extrafamilial ends: masses could be read and processions initiated there. Oral sources maintain that Córdova once boasted a private chapel in a house in the central plaza or town square. These structures were especially important in areas of highly dispersed settlement, where public churches or chapels were rare. In such cases families from neighboring ranches would come to masses and individuals often made visits in fulfillment of a vow (Cabeza de Baca 1954:53–54; Jaramillo 1941:69). Ecclesiastical records clearly distinguish these private chapels from their public counterparts (Boyd 1974:34).[6]

Plate 5

Use of communally-owned images is entailed by the next three levels.

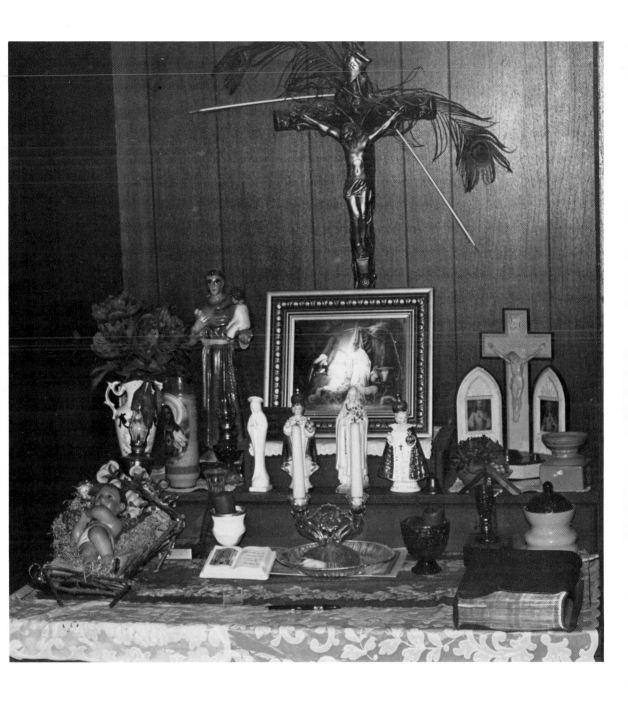

Plate 4. An Altar for Family Use in a Private Home. Polychromed wooden images used to be common in private homes, but their place has been taken primarily by plaster of Paris statues.

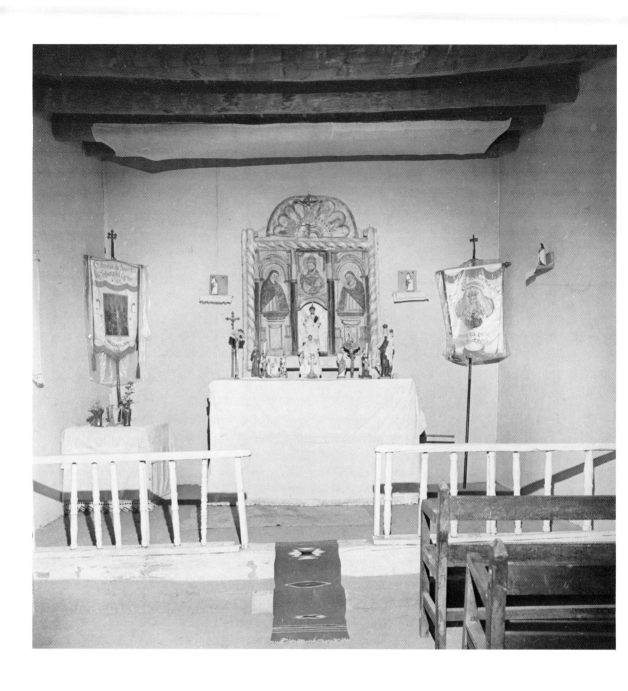

Plate 5. Interior of the St. Bonaventure Oratorio in Chimayó. This private chapel was located in one room of a private home. Photograph courtesy of the Photographic Archive, Museum of New Mexico, Santa Fe.

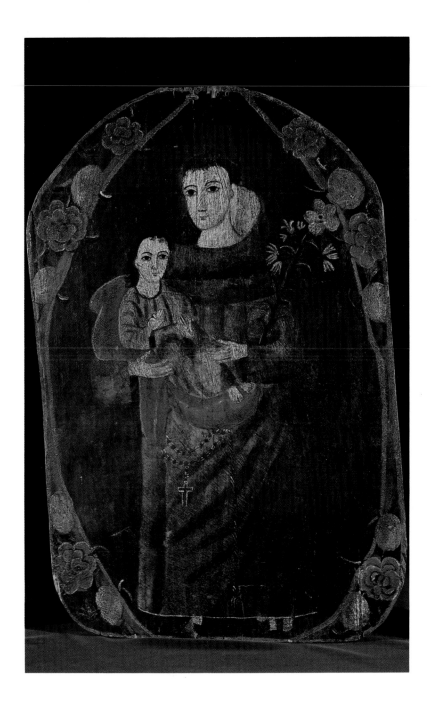

Color Plate 1. Retablo or Painting on a Board of St. Anthony with the Christ Child, Probably Executed by an Eighteenth-Century New Mexican Artist (52 x 78 cm.; 20.8 x 31.2 in.). Cady Wells Bequest in the collections of the Museum of International Folk Art, a unit of the Museum of New Mexico, Santa Fe; photograph by Blair Clark, Museum of New Mexico.

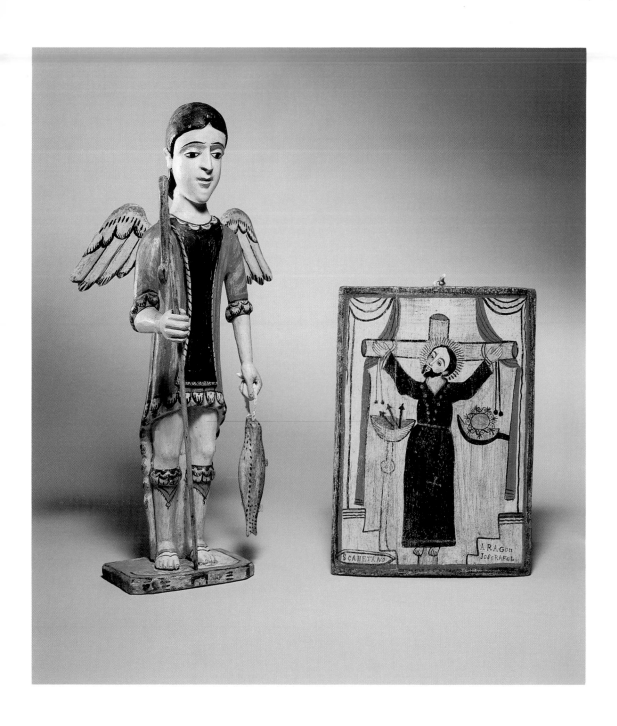

Color Plate 2. Bulto or Carving in the Round of Rafael the Archangel and a *Retablo* of St. Cajetan, the Former Attributed to and the Latter Signed by José Rafael Aragón (45 cm. in height and 20 x 28 cm.; 18 in. high, 8 x 11.2 in.). Collections of the Spanish Colonial Arts Society, Inc., in the Museum of International Folk Art, Santa Fe; photograph by Blair Clark, Museum of New Mexico.

In the third, religious and other associations frequently possessed a number of sacred representations. The brothers of the lay religious confraternities are noteworthy in this regard, but a number of other organizations were structurally quite similar and also have played significant roles in New Mexican history (cf. Córdova 1973:56). The role of images at this level of organization was not limited to voluntary associations; such entities as businesses sometimes also featured an image of their patron saint (Espinosa 1960 [1967]:83).

The last two levels were defined by cultural geography. Hispano communities like Córdova frequently consisted of more than one central plaza or (formerly) enclosed grouping of houses. Many of these settlements included a number of named plazas, and these were often associated with additional patron saints. Finally, each community was placed under the protection of at least one patron saint.[7] Córdova, for example, was first assigned to San Francisco Javier, but Saint Anthony of Padua later became the patron (SANM I: #768, SRCA). Some communities, like Abiquiú to the west, have retained the association with a former patron and celebrate two feast days (Córdova 1973:63).

Prior to the dispersion of images in this century, most community chapels and churches housed altar screens, *bultos*, and *retablos*. Although such images were considered the property of all, a number of individuals were responsible for their upkeep. Two or more sacristans served as the guardians of the building and its contents, two couples (at least in Córdova) were chosen annually to organize the feast for the patron saint and to clean the chapel, and one or more individuals often volunteered to look after particular images.

These five levels are intended to provide the reader with some idea as to the range of contexts in which traditional images have played an important role in the ritual reassertion of group identity. One should bear in mind, however, that the situation is far more complicated than this simple picture would indicate. First of all, other levels may be isolated. Beyond the community level, for example, one finds that Córdovans are included within a parish that recognizes the Holy Family as its patron. Similarly, New Mexico has depended upon La Conquistadora, an invocation of Our Lady of the Rosary, for her protection for three centuries (see Chávez 1948:307). The saints may also symbolize national unity, as Our Lady of Guadalupe does for Mexico (Wolf 1956:163). Saints may serve as symbols of ethnic identity, and this is clearly illustrated by the sentiment of New Mexico Hispanos for La Conquistadora and of Mexicans of Indian descent for Our Lady of Guadalupe. These social groups usually maintained spaces devoted to the veneration of their religious images, as did groups at the five levels previously mentioned.

Second, the transfer of images between groups at various levels of inclusiveness provides an important clue to the nature of their role in Hispano society. Images were borrowed from persons at all levels, and individuals often used the images of other individuals and groups in the course of visits to chapels and in public rituals. Indeed, the success of a number of important ritual complexes, including the Holy Week functions of the Brotherhood of Our Father Jesus, was predicated upon the transfer of images from one level of organization to another or from the possession of one group into that of another. An important example is provided by the *velorio de santos* (wake for the saints), where all owners were expected to lend their images when a wake was held in the community (Lucero-White 1936:5).[8] Such borrowing of images and the procession of the images it entailed from the place of worship of the owner(s) to that of the borrower(s) even took place between Pueblo Indians and Hispanos (cf. Brown, Briggs, and Weigle 1978:79–80).

The transfer of images between different groups of owners illustrates a direct and practical side of a much more general problem: why were the saints and their images so important in Hispano Catholicism? In addressing this question, it is useful initially to recall the preceding material on the evolution of the image-carving art in New Mexico. Between the seventeenth and early nineteenth centuries, artistic representations of the saints were increasingly severed, in stylistic terms, from their European and Mexican roots. Similarly, a process of iconographic selection occurred in which attributes familiar to New Mexicans were selected from among the elements presented by foreign prototypes.

This process may be characterized as a movement from the external focus of the early traditional art—that is, the attempt of its practitioners to imitate the fruits of more highly trained artists in Spain and Mexico—to an internal orientation or adherence to a local tradition. Some writers have suggested that this departure from academic prototypes was the direct result of the artists' inability to reproduce foreign models accurately (e.g., Steele 1974:1–26; Kubler 1964:4–8). On the contrary, this localization reflects a positive response of a group of native artists to the preferences of their people. The Puerto Rican example of the Virgin of Hormigueros illustrates the fact that the process of localization is hardly a phenomenon exclusively characteristic of Hispanos in New Mexico. Furthermore, this regionalization of widely venerated holy personages according to local cultural patterns is evident in the legends surrounding the lives and the miracles of these personages. St. Isidore, for example, who was born near present-day Madrid about 1070 and died there in 1130, is recognized as the city's patron saint (García Villada 1922; Reau 1958:III, 688). New Mexican legends portray him, however, as "a hard-working, honest rancher on a small tract of land in Agua Fría on the Río de Santa Fe, on the outskirts of Santa Fe itself" (DeHuff 1948:131) or "a small bean-and chili-rancher [who] lived near the Río Grande" (Applegate 1931:199).

A second part of the answer to this central question lies in the function of the saints and their images in Hispano life. These objects and their referents are important cultural and social mediators, and their role in Hispano society forms a central theme of the book. I use the term *mediation* (in its verbal and nominative forms) to refer to the symbolic connection of individuals, groups, concepts, social movements, and other entities. This process of relating involves more than a simple connection, as the identity of each of these entities is partly established in relation to the others and the nature of their relationship is expressed vis-à-vis the *mediator*, an element common to all of them.

A good example of this type of mediation is provided by the annual wake held until recent decades on St. Isidore's feast day, May 15, in most Hispano communities. The first part of the Córdovan observance of this ritual consisted of a procession carrying the image from the chapel to the uppermost fields, the recitation of prayers and the singing of the *alabanza* or hymn for St. Isidore, and a communal meal (turn ahead to Plate 53). This nightlong vigil stressed the binding of all Córdovans as a community through the act of seeking St. Isidore's blessing. In contrast, the morning procession back through the fields emphasized the recognition of boundaries between individual holdings and the status of the owners as landholders, an important social position (Brown 1941; Brown, Briggs, and Weigle 1978:100, 191–92). As the patron saint of *rancheros* (farmers/ ranchers), St. Isidore stood for the agricultural prosperity of the community as a whole as well as for the respect due the individual *ranchero*. Both the saint and his wake acted as mediators in the relationship between the group and its members, individuals within the group, man and nature, and so forth. These relations were not static, and the ritual annually provided an opportunity for their renegotiation.

St. Isidore shares an additional mediatory function with the remainder of the saints. Salvation is granted by God the Father; nevertheless, Christ, the Virgin Mary, and the saints have the power to intercede on behalf of humans.[9] These holy personages thus mediate in the relation between worshiper and God. Just as Christ, the Virgin, and the saints perform this task on a spiritual plane, the images embody an accessible means of evoking this mediatory power in the material sphere. The images derive their ability to mediate so effectively from their location at many junctures of the Hispano social system. For example, they are linked with a widespread religious iconography (the same personages are venerated in many areas) on the one hand, while they are tied into a set of local legends regarding the lives and miracles of the saints on the other. The images also serve as material embodiments of the legends in rituals which commemorate their referents, and the physical act of moving the images serves to bind together the various spaces, times, events, and persons that constitute the ritual (see Plate 6). The iconicity of image and referent, the *Plate 6* location of images in sacred places, and the priest's blessing of such objects enhance their potential for mediating in the relationship between supplicant, holy personage, and deity. The use of images in converting the Pueblo Indians, the importance of images in Pueblo Catholicism, and the transfer of images between Hispano and Pueblo settlements all suggest that Catholic images may serve as mediators of Hispano-Pueblo relations as well.[10]

In short, the images constitute a language, as it were, for a discourse

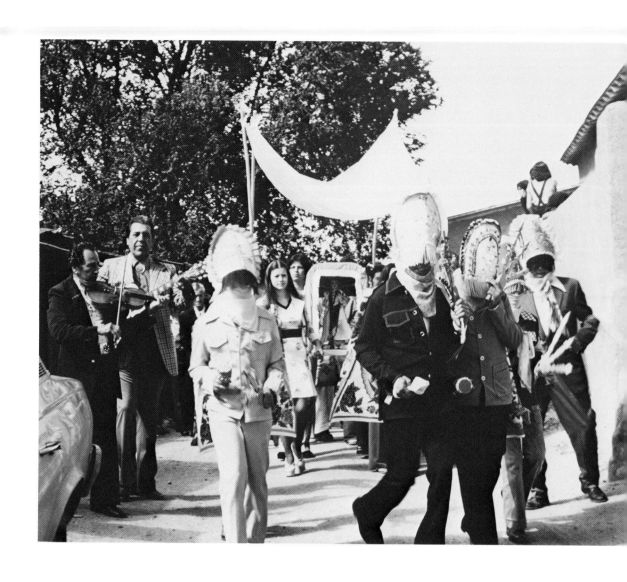

Plate 6. Procession of the Image of St. Anthony around the Córdova Chapel during the Community's Feast Day Celebration, 1977. The image is carried on an *andita* under a canopy by the sponsors of the feast. The musicians and masked dancers are reenacting the Matachines dance.

that bridges a universe of holy personages and the social universe. Just as important, however, is the means they provide for transmitting messages from one worldly realm to another. In Chapter 2 we will turn to the description of some of these images and the individuals who carved them.

2.

Beginnings: Saint Carving in Córdova from 1820 to 1917

Córdova, New Mexico has utilized the mediating potential of the saints and their images for nearly two and one-half centuries. This local devotion has existed along two lines. The beliefs and rituals associated with the images have played an important role in the lives of villagers for this entire time, but of no less importance is the prominent role of the Córdovan image carvers in the region's industry from the early 1800s through the present. A Córdovan, José Rafael Aragón, was perhaps the most popular of the nineteenth-century image makers, and his memory continues to enhance the community's pre-eminence as a carving center. An assessment of his career and of his impact on the contemporary artists entails a few remarks concerning Córdova's history.

While the exact date of settlement is unknown, Córdova is mentioned as constituting the northern boundary of the Santo Domingo de Cundiyó Grant in 1743 (SANM I: #211, SRCA). A land grant to Cundiyó in 1725 (later revoked) does not refer to any occupation of the Córdova area, and this fact indicates that settlement postdates the document (SANM I: #1041, SRCA). The earliest document uncovered so far on Córdova itself is dated 1749, and it tells of the abandonment of the valley that contains Córdova in 1748 (SANM I: #718, SRCA). Then Governor Joachín Codallos y Rabal was petitioned by fourteen citizens temporarily living in Chimayó to permit them to cultivate lands in Córdova while leaving their wives and children in the former community. They also requested a military escort. The governor decreed that the men return to their lands and that guards be placed on the high peaks to protect them (Jenkins 1974). Evidence of land conveyance in succeeding years indicates that this attempt at settlement was successful.[1]

The circuitous route by which the community acquired its present name forms the basis of an interesting tale. The original name of the settlement was Pueblo Quemado, a designation derived from the abandoned Pueblo ruin at the top of the mesa and approximately one mile west-northwest of the main plaza or town square. According to local tradition, the site was occupied by Tano Indians, and residents refer to it as *el* Alto Huachín after the last leader of the pueblo (Brown, Briggs, and Weigle 1978:55). The community acquired its present name in recognition of a prominent local family, the Córdovas, when the post office was established in 1900 (Dike 1958). The community also witnessed a change in the patron saint charged with its protection. The patron of the settlement in 1750 was St. Francis Javier, but it was later changed to St. Anthony of Padua, Córdova's present benefactor (SANM I: #768, SRCA).

Córdova's relationship to the Catholic church has always been profoundly affected by the community's status as a frontier settlement. Córdova has never boasted a resident priest; it was originally a mission of the Santa Cruz parish, as were nearby villages. Córdova was included in the Holy Family parish centered in Chimayó in 1959. Due to the number of missions that the resident clergy must visit, Córdovans normally celebrate mass only every other Sunday in their chapel. Although this situation is less than ideal, it shows considerable improvement from the early days of the settlement.

Córdova does not appear to have had any community chapel for most of the first century of its existence. Fray Francisco Atanasio Domínguez visited Córdova during his inspection of the missions of New Mexico in 1776. Although Domínguez provides a substantial account of agricultural enterprise in the settlement, he makes no mention of any chapel (Adams and Chávez 1956:83). An inventory of the chapel's furnishings appears in the Archives of the Archdiocese of Santa Fe (AASF, Patentes, Reel 54, frame 463), and Chávez dated it internally as 1821 (Chávez 1957:88.)[2] In a document of January 1, 1832, however, the residents of Quemado note that a license has been granted for a "public chapel of St. Anthony of Padua." Since this statement contains their promise to build, maintain, and furnish the chapel, it was probably built shortly thereafter (AASF, Patentes, Reel 55, frame 230). Licensing for the chapel was confirmed by Bishop Zubiría of Durango on April 17 of that year (AASF, Patentes, Reel 55, frames 222-23).[3]

Although legends have been recorded concerning the casting of the bell still housed in the chapel (Brown, Briggs, and Weigle 1978:101–5, 212–13), oral history is silent regarding the construction of the chapel or its appearance prior to the present century. A photograph of the chapel from the rear, made about 1900, reveals that the exterior has changed little since that date (Plate 7). With the exception of such features as new doors and window frames for the nave and crosses on the truncated buttresses, the only major changes executed in the present century appear to have been an enclosure of the belfry, the replacement of the earthen roof with galvanized tin, and the cement plastering of the chapel walls and cemetery fence after 1939 (see Plate 8).[4]

Plate 7

Plate 8

Similar changes have been undertaken in the interior of the chapel (see Plate 9). A wood stove and wooden floor, for example, were added before 1935.[5] A number of improvements have also been made since that date. The former lack of seating accommodations has been overcome by the addition of wooden pews, the wood stove has been moved closer to the

Plate 9

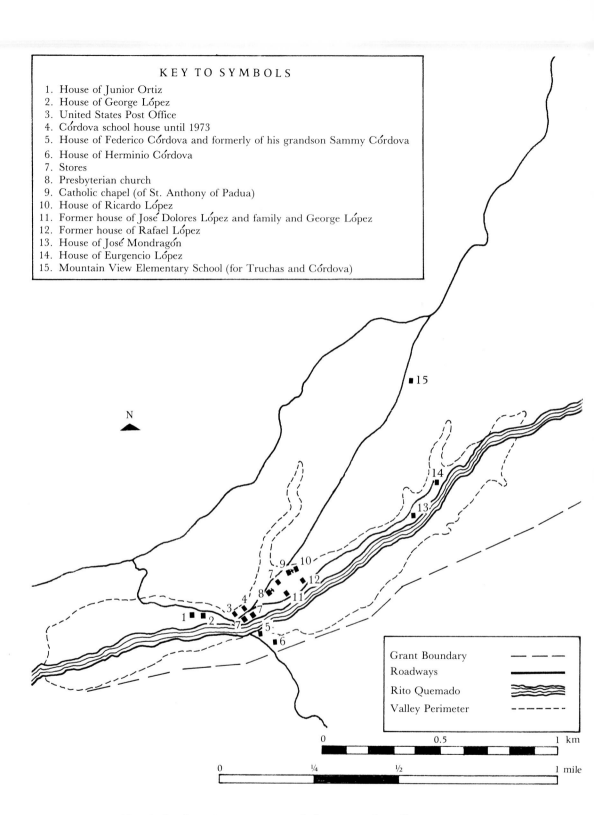

KEY TO SYMBOLS

1. House of Junior Ortiz
2. House of George López
3. United States Post Office
4. Córdova school house until 1973
5. House of Federico Córdova and formerly of his grandson Sammy Córdova
6. House of Herminio Córdova
7. Stores
8. Presbyterian church
9. Catholic chapel (of St. Anthony of Padua)
10. House of Ricardo López
11. Former house of José Dolores López and family and George López
12. Former house of Rafael López
13. House of José Mondragón
14. House of Eurgencio López
15. Mountain View Elementary School (for Truchas and Córdova)

N

Grant Boundary
Roadways
Rito Quemado
Valley Perimeter

0   0.5   1 km

0   ¼   ½   1 mile

Map 2. Córdova, New Mexico and the Quemado Valley.

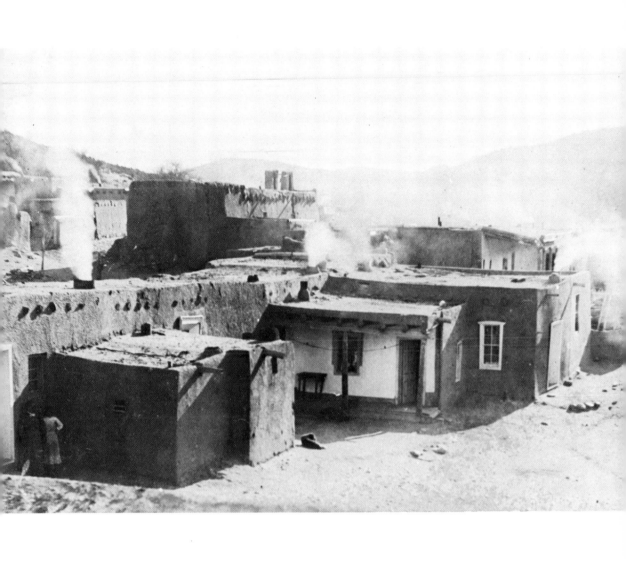

Plate 7. The Córdova Plaza about 1900, Showing a Rear View of the Chapel. Photograph courtesy of the Photographic Archive, Museum of New Mexico, Santa Fe.

Saint Carving in Córdova   23

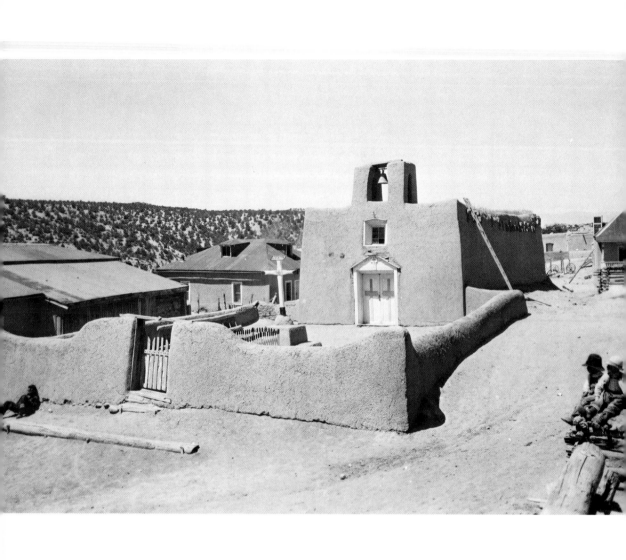

Plate 8. Exterior of the San Antonio de Padua del Pueblo Quemado Chapel, about 1935. The cement plaster and the tin roof that now grace the chapel had not been added by this time. Photograph by T. Harmon Parkhurst, from the Photographic Archive of the Museum of New Mexico, Santa Fe.

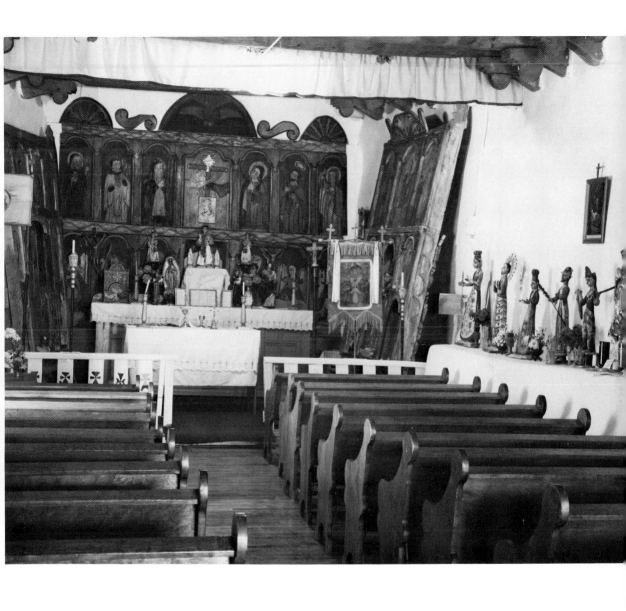

Plate 9. Interior of the Córdova Chapel, 1976.

sanctuary, and the gate has been removed from the railing separating sanctuary and nave. A major change in the appearance of the interior of the chapel has resulted from a rearrangement of the religious imagery. The *bultos* that formerly rested on tables on the sides of the sanctuary have been either removed from the chapel or placed on the buttress that forms a shelf on the right side of the nave. Conversely, the two freestanding altar screens have been removed from the nave and placed next to the main altar screen on opposite sides of the sanctuary.[6]

The polychromed images of the saints in the sanctuary and on the north buttress are some of the most visually striking elements of the chapel, and they constitute the primary focus of many chapel activities. As is the case with most of the traditional images of New Mexico, the works themselves leave few direct statements as to the identity of the artists. The one exception is the main altar screen. Although the inscription is fragmentary, the remaining words "con . . . hizo esa . . . se pintado . . . raiefal José . . . estando de Guardia el Sr Cura Don Fernando Ortis" confirm the stylistic attribution of the altar screen to José Rafael Aragón. No date is visible; nevertheless, Ortiz's residence at Santa Cruz in 1834–1838 provides evidence that Aragón was working during that period (see Boyd 1974:395). Another of Aragón's inscriptions from the Duran chapel in Talpa is dated 1851, and he probably produced images until shortly before his death in 1862.[7]

The Córdova chapel provides one of the most strikingly beautiful examples of the religious imagery of nineteenth-century New Mexico. José Rafael Aragón, the chapel's principal artist, was one of the most skilled and prolific folk artists in New Mexican history. He has also been credited with fashioning the altar screens at Llano Quemado, Picurís, the Santuario in Chimayó, the Duran chapel at Talpa, San José de Chama, San Miguel del Valle, Santa Cruz, the Carmen oratory at Llano de Talpa, and other places (Boyd 1974:396–402; Espinosa 1960 [1967]: 67–68; Carroll 1943:49–64) (Aragón's imagery is illustrated in Color Plate 2).

Two sources of information are available for the attribution of the traditional images to their respective artists. First, oral history provides provocative if conflicting information on the imagery. Testimony collected in Córdova in the 1920s, 1930s, and 1940s by Lorin W. Brown, Frank Applegate, and Charles Carroll held that both the images collected by Applegate and those displayed in the chapel were the work of a Córdovan named Miguel Aragón (Applegate and Austin n.d.; Carroll 1943). E. Boyd reported in 1946 that older Córdovans told her that a carver named Eusebio Córdova was responsible for the work (1946:64). Extensive interviewing conducted by the author in 1972–1976 revealed no mention of either of these names in connection with the *bultos*, but elderly informants gave the credit to José Rafael Aragón. George López also claims that his grandfather, Nasario López, assisted Aragón in his work.

The second line of evidence is provided by the images themselves. The link with José Rafael Aragón is firmly established by the inscription on the lower right-hand corner of the main altar screen. Stylistic characteristics separate this work, however, from that of the two side altar screens. While Rafael Aragón's eyes are crisp and almond-shaped and his brushwork firm and confident, the painter of the other two pieces was sloppier in his work and less concerned with the shading of the eyelids. Furthermore, the boldness of Rafael's palette is not matched by that of the other artist. The apparent intent of the image maker who produced these *retablos* to copy the work of Rafael Aragón, along with his failure to duplicate his predecessor's mastery of the medium, lends support to the suggestion that the former was a "disciple" or "imitator" of Rafael Aragón (Boyd 1946:47; Espinosa 1960 [1967]:69).

Although the subject of the execution of the altar screen has been treated with some eloquence in the literature, the attribution of the *bultos* is far more clouded. Carroll (1943:63) states that the *bultos* were the work of Miguel Aragón. In 1946 Boyd (1946:47–52) went to great lengths in arguing that the Córdova reredos and *bultos* were not produced by the same hand. The discussion of Rafael Aragón that she published in 1974 does not reiterate these conclusions, however, and the caption for a plate illustrating an image from the Córdova chapel attributes the piece to Rafael Aragón (1974:403).

A detailed examination by the author of the Córdova *bultos* in 1976 revealed that they are the work of several hands. While the treatment of the eyes and the painting on what Boyd believed to be a Virgin of the Immaculate Conception (see Plate 10) and on a figure of St. Peter identify the work as that of Rafael Aragón, several of the *bultos* are easily identified as the work of Aragón's follower. In addition to the two bultos by Rafael Aragón, seven were produced by Aragón's follower and five by an altogether different artist. Four were repaired and painted by José Dolores López. Of the latter, two appear originally to have been produced by Rafael Aragón.

At present one can merely speculate as to whether Rafael's follower was Miguel Aragón, Nasario López, or someone altogether different. The fact that the stylistic differences evident between Aragón's main altar screen and those of his follower are also represented among the *bultos* lends support to the notion derived from contemporary local tradition that both Aragón and another image maker worked in the nineteenth century. The presence of a number of *bultos* by different hands further demonstrates the fact that other individuals were involved in the production of Córdova's images. The notion that a third carver may have resided in the village is suggested by the discovery that one of the crucifixes and a Virgin of Guadalupe were painted by the same artist. Thus it is possible that José Rafael Aragón, Miguel Aragón, and Nasario López were all resident image makers, although the anonymity of all except the first artist's works prevents us from verifying this possibility.

The possible participation of Miguel Aragón and/or Nasario López in the production of the chapel images is further clarified by the documentary record. José Miguel Aragón was baptized in Santa Cruz parish on

Plate 10

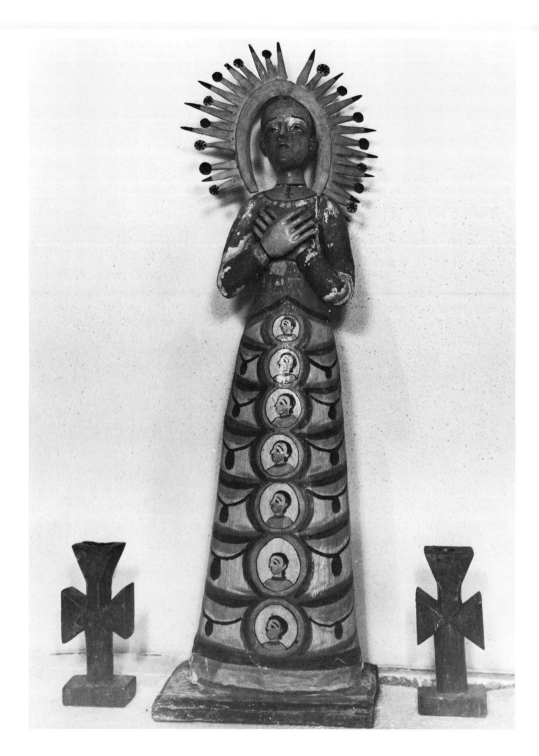

Plate 10. A Nineteenth-Century Polychromed Image by José Rafael Aragón (height 92.5 cm. or 37 in.). Although Boyd (1974:403) believed it to be an Immaculate Conception, Córdovans maintain that it is Our Lady of Sorrows. From a private collection.

28   *Beginnings*

September 10, 1843 and was listed as a nine-day-old son of Rafael Aragón and Josefa Córdova of San Antonio del Quemado (AASF, Baptisms, 10 September 1843, SRCA). Nasario Guadalupe López was born in 1821, and López and his wife, María Teresa Bustos, baptized their first child, José de la Cruz, in 1856 (AASF, Baptisms, 4 May 1856; Burials, 28 June 1891, SRCA). That the painter of the side altar screens in the chapel was at work about 1850 is suggested by the fact that he used both hand-adzed and milled boards in some of his other works, the latter becoming common after the American conquest of New Mexico in 1846 (Boyd 1946:46; Espinosa 1960 [1967]: 69). Although both Miguel Aragón and Nasario López could have been carving shortly after this time, the fact that López was born thirteen years earlier than Aragón seems to indicate that he is the more likely candidate, especially since Aragón would have been only nineteen years old when his father died. López's death in 1891 demonstrates that he could have been at work nineteen years longer than Aragón. This longevity suggests that if one of the two is responsible for the large number of later works in the same style in the Santa Cruz area, López was the artist (AASF, Burials, 28 October 1872 and 28 June 1891, SRCA).

Nevertheless, Córdova residents have claimed on the basis of independent evidence that Nasario López was an image maker. Wilder and Breitenbach (1943: text opposite plate 32) claim that the expertly executed Death cart in the Taylor Museum's collections was said to have been carved by the grandfather of José Dolores López (see Plate 11). *Plate 11* Córdovans assert, however, that this attribution is erroneous because the piece was carved by José Dolores' father, Nasario López. It is also believed that Nasario and all of his sons were carpenters and weavers.

Regardless of the identity of specific artists, it is apparent that the Aragón and López families in Córdova, which were related by marriage,[8] were known in the community as specialists in image making. Toward the end of the century, however, producers of polychromed images were becoming scarce in New Mexico. At this point the use of tempera paints on locally produced wooden figures had largely given way to the importation of mass-produced statues. Local manufacture of *retablos* had been primarily displaced by an influx of lithographs and chromolithographs several decades earlier (Lange 1974). The arrival of the railroads in the last two decades of the century virtually amounted to a *coup de grace*.

Nevertheless, the Córdovan materials show that the cultural elements that had molded the image-making art in the nineteenth century were still present even if they were less apparent in the twentieth. The unique constellation of events that led to a revival of the image-carving tradition began with the birth of José Dolores, the last child of Nasario López and María Teresa Bustos, in Córdova on April 1, 1868 (AASF, Baptisms, 5 April 1868, SRCA).

Oral history provides little information on José Dolores' childhood and early adulthood. Nasario died when José Dolores was twenty-three, and the young López had been herding sheep for a wealthy owner from Santa

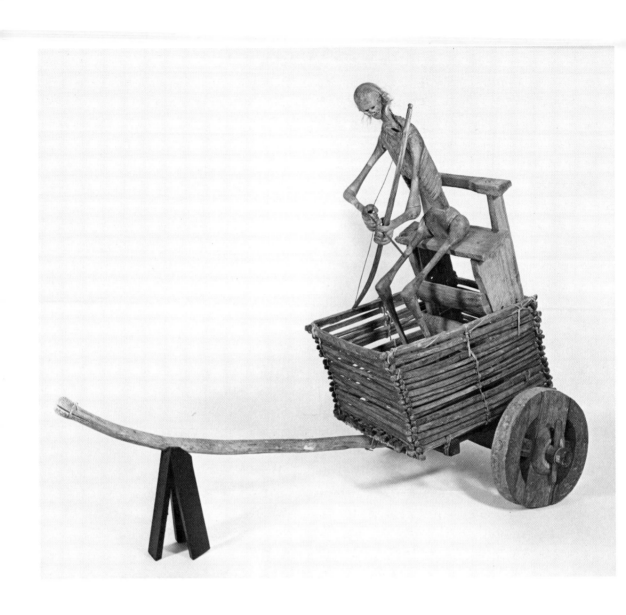

Plate 11. A Death Cart Said to Have Been Made by Nasario López (height of
figure 90 cm. or 36 in., total height 127.5 cm. or 51 in.). Taylor Museum
Collection of the Colorado Springs Fine Arts Center: Gift of Alice Bemis Taylor;
photograph courtesy of the Colorado Springs Fine Arts Center.

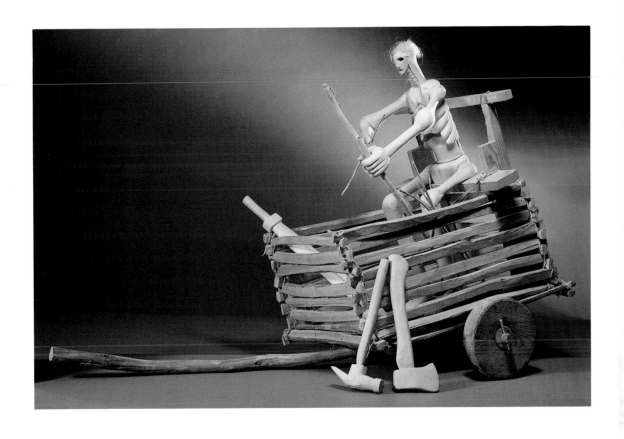

Color Plate 3. Skeletal Figure of Death Riding in a Cart by the López Family (total height 90 cm., cart is 67 cm. in length, 42 cm. in width, and 33 cm. in height; total height 36 in., cart 26.8 x 16.8 x 13.2 in.). In the collections of the International Folk Art Foundation in the Museum of International Folk Art, Santa Fe; photograph by Blair Clark, Museum of New Mexico.

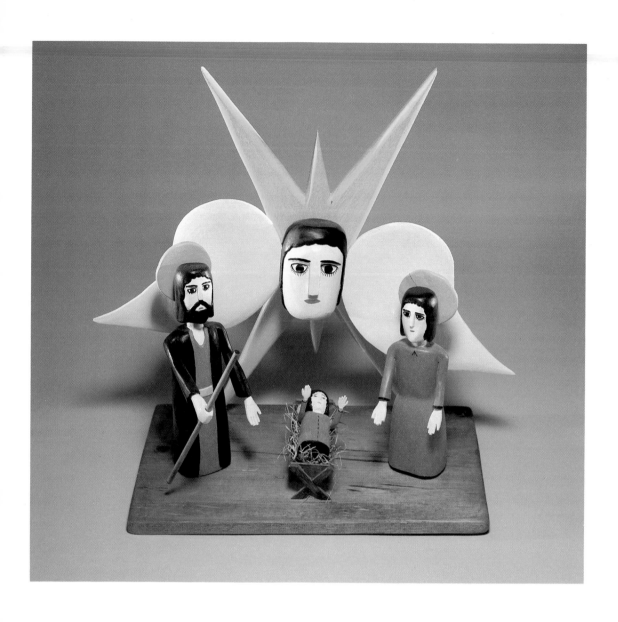

Color Plate 4. Nativity by Luis Tapia (total height 49.4 cm. or 19.5 in., base 43.0 cm. x 28.4 cm. or 17 x 11.25 in.). Museum of International Folk Art, a unit of the Museum of New Mexico, Santa Fe; photograph by Blair Clark, Museum of New Mexico.

Fe for several years by that time (AASF, Burials, June 28, 1891). He left the sheep camps when he married Candelaria Trujillo in 1893 (AASF, Marriages, November 21, 1893, SRCA). The couple moved up to the Llano de los Quemadeños, an area east of Córdova that was settled by Córdovans, to escape an apparent shortage of irrigable land. They returned to Córdova after a dry spell in 1913, bought land, and remained there. This second attempt seems to have been more fruitful; López came to own land in Truchas, the Llano de los Quemadeños, Las Joyas, and several parts of Córdova. His maintenance of a herd of about one hundred goats further provided his family with meat, dairy products, and a small income from the sale of milk, cheese, and kid. López is shown as he appeared later in life in Plate 12.

Plate 12

One element of José Dolores' life that was of great importance to his later revival of the image-carving art was his trade as a carpenter. José de la Cruz and José Fernández, José Dolores' brothers, were referred to as *carpinteros*, indicating that they exercised the full range of skills required of the carpenter at that time. José Dolores fell short of this designation, however, as he concentrated his efforts on furniture, window and door frames, niches, roof beams and corbels, crosses for grave markers, coffins, and chests, and did not raise roofs (see Plate 13). His furniture repertoire consisted mainly of *relojeras* or shelves for clocks, *rinconeras* (corner cupboards), *almarios* or niches with carved doors, chests, freestanding dish cabinets and clothes closets, niches, hanging shelves, and chairs. Carpenters were specialists (Ahlborn 1958:15–16), and José Dolores' competence in such aspects of the trade as the construction of joints without nails or glue is clearly reflected in his later work. Although it appears to have been well executed, José Dolores' carpentry was not exceptional. He adhered to currently popular motifs, including recent Mexican imports, and his works were not sold to Anglo-Americans. The *trastero* or freestanding dish cupboard pictured in Plate 14, for example, was fashioned by José Dolores López for family use, and it continues to be a functional piece in the house of a neighbor. Well built if not unique, it is representative of the homemade, utilitarian items that were common near the turn of the century. The cupboard was repainted periodically, and so we do not know whether Mexican motifs such as those exhibited by the López furniture in Plate 13 originally graced it.

Plate 13

Plate 14

Two other facets of José Dolores' life influenced his development of the contemporary carving art. First, the López family reports that José Dolores was skilled in filigree jewelry while it was still in fashion toward the end of the last century. The Lópezes further state that these designs influenced the chip-carving that José Dolores later used on his wood carvings. Second, he filled a number of religious offices in his community, including that of *hermano mayor* of the *cofradía* (the annually elected head of the local chapter of the Brotherhood of Our Father Jesus) and the sacristan of the chapel. Both of these positions involved extensive contact with the village's religious images.

In short, many of the elements that shaped the emergence of the art of

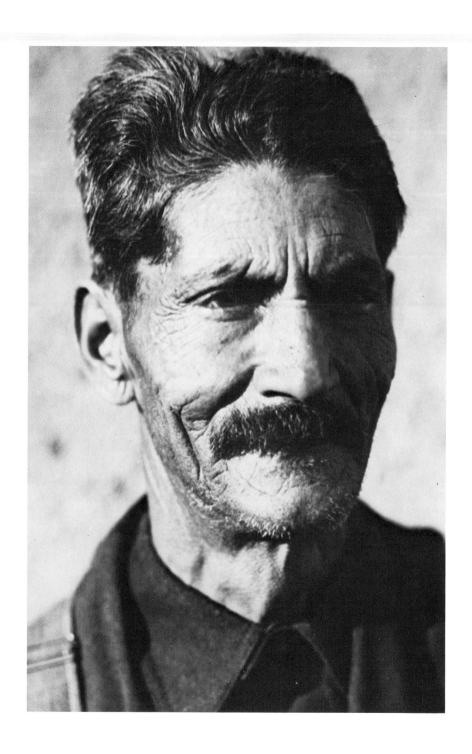

Plate 12. José Dolores López, a Portrait by Ansel Adams, about 1928. Photograph by Ansel Adams, reproduced from a copy in the E. Boyd Collection, State Records Center and Archives, Santa Fe.

32   *Beginnings*

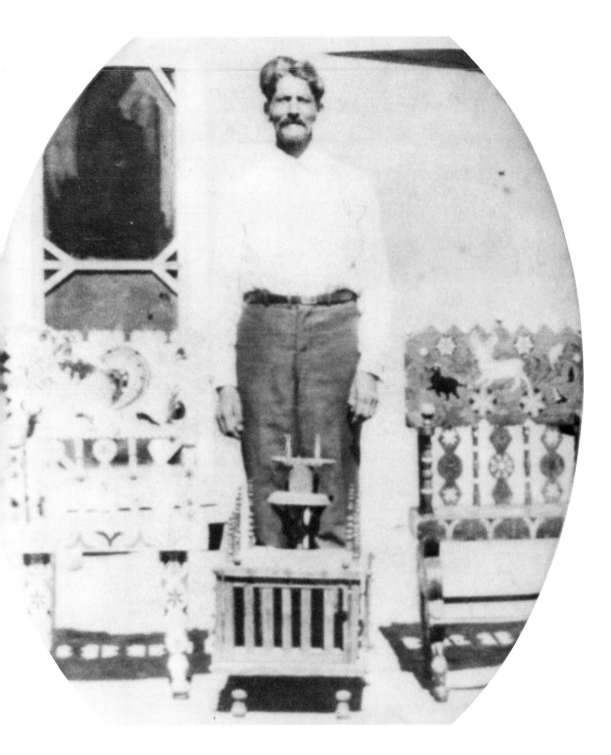

Plate 13. José Dolores López with Examples of His Painted Furniture (Left and Right) and Carved Furniture (Center). Photograph courtesy of Mr. and Mrs. Richard E. Ahlborn, from a negative in the Photographic Archive of the Museum of New Mexico, Santa Fe.

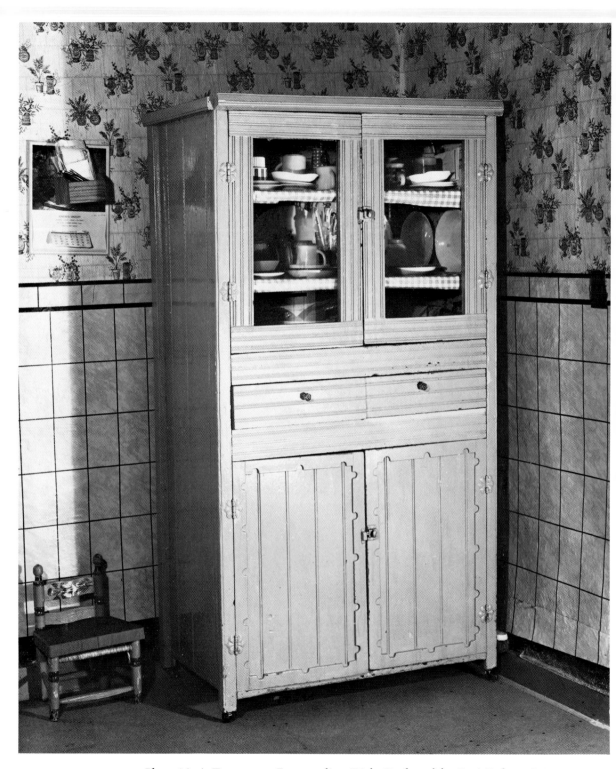

Plate 14. A *Trastero* or Freestanding Dish Cupboard by José Dolores López (approximately 1.8 m. or 6 ft. in height). From a private collection.

the traditional image carver in New Mexico in the eighteenth century were still present in Córdova in José Dolores López's day. In addition to being intricately involved in the religious life of his community, José Dolores was a skilled woodworker and had painted wooden objects. Furthermore, Hispano culture recognizes a category of behavioral characteristics thought to be inherited by all consanguines in a particular family. José Dolores López was thus characterized as having had the art of the image carver "in the family" or "in the blood."

The local production of traditional polychromed figures was largely dormant at this time, however, and José Dolores López's talent remained latent. In short, although many of the requisite components were present, the re-emergence of image carving in Córdova seems to have been prevented by the lack of a suitable catalyst. As will be described in the next chapter, however, a catalytic agent was soon to appear.

3.

The "Discovery" and "Encouragement" of José Dolores López

The transition from traditional to contemporary art forms was initiated by a personal hardship that José Dolores López suffered in 1917. Although New Mexico had been under American dominion since 1846, most Córdovans' understanding of the nature of their obligations to the new government was still imperfect in the early part of this century. Accordingly, José Dolores became distraught when his oldest son Nicudemos was called up to fight in World War I. He firmly believed that a trip across the ocean was not only unnecessary but was a journey from which a person would never return. Feeling his loss deeply, José Dolores could not sleep until eleven or twelve o'clock at night. He was a farmer and livestock keeper, rising with the first light of day, and so this deep melancholy threatened his health.

In order to pass the time and to turn his thoughts away from his son, José Dolores began to whittle a piece of wood. He was greatly relieved when he received a letter from Nicudemos in basic training camp in Kansas. Beyond reporting that he was safe and sound, Nicudemos conveyed to his father his newly found feeling of identity as an American. Enclosed was a picture of Nicudemos' company.

This correspondence not only lifted José Dolores' spirits but instilled in him a sense of patriotism (Brown, Briggs, and Weigle 1978:204). His new hobby provided him with a means of preserving this moment of exaltation. He cut a rectangular frame, using a saw to inscribe a simple repeated *Plate 15* motif (see Plate 15). Letter and picture were placed inside, and the frame was hung above the fireplace in his best room (1978:204). As with his later work, his signature and the date were penciled onto the bottom.

By the time Nicudemos returned home in 1919, José Dolores had expanded his hobby to fill every available moment. Residents say that López did not sell any of his early works. Rather, his initial efforts were concentrated on addressing the needs of his fellow villagers in a number of ways.

First, José Dolores began providing gifts for village families, and according to Brown, every married couple received a clock shelf or lamp stand, carved and brightly painted, with the initials of the couple prominent and "JDL" not so conspicuous (1978:204–205). Although his repertoire at this time consisted essentially of the items included prior to 1917, his style was considerably altered by the carving ornamentation. This difference is illustrated by a comparison of López's painted furniture in Plate 13 and his *trastero* or freestanding dish cupboard in Plate 14 with a modern photograph of the middle (carved) niche (see Plate 16). Like most of his later work, the niche is garnished with extensive chip-carving and with his name and place of residence. More unusual, however, are the two-toned effect and the stylized Indian and arrowhead. His gifts also took the form of picture frames. He would buy a picture of the Virgin or of a saint, carve a frame, and provide a glass to protect it. Upon his return, Nicudemos encouraged his father to continue carving.

Plate 16

Second, López's first carvings were not religious articles, but it was not long before he integrated into the religious life of the community the art form that he had innovated. As sacristan of the chapel, one of López's first tasks appears to have been the repair of a number of traditional polychromed images that had suffered paint loss and breakage. Six objects now visible in the chapel have been partially overpainted by López. Unlike his predecessors, José Dolores did not make his own paints. His materials consisted instead of commercial house paints, which were then available in nearby general stores. His brushwork lacked the experience of Rafael Aragón—his palette was limited and his detail work quite crude. Naturally, his efforts were concentrated on the heads and hands of images, as these fragile appendages were easily broken. Flesh parts were cast in a dense white, while eyebrows, eyelashes, and pupils received an inhuman blue. A course blotch of red constituted the lips, coal black provided the only hair color, and one figure was adorned with cheeks and

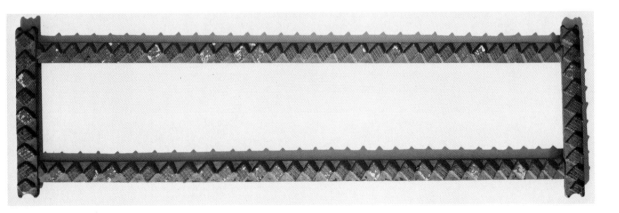

Plate 15. A Carved Picture Frame by José Dolores López, Said to Be His First (approximately 90 x 32.5 cm. or 36 x 13 in.). From a private collection; photograph by Alan Pitcairn.

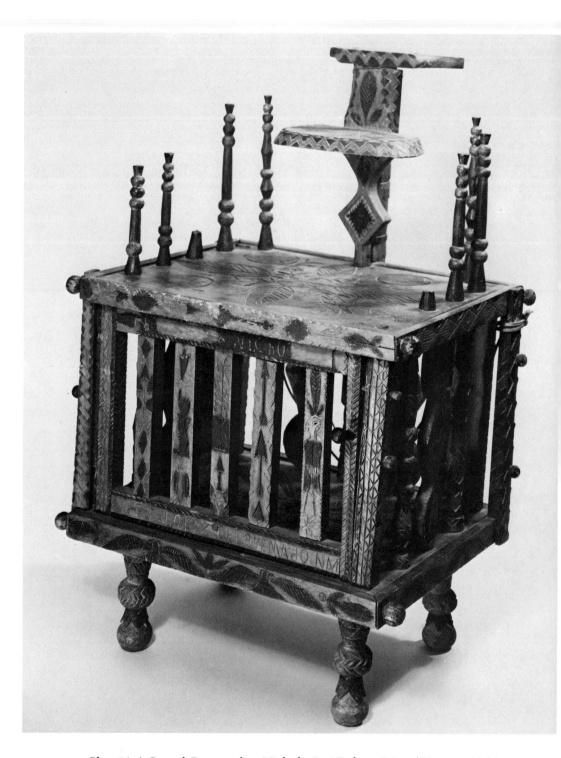

Plate 16. A Carved, Freestanding Niche by José Dolores López (63 cm. or 25.2 in. in total height, box 40.4 x 39 x 29.5 cm. or 16.2 x 15.6 x 11.8 in.). In the collections of the Museum of International Folk Art, a unit of the Museum of New Mexico, Santa Fe.

chin of light pink. While his technique may have been unrefined, his devotion was nevertheless appreciated by the congregation, for he was allowed to repair and repaint the head and hands of the chapel's patron saint (see Plate 17). His other subjects consisted of an additional Saint Anthony, three images of the Holy Child of Atocha, and a tabernacle. José Dolores also repaired or supplied bases and niches for these figures. The Saint Anthony to the right of the altar is conspicuously labeled with the date, 1921, and with the initials "J.D.L."

Plate 17

Third, López also produced a number of articles for the chapel and for the *morada* or chapterhouse of the *cofradía*.[1] These items are of three classes: large pieces for the chapel, accessories for chapel and *morada*, and at least one image. First, López utilized his carpentry skills in producing such features as the door to the chapel, its wooden frame, and the large cross in the chapel cemetery. Although the wooden frame and doors were removed and the cross was repainted years ago, they are visible in Plate 8. The beautiful railing in the *morada* is also José Dolores' work. Second, López produced a number of items for use in both chapel and *morada*. Both of these structures contain beautiful candelabras by José Dolores, and they are still in use. The brightly painted Bible stand in the chapel (see Plate 18) is another example of his ingenuity, and its conspicuously painted date of 1919 indicates that López's labors in the chapel followed his initial inspiration rather closely. Finally, José Dolores carved and painted at least one image for community use. Intricate painting and chip-carving grace a crèche that López provided for the chapel (see Plate 19). Earlier in this century it was customary to place a crèche upon the altar during the Christmas season, and López's nativity may have served frequently in this capacity. Although this piece may have been utilized as a prototype for contemporary versions, it lacks the figures of St. Joseph, the Virgin Mary, and the animals that complement more recent attempts. It also appears that López carved and painted a few images for use in worship by Hispanos from other localities. One of his sons reports, for example, that López made a polychromed Virgin for a *morada* in Chimayó and that it was donated to the group. The diminutive size of a beautiful polychromed Virgin by López indicates that it may have been made as a gift to an individual (see Plate 20).

Plate 18

Plate 19

Plate 20

It is not clear, however, whether or not José Dolores sold polychromed images to Hispano Catholics. All contemporary residents who were asked about this responded in the negative. A set of unpublished notes by E. Boyd cites Apolonio Rodríguez's description of a visit with "an old man" in Córdova in 1954. Rodríguez reported his informant's statement that José Dolores made a "selling trip" to Colorado "a long time ago" with about one hundred painted images of the saints. His sales were said to have been made largely to the brothers of the Conejos chapter of the Brotherhood of Our Father Jesus in the San Luis Valley. The report is backed up by a tentative identification of a *bulto* in the Taylor Museum as López's work (Boyd 1954b). It is unfortunate indeed that such an interesting question cannot be more easily answered.

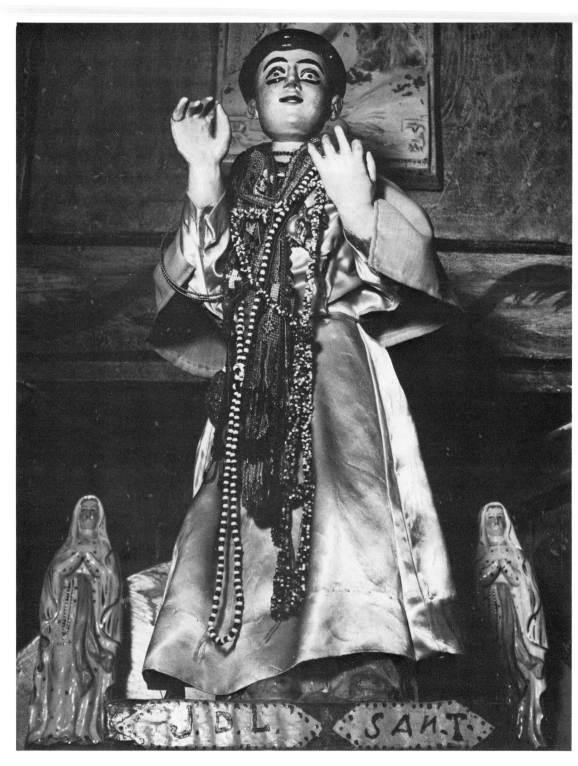

Plate 17. Image of St. Anthony of Padua, Patron Saint of Córdova (55 cm. or 22 in. in height). From a private collection.

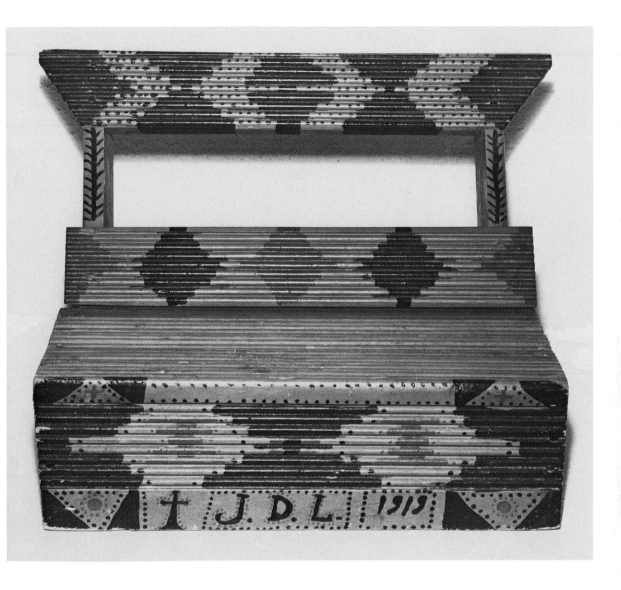

Plate 18. A Painted Bible Stand by José Dolores López (total height 28.8 cm. or 11.5 in.; base 36.3 x 11.3 x 31.3 cm. or 14.5 x 4.5 x 12.5 in.). Blue, black, and red paints rather than chip-carving grace the stand; note the date 1919 and López's initials on the bottom. From a private collection.

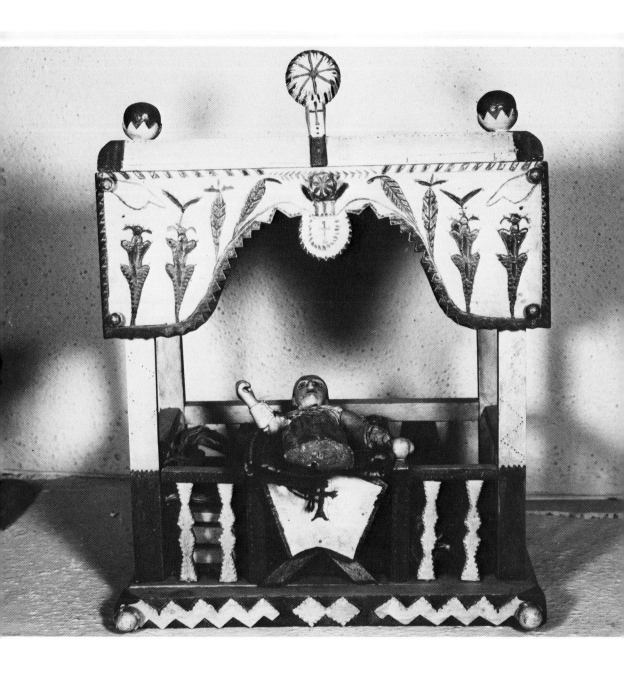

Plate 19. Polychromed Crèche by José Dolores López (stable, 40.8 cm. or 16.3 in. total height, length, 32 cm. or 12.8 in.; length of Christ Child 20 cm. or 8 in.). From a private collection.

42   *Beginnings*

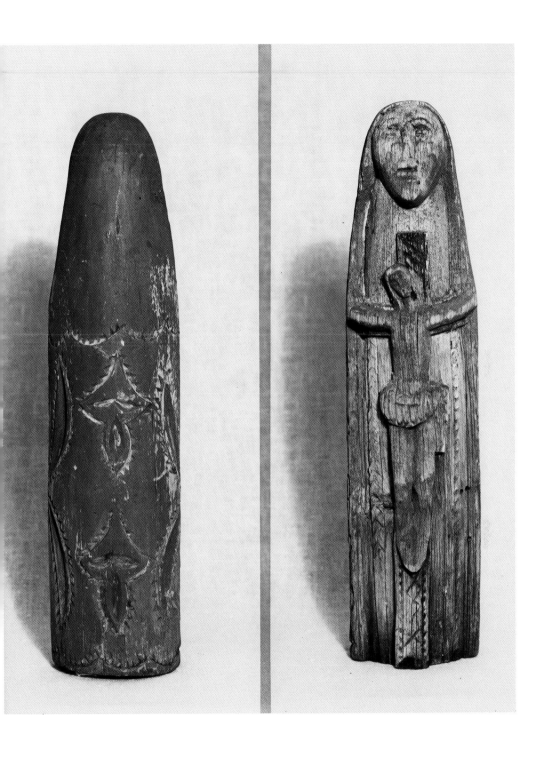

Plate 20. Polychromed and Chip-Carved Virgin with Crucifix by José Dolores López (24.4 cm. or 9.8 in. in height). Although the paint has faded considerably, the reddish brown of the skin, the blue of the cloth, and the black cross are clearly visible. From a private collection.

Nevertheless, José Dolores López's artistry did not long remain an exclusive possession of his own ethnic group. As removed as Córdova must have been from the social life of such centers as Santa Fe in the early part of this century, the influence of these places made itself felt in the community. Indeed, the late teens and early twenties found a number of outsiders engaged in occasional pilgrimages to Córdova, and these trips were generally made during Holy Week. The profound effect that outsiders' discovery of José Dolores exerted on the development of the industry renders them major actors in the artistic drama and merits a brief description of their entrance on the scene.

An intrinsic feature of twentieth-century American society is the appropriation of the material and cultural goods of one group by the members of others. As Grimes (1976:34) has recently noted, the Southwest has become a mecca for persons who firmly believe in drawing upon the symbolic resources of other cultures. Artists seem to have exceeded other groups in asserting the legitimacy of this process with respect to their own interests (Grimes 1976:34). In the case of the founders of the Taos and Santa Fe art colonies, this orientation toward Pueblo Indian and Hispano cultures formed a part, in the words of one of them, of a "great enthusiasm for the discovery of fresh material" (Blumenschein 1926:190).

The cultural diversity of northern New Mexico made it a natural target for persons with such interests. As Coke (1963:9) states, "The customs of both the Indians and [the] Spanish Americans played a part in creating an exotic atmosphere unlike that found in any other part of the United States."[2] Although the non-Western appeal of the Pueblos predominated early, the 1920s signaled an emergence of interest in a greater variety of subject matter (1963:110). As more attention was focused on the Hispano component of the population, two elements of its cultural matrix were selected by the Anglo-Americans as central foci.

First, artists such as Oscar Berninghaus, Fremont Ellis, Marsden Hartley, B. J. O. Nordfeldt, and Howard Schleeter depicted traditional polychromed images in their paintings (Coke 1963). A number of artists were involved in the study and preservation of "native" art and architecture, the extent of which is suggested by the book-length manuscript of Applegate and Austin (n.d.). The artistic values offered by these cultures, however, had little influence on the painters' own styles (Coke 1963: 107).[3]

Second, the public rituals of the Brotherhood of Our Father Jesus proved quite fascinating to many Anglo-American visitors to the villages, even though the brothers' beliefs were not shared by the observers (Bodine 1968:149; Weigle 1976:75–76). Indeed, the increase in rules of discretion and separateness enacted by the brothers was partly stimulated by Anglo-American encroachment. As Weigle (1976:90–91) notes, greater seclusion of the organization's activities served further to titillate the hordes of "Penitente hunters."[4] The works of Nordfeldt and Austin provide examples of how this fascination was turned to artistic ends (Coke 1967; 1972:57–61; Austin 1924:349–72; 1931:226–32).

Córdova was deemed a paradise for many of these pursuits. Linguistic and cultural barriers created the need for a mediator, however, and Lorin W. Brown was instrumental in this regard during the 1920s and 1930s. Born in Elizabethtown, New Mexico and of Anglo-American, Pueblo, and Hispano parentage, Brown joined his mother, Cassandra, in Córdova in 1922. Cassandra Brown entered Córdova to fill a vacancy in the local school; she became a resident for more than a decade and married into the López family. Lorin Brown took over her job when she vacated it about 1922; he also ran a general store and post office, sold game and fish licenses, and taxied Córdovans to town. Having moved to Santa Fe in 1931, Brown periodically returned to Córdova in connection with his employment as a contributor to the New Mexico Writers' Project from 1936 to 1941 (see Brown, Briggs, and Weigle 1978:3–34).

During much of his residence in Córdova, Brown served as a liaison between the community and Santa Fe artists and writers. His frequent guests during Holy Week included Mary Austin, Frank Applegate and his wife, the members of the Cinco Pintores (a group of artists), Aileen Nusbaum (a former director of the Writers' Project), Fremont Ellis, and others. Brown has recently recorded his recollections of these visits (Córdova 1972:9):

> For the most part, my guests were annual visitors—writers, artists, and friends from families with whom we were intimately acquainted in Santa Fe. In season, many were also my guests on pre-arranged fishing and hunting trips. We were a close-knit group, thoroughly enjoying the flow of conversation, which was as varied as the group itself.

The group would gather at Brown's house on Maundy Thursday. Although the major event was the observation of brotherhood processions, much of the evening was apparently spent roasting apples and piñon nuts over an open fire and engaging in conversation. Some of the guests stayed through the Tenebrae services of Good Friday night.

The most important aspect of this event for the present analysis was the contact between the visiting artists and writers and the native Córdovans. Over the years, several of the guests became fond of a number of villagers, and these visitors would ask Brown to take them to their friends' homes. A regular on these rounds was Guadalupe Martínez. As the caretaker of the images in the chapel, "Aunt Lupe" would give a tour of her charges (Córdova 1972:9–10). Her popularity extended beyond the confines of Brown's group; the guides of tours of northern New Mexico made her home "a regular stopping place" (Brown, Briggs, and Weigle 1978:137). Like José Dolores López, Martínez spoke no English, so Brown or his stepfather would translate.[5]

An inevitable outcome of this intercourse was the "discovery" of José Dolores López's carving art. The village-wide distribution of López's furniture, his participation in brotherhood activities, and his lively wit and outgoing nature would have made him a worthy find for an Anglo-

American visitor in search of the unique. Brown reports that he introduced Frank Applegate to López shortly after the former's arrival in New Mexico and that Applegate then acquainted José Dolores with Mary Austin. Since Applegate entered New Mexico in 1921 (Coke 1963:121), this places the "discovery" of José Dolores nearly half a decade after his innovation of the contemporary carving art. Applegate's and Austin's interest in López is reflected in their citation of his work in their survey of Spanish colonial arts and crafts (n.d.:159–60).

López's flamboyance and originality of artistic expression impressed Applegate and his friends. They found a man who was accomplished in several aspects of traditional Hispano technology and was related, although affinally, to the Aragóns, but who was far less constrained by nineteenth-century stylistic conventions. Although Applegate and Austin did not record their aesthetic evaluation of López's works in great detail, they did laud his combination of "the austere lines and expressiveness of the best modern sculpture" and a pervasive utilization of "the authentic folk touch" (n.d.:160).

In light of the disparity between the two groups' motives, native languages, and cultural backgrounds, the efflorescence of the wood-carving industry exhibits a remarkable serendipity. At about the same time that José Dolores López began selling to Córdova visitors, a number of Santa Fe artists, writers, and patrons of the arts initiated a series of changes that quickly and dramatically expanded the market for the works of López and other Hispano artists. The effect of Applegate and his friends on the industry was not, however, confined to an augmentation of commercial demand; their influence was quite substantial in determining the direction that the various genres would eventually take.

Austin, Applegate, and a number of other individuals shared a relatively well-formulated ideological position with respect to what they saw as the decline of Spanish colonial arts and crafts. One of their primary tenets was that enlightened patrons were indispensable in rekindling the dying embers of "native" (i.e., Hispano) art.[6] The faith of the patrons in their ability to accomplish this mission has been aptly summarized by Austin (1932:357, 358) in her autobiography: "About that time Frank Applegate and I had gone so far with the Spanish colonial arts that it seemed worthwhile to attempt their revival. . . . I . . . set the revival of the Spanish colonial arts in motion." Although attitudes toward Pueblo Indian arts were quite similar, the latter group received the bulk of the attention (McCrossen 1931:456; Mauzy 1935:65). Efforts to revitalize Hispano work centered on the "discovery" and "encouragement" of artists, and Applegate and Austin were prime movers in the search (McCrossen 1931:456).

An equally important tenet of this movement was that selectivity must be exercised in such encouragement. Reports written by leaders of the revitalization effort indicate that their goal was the isolation of purely "traditional," "colonial," or "Spanish" crafts from syncretic innovations (Anonymous 1926:104; El Pasatiempo 1931:4). The patrons defined the category of "traditional" Hispano art and determined which works conformed to this definition on the basis of their own historical assessment and aesthetic judgment rather than upon the Hispano artists' understanding of their heritage. Other central concerns of the Santa Fe patrons involved the quality and the originality of craftsmanship. An anonymous contributor to *El Palacio*, a central forum for the group, aptly summarized this position: "Mary Austin and Frank Applegate and a number of others have worked faithfully for the revival of these handicrafts and with great wisdom, encouraging the people not only to copy old designs but to create new ones in the same spirit of originality and play as did their ancestors" (1930:106).[7] The movement's ideological platform led to two primary modes of influencing the industry: the provision of new markets and the creation of competition between artists.

The first realization of these dreams took the form of the "revival" of the Santa Fe Fiesta in 1919. This early fall festival was intended to be "an event of national significance contributing to the renaissance of Indian arts, furthering a true appreciation of Indian drama and ceremonies, a perpetuation of Spanish folklore and traditions, and a better knowledge of Southwestern history . . ." (Anonymous 1924:24). Although more attention seems to have been paid the "Indian Fair," the first and subsequent fiestas included a "Spanish Market" or "Spanish Fair," which was housed in booths of aspen poles and cedar and piñon brush roofing (Anonymous 1919:103–28).

A more concerted effort to focus attention on Hispano arts came in 1925. A meeting called by Applegate and Austin in Santa Fe resulted in the formation of the Spanish Colonial Arts Society. Austin became the director, and Applegate was placed in charge of arts and crafts (*El Pasatiempo* 1931:4). Incorporated in 1929, the society is still active in fostering "traditional" Hispano work today.[8] One of the first courses of action adopted by the society complemented the annual Spanish Fair or Spanish Market during the Santa Fe Fiesta by adding to it the "Spanish Colonial Arts and Crafts Exhibition."[9] Although the market was held outdoors, first on the north edge of the plaza and later underneath the *portal* or awning of the Palace of the Governors, the exhibition took place within the Museum of New Mexico itself (Anonymous 1919:103; 1928:183).[10]

The commercial success of the annual exhibition led to the establishment of the Spanish Arts Shop by the society in Santa Fe's Sena Plaza in 1929.[11] The shop was managed for two years by Preston and Helen McCrossen and then for the remaining two years of its existence by Nellie Dunton (*El Pasatiempo* 1931:4; Mauzy 1935:67). Because its inventory consisted entirely of Hispano work, it provided a less ephemeral forum for the artists than that afforded by the fiesta activities. The staff of the Spanish Arts Shop influenced the development of the art through their selection of the artists represented and the articles chosen for sale. Similarly, the goods displayed in their shop helped to shape both artists' and customers' perceptions of what constituted "native" (i.e., Hispano) arts and crafts. They also influenced the artists more directly in the course of their periodic trips to the communities in which the artists lived, when the staff delivered materials and picked up finished products (Nestor 1978:9).

Plate 21

In June, 1934, shortly after the closing of the Spanish Arts Shop, Leonora Curtin (Paloheimo) subsidized the establishment of a non-profit "Native Market" on Santa Fe's Palace Avenue (see Plate 21). The market was first managed by Dolores Perrault, an employee of the New Mexico Department for Vocational Education, and later store managers included Pamela Parsons, Katherine C. Page, Eleanor Bedell, Roy Schoen, and Margaret Nelson (Nestor 1978:21). Nevertheless, artists, writers, and upper-middle-class Santa Fe *aficionados* also volunteered their time in steering the course of the market and thus of Hispano art. Such assistance included the staffing of a panel of judges who imposed "high standards of workmanship [that] were demanded in every article purchased for sale" (Mauzy 1935:68; also see Coan 1935:15).

The market was later relocated in 1937 in "El Parian Analco," a re-creation for tourists of a public market as it would have been in the 1880s and 1890s. Located three blocks south of the Santa Fe plaza, the facility included restaurants, crafts booths, a bar, and entertainment services in addition to the market. The Native Market was managed in its new location by Janette Lumpkins until its closing in 1939 (Nestor 1978:35–36; 46). Offshoots of the market included a branch (Tucson Native Market), a mail order business in Santa Fe, and an Alianza de Artesanos, a group of artists who kept the market facilities in operation for about six months after Leonora Curtin turned over its management to the group (1978:31–32; 52–53).

Although the Native Market bore a great resemblance to previous efforts to "revive" Hispano arts, it was also characterized by a number of differences. Leonora Curtin's motivating force in developing the market was to further the financial self-sufficiency of both the market and the craftsmen: "I therefore, in the Native Market, tried to discourage sentimentality and to uphold sound business principles" (quoted in Nestor 1978:18). The other departures of the market from previous efforts stemmed largely from this aim. A number of Hispanic artists were paid to display dyeing, *colcha* embroidery, weaving, carding and spinning, tinwork, furniture-making, and wood-carving techniques. These workers were employed primarily as a means of promoting sales; nevertheless, "village craftsmen who brought in their goods to the Native Market were given advice and instructions by these experts when they were needed" (1978:21–23).[12] As was the case with the Spanish Arts Shop, managers of the Native Market traveled to the vocational schools and to artists' homes in order to deliver raw materials (when necessary), pick up finished work, and to ". . . offer advice on techniques and designs" (1978:21).

Although the market's management subscribed to the familiar aesthetic canons of "tradition," "originality," and "quality," it was also most

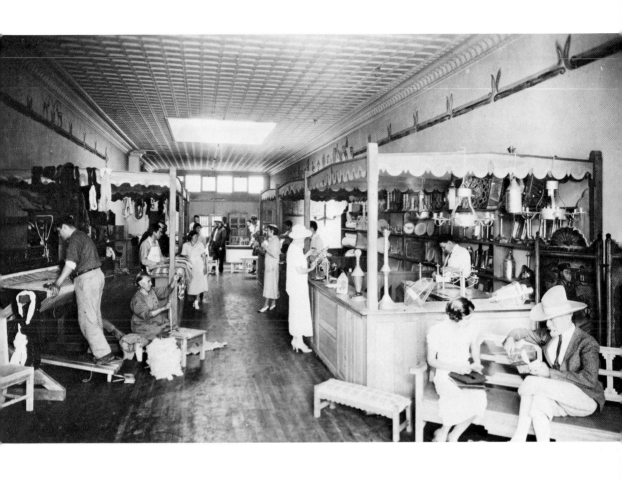

Plate 21. Interior of the Native Market, Santa Fe. The Hispano artists are at work; Dolores Perrault and artist Sheldon Parsons examine Hispano work in the foreground. Photograph by T. Harmon Parkhurst, courtesy of the Colonial New Mexico Historical Foundation.

anxious to respond to market tastes. Leonora Curtin's role in this process has been summarized as follows:

> Miss Curtin also provided numerous contacts for the store out of state, acting as a sales representative wherever she went. In addition she offered personal advice and guidance of the most practical kind, *seeing the Market as a sort of laboratory for the development of saleable products*. Correspondence shows, for example, that when clients complained about the finish on Native Market trays she did research and came up with a prescription for lacquer which worked. [Nestor 1978:32; emphasis mine]

Finally, previous efforts to induce competition among the artists and to encourage responsiveness to market tastes were surpassed in the operation of the Native Market.[13] A more direct attempt was made, for instance, to convince the Hispano artists to "produce more goods in less time for higher profits" (1978:33).

Unfortunately, the influence that this group of patrons exercised over the development of Hispano art has seldom been recognized in the extant literature. Hispanos during this period were considered to have lost interest in and knowledge of their own culture (i.e., material culture and folklore). Upper-middle-class Anglo-Americans and Hispano urbanites therefore considered themselves to be the logical agents for instilling ethnic pride among Hispanos and for reacquainting them with "forgotten" realms of Hispano folklife. As the noted writer Charles Lummis put it: "Outside appreciation is teaching [our Spanish people] to value more highly their own songs, dances, customs and arts" (quoted in Barker 1926:324).

Indeed, the Santa Fe patrons were in one sense appropriate leaders of the "revival" movement in Hispano arts. At a time when overt Anglo-American racism against both Hispanos and Indians was marked, the Anglo-American members of this movement were among the more sensitive and well-intentioned of the newcomers. Nevertheless, the "revival" involved a classically patronizing formula—the appropriation of control over an ethnic resource primarily by members of a superordinate society. Accordingly, the patrons attempted to direct the evolution of the art according to a set of principles that emanated from the concerns of their cultural milieu rather than from those of the Hispano artists.

The writers, artists, and other members of the Santa Fe intelligentsia who "revived" Hispano art were generally of at least upper-middle-class standing. As is the case in other parts of the United States (and elsewhere), one means of acquiring prestige in this class was the support of artists and musicians. This is usually accomplished through donations of both funds and volunteer labor (especially in serving on boards of directors, giving tours or lectures, and staffing the sales counters of non-profit shops). Beyond the support of professional artists and musicians, upper-middle-class patrons often aided working-class and ethnic groups who lacked professional training in "cultural" activities (i.e., folk music, theater, arts and crafts, etc.).

This second form of patronage proved especially important to Santa Fe patrons between 1919 and the beginning of World War II. The area offered little in the way of symphonic, operatic, and theatrical resources in comparison to the urban backgrounds of many newcomers and visitors. The patrons thus exploited the ethnic diversity of the region and its reputation as a mecca for artists and writers in fulfilling their need to foster artistic pursuits. Beyond the impressiveness of the landscape, the "exotic" quality of Hispano and Indian cultures and the appeal of the two artistic colonies (Taos and Santa Fe) fueled local efforts to create the image of New Mexico as a magical or spiritual "land of enchantment." To be unique, and thus to be distinguished from middle-class America, was a prime concern of the Santa Fe intelligentsia. This group's efforts to "revive" Hispano arts doubly served to satisfy their desire for uniqueness; it allowed them to exploit a set of cultural products that differed considerably from those of mainstream America and could enhance personal prestige while creating a distinct image of their region. This image further served to bolster their own collective self-image as well as to attract business. The movement thus emanated from and contributed to the concerns of Santa Fe's Anglo-American and Hispano upper middle class.

Needless to say, these concerns were hardly shared by early twentieth-century Hispano villagers such as José Dolores López. Anglo-American individualism contrasted sharply with Hispano emphasis on the integration of the individual within society. The Santa Fe patrons harbored a lofty ideal for their movement—the artistic, social, and economic "rehabilitation" of the Hispano people. As Austin (1932:359) noted "it was in the rebuilding of that shattered culture that the Society for the Revival of the Spanish Arts was concerned." Through a crafts "revival," it was believed that the self-confidence of a people could be restored and pride in an ethnic heritage could be instilled. This assessment of the demise of Hispano culture was surely greatly exaggerated. Moreover, the "revival" was initiated and administered primarily by persons of a different social class and, or cultural background. This difference generated a number of profound contradictions in the role of the patrons in the arts.

First, the patrons predicated their efforts, in Mary Austin's words (1932:336), upon the "possibility of the reinstatement of the hand-craft culture." Nevertheless, the majority of the patrons, including such principals as Applegate and Austin, were members of a society that conquered the area. In addition to supplanting Mexican with American governmental structures, the conquerors imposed an economic system predicated upon the replacement of handmade goods with mass-produced goods and the conversion of self-sufficient farmers and ranchers into dependent wage earners. Moreover, the Santa Fe patrons participated more directly in urging the artists away from a subsistence economy as well; they urged a close integration of Hispano art production with market tastes and fostered sales to customers from distinct cultural and religious backgrounds.

Second, although the patrons wished to enhance pride in the Hispano heritage, it was they who decided which areas of Hispano culture were to be "revived" and which direction the "revival" was to take. Their perceptions differed considerably from those of the Hispano artists, and the process of "discovery" and "encouragement" resulted in the transformation of many an artist's technique, style, and subject matter. Canons were ostensibly set according to the norms of Hispano art of the Spanish colonial or traditional period. Nevertheless, many of the objects produced in the course of the "revival" were either unknown during the colonial period or were put to a non-traditional usage by modern customers. Much of the repertoire of the period resulted from the imposition of currently popular "traditional" designs on objects such as lazy susans and record racks, which certainly had no Spanish colonial counterparts.

Finally, the Santa Fe patrons aspired to ameliorate the self-respect of Hispano artists and Hispanos in general. Unfortunately, such self-respect was not promoted by the patronizing manner in which many of the patrons interacted with the artists. Like José Dolores López, many of these individuals were descendants of highly skilled and prolific nineteenth-century artists, and they saw themselves as having the requisite talent "in the blood" or "in the family." Others had been surrounded by handmade Hispano products all of their lives. Most of the patrons, on the other hand, were newcomers. They took it upon themselves, however, to inform the Hispanos that they had lost track of their own traditions and sought to teach them both the characteristics of Hispano art and the way in which it was to be adapted to the modern world. The annual fiesta prize competition and the quality test of the Spanish Arts Shop and Native Market judges provided effective forums for the regular reassertion of the current definitions of each type of Spanish colonial arts and crafts.

The evolution of José Dolores López's wood carving provides a fitting example of the influence of the Santa Fe patrons on the artists. As noted above, his carving began as a response to the shock of his son's having been drafted to serve in World War I. Similarly, his hobby was first utilized in meeting the needs of López, his family, and his neighbors. Nevertheless, his contact with the Santa Fe patrons produced a number of changes that directed his work away from the local market.

First, Frank Applegate persuaded López to sell his works at the Santa Fe Fiesta in the early 1920s. Oral sources indicate that López anticipated the annual fiesta far in advance; he began compiling his inventory for the fall competition during the previous winter. He made most of his year's sales during the fiesta, and many orders were received at that time as well. Federico Córdova, a schoolteacher and justice of the peace, would take his uncle José Dolores, López's daughter Liria, and George López's wife, Silvianita, to Santa Fe on the first day of the fiesta. Carvings were brought in boxes and wash basins, and they were set up on a table for sale. López was later persuaded to sell his work in the Spanish Arts Shop and the Native Market (cf. Hare 1943).

Second, Frank Applegate and other patrons soon induced a change in José Dolores' technique. The furniture produced for Córdovans was generally finished with house paints, and bright colors were often complemented with current Mexican designs (refer back to Plate 13). López's polychrome technique proved to be rather too gaudy for the Santa Fe market, however, and it was suggested that he leave his work unpainted. Although López did sell a few pieces of polychromed furniture in Santa Fe (Boyd 1972: Personal communication), he largely heeded the patrons' advice and concentrated instead on chip-carving and incised designs.

Third, the promptings of the Santa Fe patrons also produced a change in the range of items that he produced for sale. He sold few of such traditional Hispano pieces as *relojeras*, or shelves for clocks, and clothes closets. On the other hand, he received many orders for non-traditional pieces such as lazy susans, record racks and, much later, screen doors, which he incorporated into his repertoire. Whether on the basis of personal inspiration or at the request of a patron, López began to market carved animals and his own versions of Swiss and German toys (see Boyd 1974: 471). In any case, the birds and animals were captured in interesting poses and often bore personifying facial expressions, and they proved quite appealing to both tourists and Santa Feans.

Finally, Frank Applegate induced López to produce unpainted representations of the saints, the Virgin, archangels, and Biblical personages. Although José Dolores only carved these figures during the last decade of his life (see below), his current fame is largely based on these representations. These images also constituted a dominant element in the work of José Dolores López's descendants. Since the carving of images formed an element of Hispano life as early as the seventeenth century, it would appear at first glance to be an easily comprehensible and traditionally sanctioned pursuit. Because of the fact that López and his followers sold such images primarily to Anglo-Protestant customers, however, a rift was formed between such sales and the activity of the eighteenth- and nineteenth-century image carvers. Thus, both the images themselves and the questions raised by their production in the twentieth century constitute a major focus of the work.

Because the López family has never kept any record of the carvings that its members have produced and sold, the exact chronology of José Dolores' artistic development is difficult to ascertain. Scattered published references and oral sources do concur, however, in the assertion that López did not produce images of the saints for sale prior to the late 1920s. From 1917 to about 1929, therefore, his work consisted primarily of furniture and, at a slightly later date, carved birds and animals. The highchair featured in Plate 22 provides a good example of López's unpainted furniture. Such pieces were generally made of pine, and the surface was often finished with varnish. Each section was separately carved, and then they were doweled and/or nailed together. This piece was

Plate 22

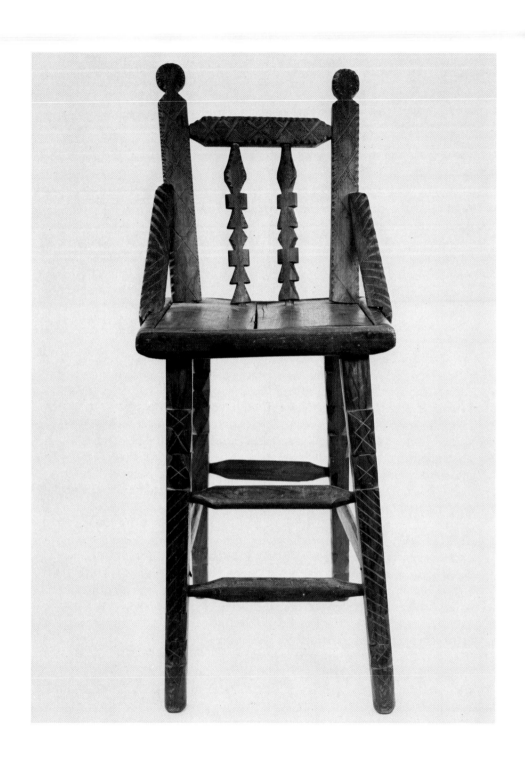

Plate 22. Carved Highchair by José Dolores López (59 cm. or 23.6 in. high and 26 cm. or 10.4 in. deep). The highchair is made of red cedar and pine. In the collections of the Spanish Colonial Arts Society, Inc., in the Museum of International Folk Art, Santa Fe.

54   *Beginnings*

produced as a gift for Fidel, Nicudemos López's son, and was presented to him as a Christmas present when he was one year old. It is accordingly signed by José Dolores and further labeled with the initials "F.L." and the date, December 27, 1924.[14]

Some items, such as the striking lazy susan shown in Plate 23, contained ornamental embellishment in the form of birds, leaves, and the like. The appreciation that this work received in the outside world was largely due to the simple repeated motifs, marginal patterns, and paneled decorations on the surface. Chip-carving was accomplished with a penknife. López incised similar designs on the chests that he produced for the tourist trade. The effect of pieces such as the one pictured in Plate 24 was enhanced by a black oil stain.

The artistic creativity that the Santa Fe patrons admired in José Dolores was quite apparent as well in his carved birds and animals. One group of small figures that López produced consisted of individual birds, squirrels, cats, pigs, and mice. As demonstrated by the birds shown in Plate 25, such pieces were heavily decorated with chip-carving. The designs served to articulate anatomical features of the species represented as well as to introduce purely decorative elements. The originality of López's works, a characteristic highly valued by his patrons, was often enhanced by the addition of a personifying facial expression or an identifying caption. Personification was also apparent in the second category of animal carvings, those involving multiple figures. Plate 26 illustrates *The Animal Musicians;* here López's humor was expressed only at the expense of many hours of labor. In addition to the seated animals, each of which plays a different instrument, a squirrel approaches a bird atop the pole. Similarly, the stylized pine tree in Plate 27, a good example of López's polychromed figures, is graced with three woodpeckers, each of a different species, and a chipmunk. The visual effect is heightened by the interplay of parallel and intersecting lines. López often placed birds and animals atop the branches of trees (see Plate 28). The prototypes for a third set of López's bird and animal carvings were Swiss and German toys (Boyd 1974:471). The birds in Plate 29, for example, are seated on an elaborate leaf. By operating strings on the bottom of the leaf, the impression is given that the birds are pecking the wheat. Here José Dolores came even closer to realizing his apparent goal of bringing the figures to life.

Another innovation was, however, soon added to López's repertoire. Many screen door frames were ordered by Santa Feans, including several for Mary Austin's home, and frames were shipped to other parts of the country as well. Oral sources assert that work on screen door frames constituted the majority of López's carving activity after he suffered a serious accident around 1933. Widely divergent examples of his frames are provided by the piece illustrated in Boyd's *Popular Arts of Spanish New Mexico* (1974:261) and by Plate 30. The former frame, in which José Dolores' initials are dominated by a menagerie of trees, birds, animals, and the like, still graces the doorway of a private home. The latter example was carved by López in 1929 for use in his own home, and it once

Plate 23

Plate 24

Plate 25

Plate 26

Plate 27

Plate 28

Plate 29

Plate 30

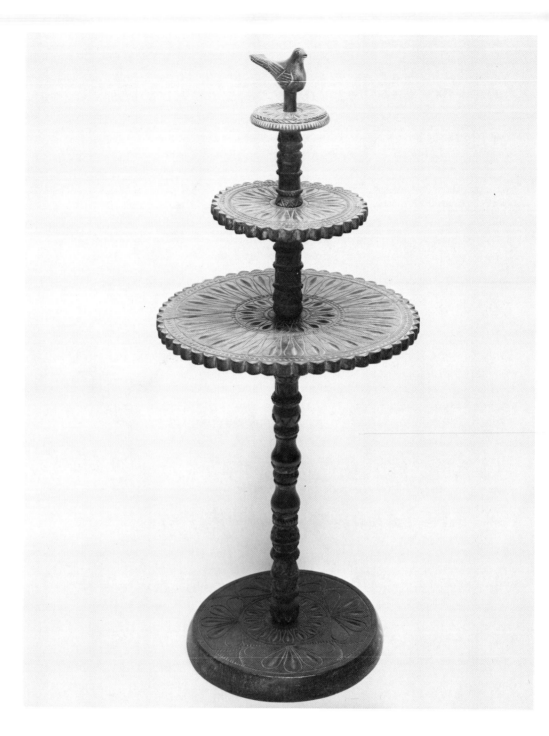

Plate 23. Ornate Lazy Susan by José Dolores López (118 cm. or 47.2 in. in height, largest tray 50.5 cm. or 20.2 in. in diameter). This piece was produced for sale at the Spanish Market of the Spanish Colonial Arts Society, about 1929. In the collections of the Spanish Colonial Arts Society, Inc., in the Museum of International Folk Art, Santa Fe.

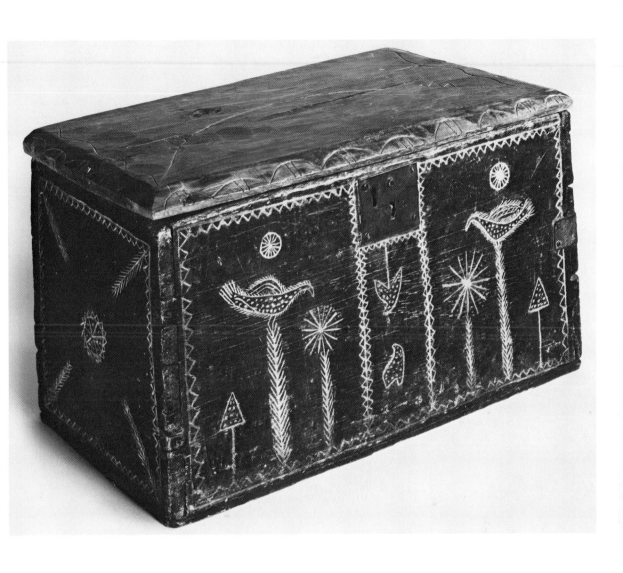

Plate 24. Incised and Stained Box, Possibly by José Dolores López (box 20.5 x 40 cm. or 8.2 x 16 in.). Note the bird and flower designs favored by López. In the collections of the Museum of International Folk Art, a unit of the Museum of New Mexico, Santa Fe.

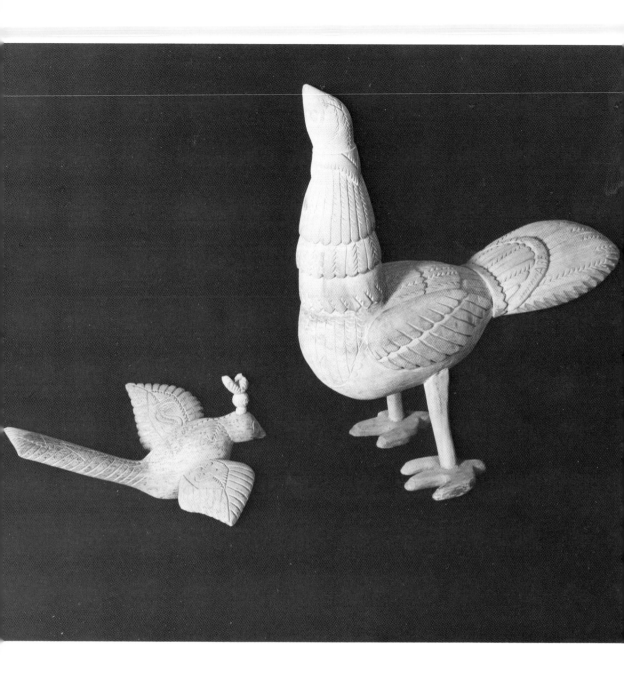

Plate 25. Rooster and Flying Bird by José Dolores López (rooster 35 cm. or 14 in. in height; bird 22.5 cm. or 9 in. in height, with a wingspread of 28 cm. or 11.3 in.). The rooster bears the words "Bird of Paradise" in Spanish on its tail. Both objects in the Taylor Museum Collection of the Colorado Springs Fine Arts Center: the rooster is a permanent loan from the U.S. Government, and the flying bird is a gift of H. H. Garnett; photograph courtesy of the Colorado Springs Fine Arts Center.

58   *Beginnings*

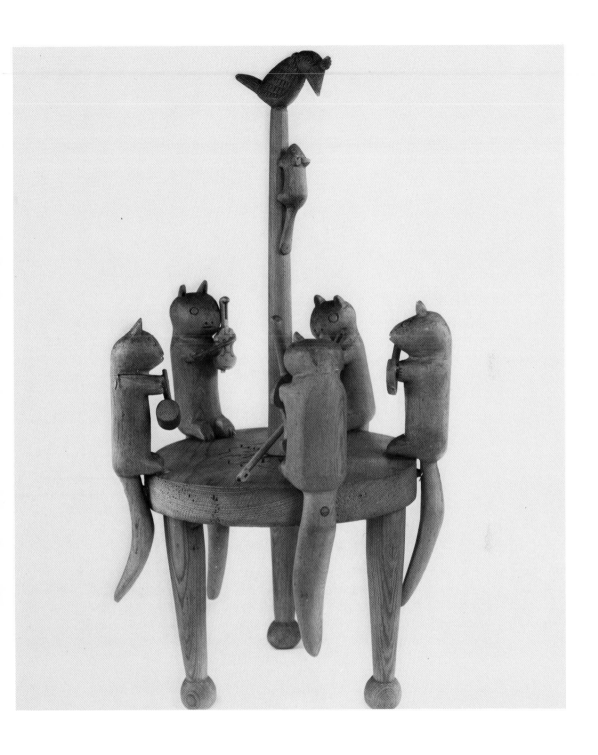

Plate 26. The Animal Musicians by José Dolores López (height 42.5 cm. or 17 in.).
In the collections of the Spanish Colonial Arts Society, Inc., in the Museum of
International Folk Art, Santa Fe.

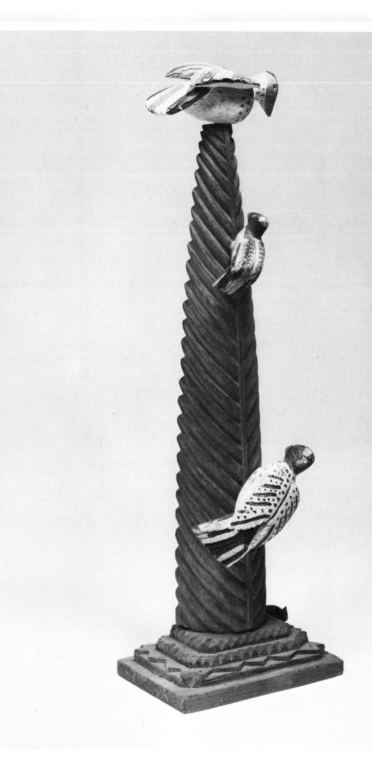

Plate 27. Pine Tree With Woodpeckers by José Dolores López (42.5 cm. or 17 in. in height). Photograph courtesy of the Denver Art Museum, Denver, Colorado.

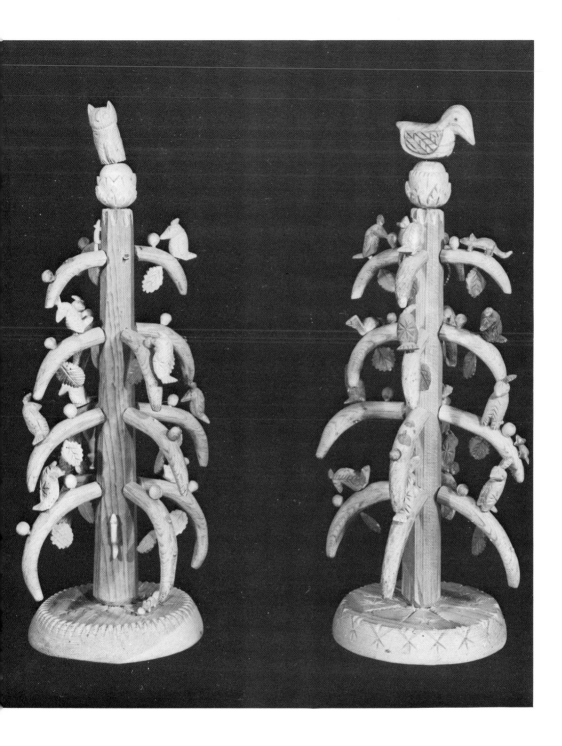

Plate 28. Two Trees by José Dolores López. Note the use of curved branches and the many animals in this early example of his work. From a private collection; photograph by Ernest Knee.

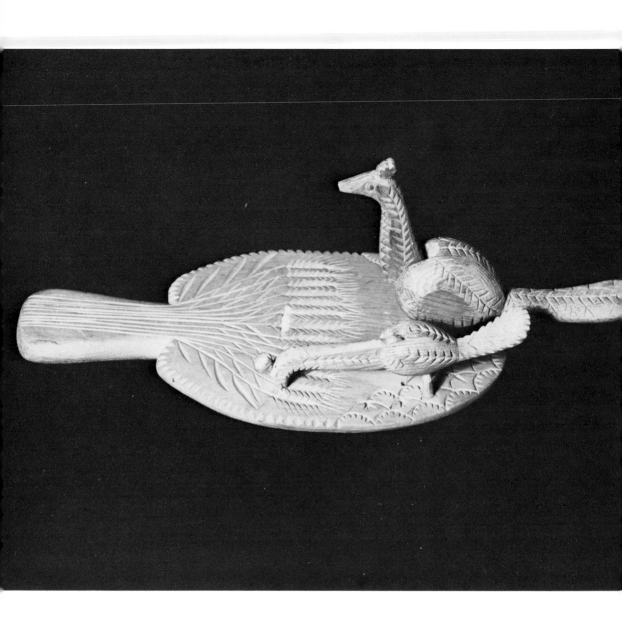

Plate 29. Birds in the Wheat, a Pecking Toy by José Dolores López (leaf 20 cm. or 8 in. in length, birds 15 and 10.5 cm. or 6 and 4.2 in. long). The birds' heads can be made to bob up and down when strings under the leaf are pulled. Collections of the Spanish Colonial Arts Society, Inc., in the Museum of International Folk Art, Santa Fe.

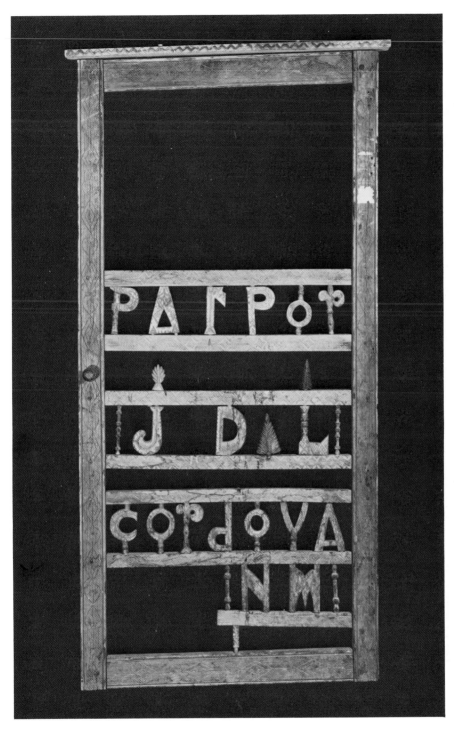

Plate 30. Screen Door Carved by José Dolores López for Use in His Own Home (height, 190.5 cm. or 76.2 in., width 96.7 cm. or 36.7 in.; date 1929). In the collections of the International Folk Art Foundation in the Museum of International Folk Art, Santa Fe.

boasted blue letters and green floral inserts. The conspicuousness of the artist's initials assisted customers in identifying his house.

Contrary to the assertions of other writers (e.g., Boyd 1974:468), López did not begin carving images of religious figures in 1917. López gained his initial reputation in Santa Fe through his furniture and animals, as attested by his first prize for a wall rack in the carved furniture category of the second annual prize competition of Spanish colonial arts in 1927 (Anonymous 1927:337). A full-page spread on López in the 1931 fiesta issue of the *Santa Fe New Mexican* lauds his continued success in securing awards but makes no mention of image carving.

López's impetus for image carving sprang from two sources. First, another Hispano artist, Celso Gallegos (1864–1943) had achieved great success in the fiesta market with his images by the late 1920s (see Plate

Plate 31 31). Gallegos, a resident of nearby Agua Fría, took first prize in the figure-carving section of the 1926 and 1927 Spanish colonial arts competitions as well as in later years (Anonymous 1927:337; *El Pasatiempo* 1931:6–9). Gallegos was cited in *El Pasatiempo* (1931:6) as being "one of the best known and beloved of the native craftsmen, and one of the most skilled." Gallegos carved both images and animal figures, and his media included both wood and stone. One of his stone carvings is shown in Plate

Plate 32 32. His early accomplishments in image carving certainly had an impact on López. The two artists were both pious, both were related to traditional image makers, and both served as sacristans. This mental picture of the pious carver of holy representations proved most attractive to the Anglo-American patrons.[15] Second, Frank Applegate's influence was the more direct, for it was he who encouraged López try his hand at making *bultos* (Hare 1943:21). This provides another example of the degree to which the Santa Fe patrons influenced the work of the Hispano artists.[16]

Although a full-page story on López in the 1931 *El Pasatiempo* does not mention his carving of any images, an anonymous contribution to *El Palacio* in September 1932 indicates that López had finished his portrayal of Adam and Eve in the Garden of Eden by that time (Anonymous 1932:120). In the case of these figures, José Dolores' prototypes for the group were contained in "an old book of French drawings which López displays with pride to his visitors" (Anonymous 1933:126). It is of interest that José Dolores López's use of filigree ornamentation and his reluctance to paint his images represent important stylistic departures from eighteenth- and nineteenth-century precedents.

Whether more than one complete set of carvings in this scene was ever completed is not known. An example of the Temptation in the Garden is present in the collections of the Taylor Museum, and this work is illus-

Plate 33 trated in Plate 33. The composition consists of three separate pieces, each with its own base. The underbrush in the foreground is termed the "Garden" by contemporary López family carvers. In the middle, Eve hands Adam the apple, while the Devil looks on from inside the tree in the background. Both tree and garden are composed of individually carved

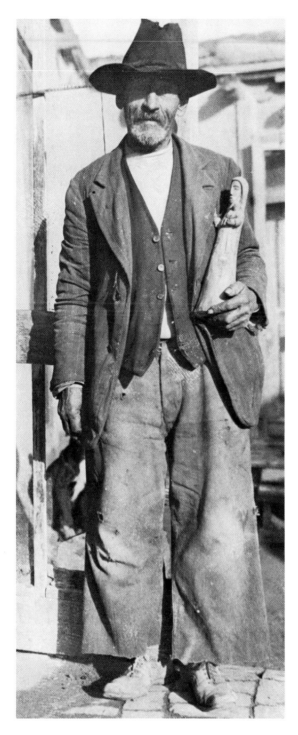

Plate 31. The Image Carver of Agua Fría, New Mexico, Celso Gallegos. From Arthur L. Campa, *Hispanic Culture in the Southwest*, p. 270. Copyright 1979 by the University of Oklahoma Press, Norman, Publishing Division of the University.

José Dolores López   65

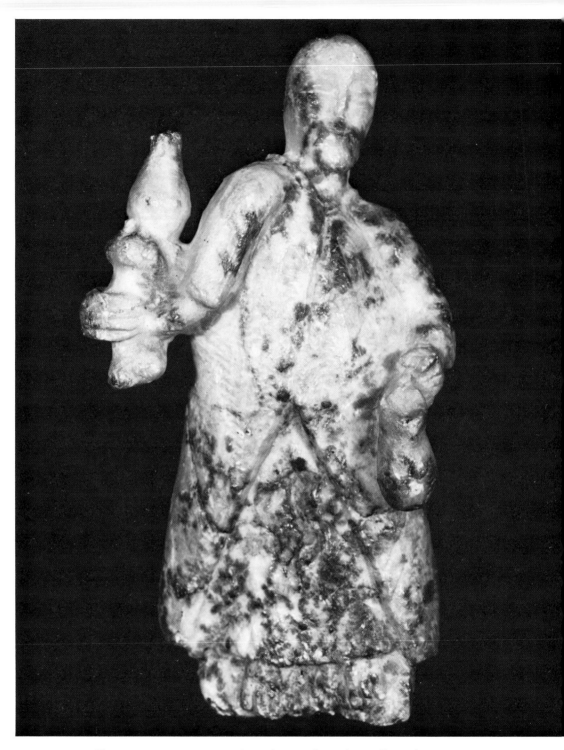

Plate 32. A Stone Carving of a Male Saint by Celso Gallegos (16 cm. or 6.4 in. in height). Cady Wells Bequest in the collections of the Museum of International Folk Art, a unit of the Museum of New Mexico, Santa Fe.

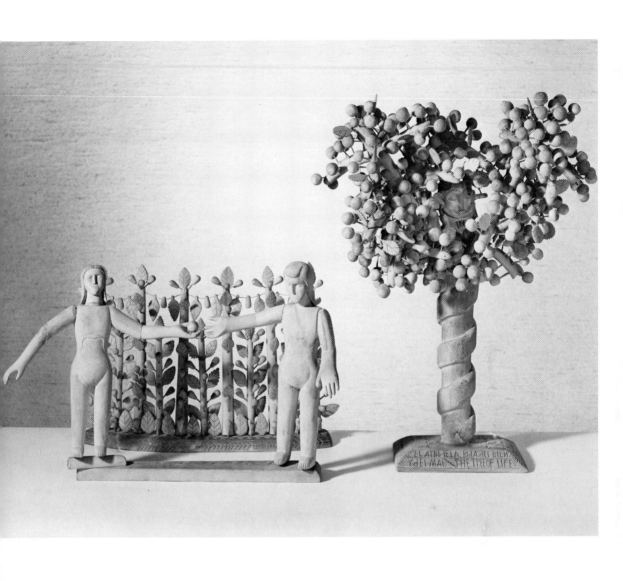

Plate 33. Adam and Eve in the Garden of Eden by José Dolores López (Adam and Eve 29 cm. or 11.5 in. in height, tree 52.5 cm. or 21 in. in height). "The Tree of Life of the Good and the Bad" is inscribed in English and Spanish on its base. Taylor Museum Collection of the Colorado Springs Fine Arts Center: Gift of Alfred I. Barton; photograph courtesy of the Colorado Springs Fine Arts Center.

José Dolores López   67

leaves, branches, and fruit, and the parts were doweled together once they were finished.

Plate 34   The episode is concluded in *The Expulsion*, featured in Plate 34. Here the figures are even more expressive, the stern countenance of the angel conveying the gravity of the situation; his sword (now missing) and the cross on his wings relate the divine sanctity of his mission. Adam and Eve conceal their embarrassment by hiding their faces while outstretched hands convey their submission. The didactic style of the figures in the Garden of Eden is further emphasized by the inscription on the base of the tree, which identifies the subject.[17] López used *poñe*, a bush whose wood is harder than aspen, in doweling the joints in his carvings. This enabled him to give his figures highly expressive gestures.

López's religious subjects were hardly confined to those contained in the Book of Genesis. His strikingly beautiful St. Peter as well as his Michael the Archangel and the Dragon similarly demonstrate López's pedagogic orientation. The large and elegant Michael the Archangel pic-

Plate 35   tured in Plate 35 bears the saint's name in Spanish on his helmet and
Plate 36   sword, while the Devil is clearly labeled in English. St. Peter (Plate 36) provides one of the most elaborate examples of López's inscriptions on images. The dove carved onto St. Peter's mitre is labeled "The Holy Spirit," and "San Pedro" decorates the other half of the mitre. The Bible in his right hand features a cross and the words "The Book of the Life of Jesus" on the outside with some pen-and-ink script on the inside; the key is marked "Saint Peter, the Door of Heaven." Both St. Peter and Michael the Archangel bear the signs of the cross, indicating the divine sanctity of their tasks. The name of the artist and his place of residence are also conspicuous on both images.

José Dolores López's more ambitious works were individually con- ceived and executed. As is evident from the representations of Michael

Plate 37   the Archangel shown in Plates 35 and 37, López's portrayals differed substantially from each other. Nevertheless, his images do share three features: much care is evident, first in the crispness of the chip-carved detail and second in the integration of facial and bodily gestures. This is

Plate 38   clearly exemplified in López's image of St. Peter (see Plate 38). The saint's eyes appear to be focused on the Bible, while his mouth conveys the impression that an act as serious as a pronouncement of salvation or damnation is soon to be made. His images, like well-executed three- dimensional art in general, were created with a concern for the reciprocal relations between graphic ornamentation and plastic design. Finally,

Plate 39   López was a master of finesse and delicacy, as is evident in Plate 39.

José Dolores López's *Nacimiento* (manger scene) contains the most individual pieces of any of his works and far more than the simple polychromed crèche he made for the Córdova chapel. The stable itself has

Plate 40   intricately carved roof beams and corbels (see Plate 40). The detailed chip-carving and sculptural finesse of López's larger images are matched by each of the three kings, Joseph, the Virgin Mary, and the Christ Child in this set. Care was taken to detail attributes in order to permit the

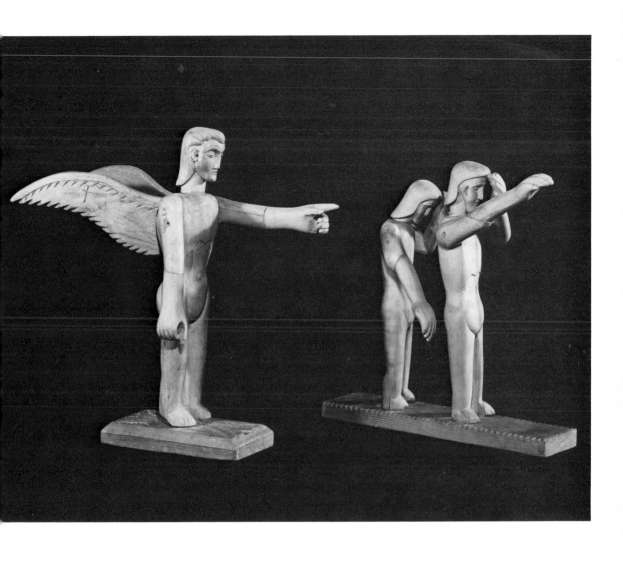

Plate 34. The Expulsion from Paradise by José Dolores López (base of Adam and Eve, 34 x 10 cm. or 13.6 x 4 in., Adam 32 cm. or 12.8 in. in height). Note that the angel's sword is now missing. In the collections of the Museum of International Folk Art, a unit of the Museum of New Mexico, Santa Fe.

José Dolores López 69

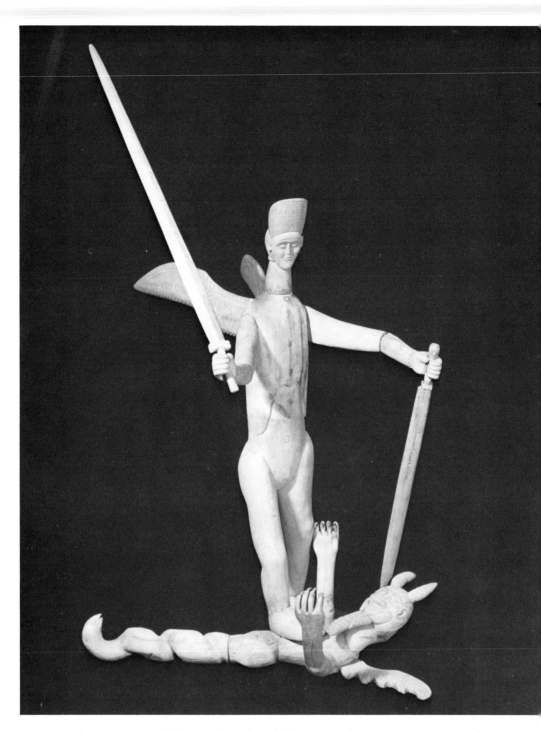

Plate 35. Michael the Archangel and the Dragon by José Dolores López (St. Michael 1.10 m. or 3.7 ft. in height; the dragon is 86.5 cm. or 35 in. in length). The modeling of the figures as well as their size is especially noteworthy. Taylor Museum Collection of the Colorado Springs Fine Arts Center: Gift of H. H. Garnett; photograph courtesy of the Colorado Springs Fine Arts Center.

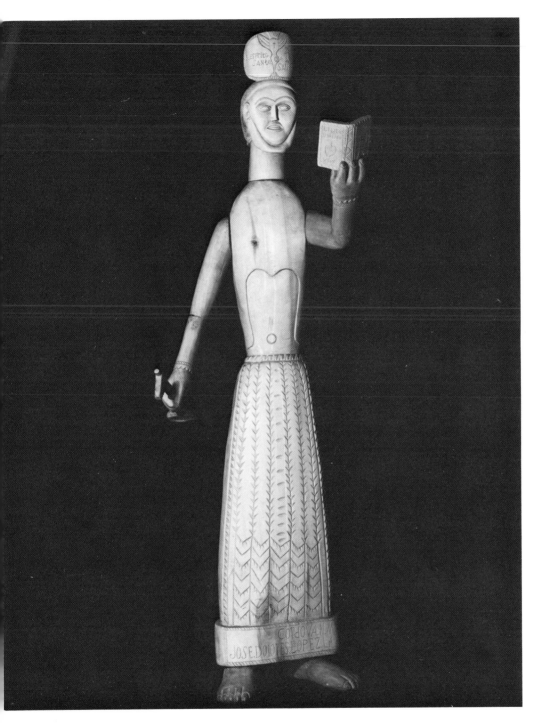

Plate 36. St. Peter with His Key and Bible by José Dolores López (height 1.35 m. or 4.5 ft.). This figure is interesting because of its impressive size, carefully articulated facial features, and symmetrical chip-carving. From the collection of Mr. and Mrs. Richard E. Ahlborn, on loan to the Museum of International Folk Art, Museum of New Mexico, Santa Fe.

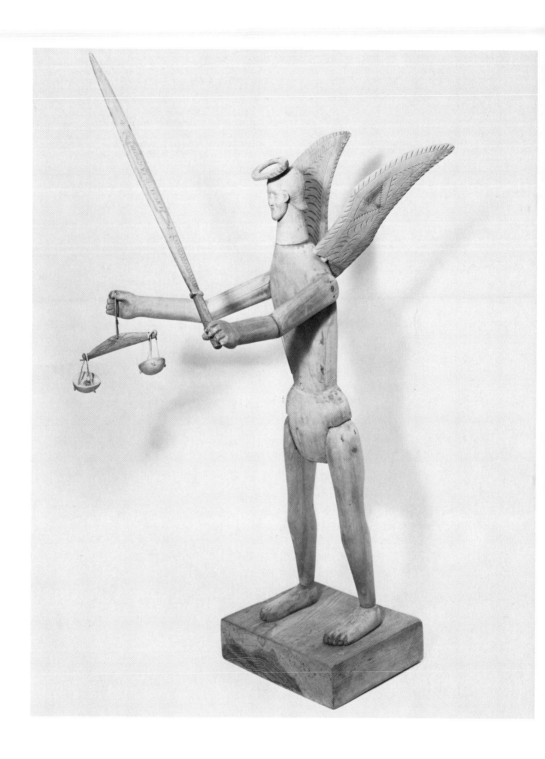

Plate 37. *Another Version of Michael the Archangel* by José Dolores López (95 cm. or 38 in. total height, wings 36.5 cm. or 14.6 in. long). From the Lepard Family Collection, on loan to the Museum of International Folk Art, Museum of New Mexico, Santa Fe.

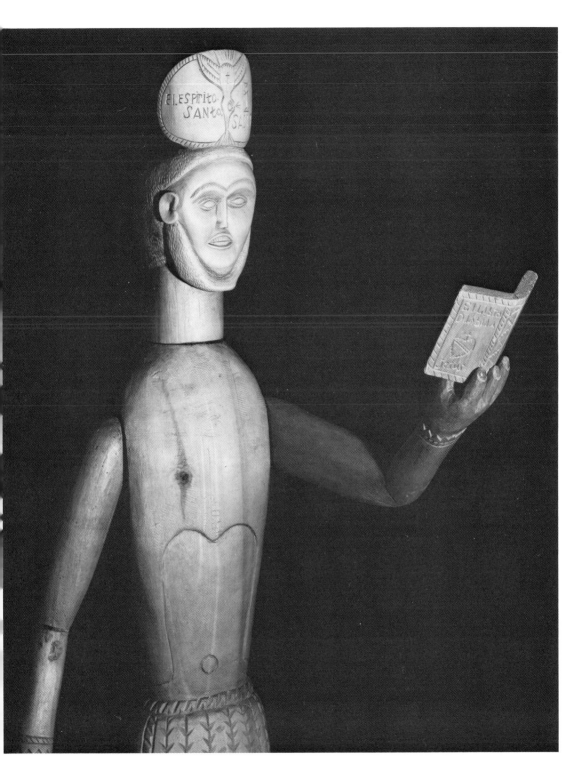

Plate 38. Detail of Plate 36, Image of St. Peter by José Dolores López.

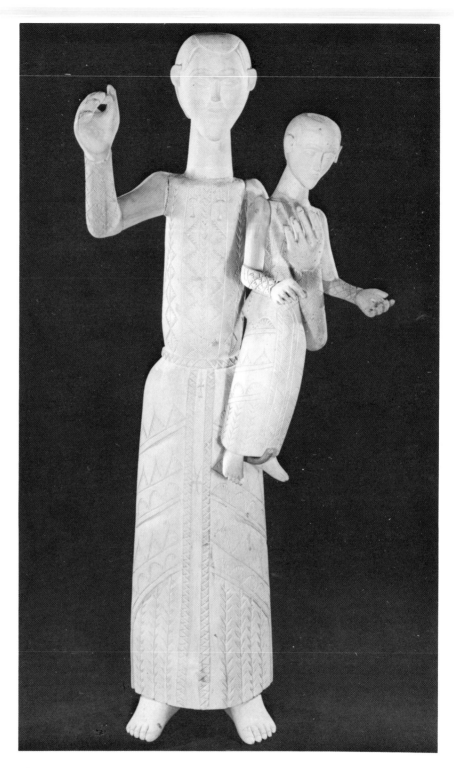

Plate 39. St. Anthony by José Dolores López. From a private collection; photograph by Ernest Knee.

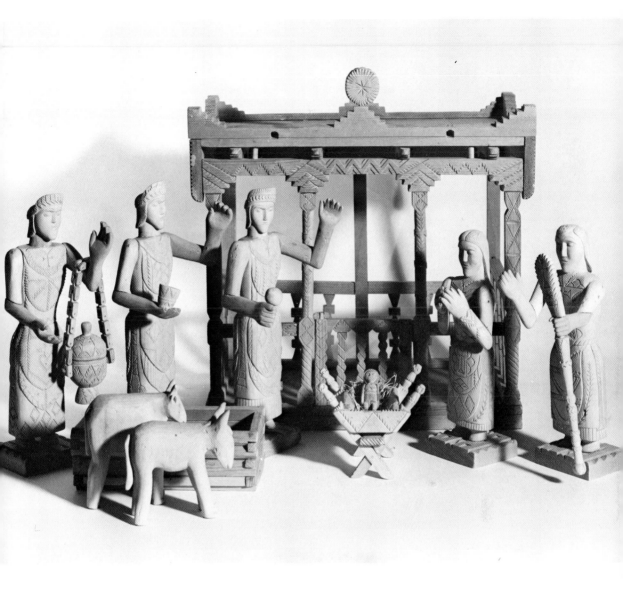

Plate 40. José Dolores López's Elaborate Manger Scene (base of stable 30 x 45 cm. or 12 x 18 in., figures 30 cm. or 12 in. in height). Taylor Museum Collection of the Colorado Springs Fine Arts Center; photograph courtesy of the Colorado Springs Fine Arts Center.

viewer to distinguish the characters. The set also contains a trough, a manger, and two animals.

Several more prototypes for López's works have come to light. José Dolores is said to have produced a number of figures of Death riding in a cart. These may have been modeled after the Death cart made by López's father, Nasario, which was kept in José Dolores' home before its sale (Wilder with Breitenbach 1943:40; refer back to Plate 11). José Dolores' versions demonstrate the influence of his father's style; they lack, however, the thin coat of gesso followed by light brown stain that graces Nasario's version. One of José Dolores López's more unusual representa- *Plate 41* tions of Death is shown in Plate 41.

López was also influenced by the work of José Rafael Aragón. Several of López's carvings depict subjects that were unusual for traditional image makers and had been portrayed by Aragón as well. López's *Flight into* *Plate 42* *Egypt* (Plate 42) and two polychromed *retablos* of the same subject by Aragón (illustrated in Boyd 1974:410 and Houghland 1946:24) show some similarities. Aragón also made one atypical horizontal panel in three sections showing Eve's creation from Adam's rib, the Temptation, and the Expulsion, which López might have seen in his youth (Boyd 1974:471). López's *St. Peter* (Plates 36 and 38) was also modeled on an image by Aragón that was located in the Córdova chapel.

López's *Our Lady of Light*, one of his most beautifully ornamented *Plate 43* works, provides a most striking example of this influence (see Plate 43). It appears that a painted image by José Rafael Aragón (refer back to Plate 10) offered a prototype for the halo of López's *Our Lady*. Boyd (1974:403) believed that Aragón's image was a representation of the Immaculate Conception; contemporary Córdovans consider it to be Our Lady of Sorrows. The seven heads on her gown, which they claim represent the Seven Joys and Sorrows of Mary, have led them to call her "Our Lady of the Seven Sorrows."[18]

A comparison of the images by Aragón and López reveals much about López's technique. While his intent was to portray an element present in Aragón's version, López transposed this feature into his own mode of *Plate 44* expression. As Plates 44 and 45 show, José Dolores suggested Mary's halo *Plate 45* with his filigree designs, whereas Aragón used his palette, and José Dolores used additional surface ornamentation to fill in the broad spaces that had been polychromed by Aragón. The result is a much more complex and intricate halo. George López relates that the smaller images of Our Lady of Solitude that both he and his father carved were modeled after Aragón's image (see Plates 51 and 52).

It is remarkable that José Dolores López devised and carved these images in less than a decade. His entire carving career was confined to the end of his life, even though he appears to have acquired all of the prerequisite skills much earlier. His great volume of carving during the last years of his life may be accounted for in part by his reduced economic responsibilities. His early carving was concentrated during the more

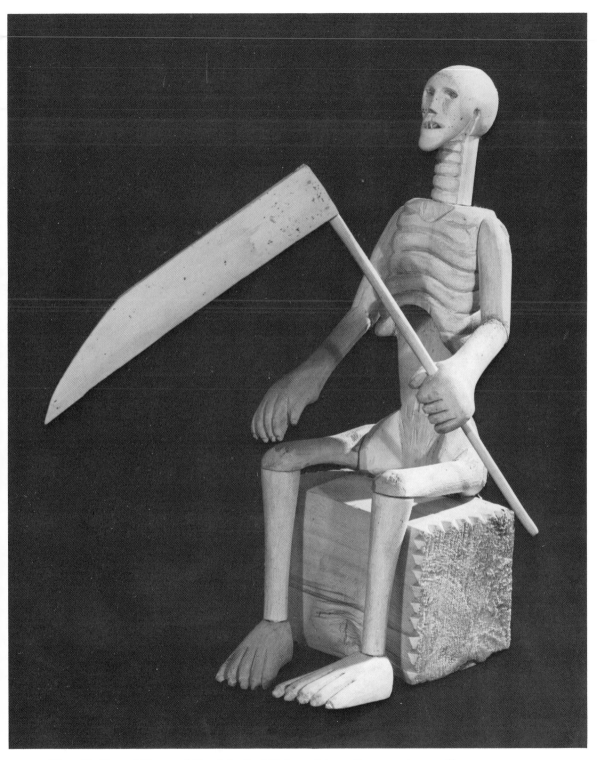

Plate 41. Carved Figure of Death by José Dolores López. From a private collection; photograph by Ernest Knee.

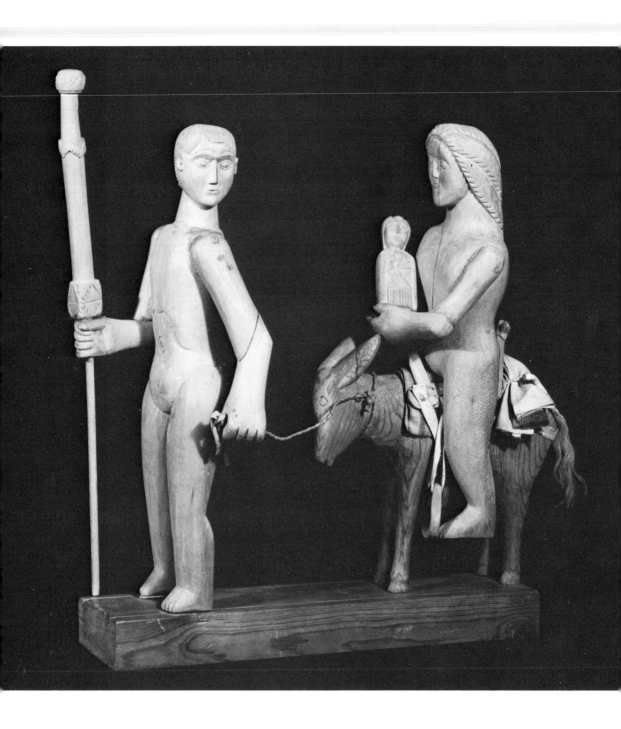

Plate 42. The Flight into Egypt by José Dolores López (base 7.8 x 32 cm. or 3.1 x 12.8 in., figure 32 cm. or 12.8 in. in height). In the collections of the Spanish Colonial Arts Society, Inc., in the Museum of International Folk Art, Santa Fe.

78   *Beginnings*

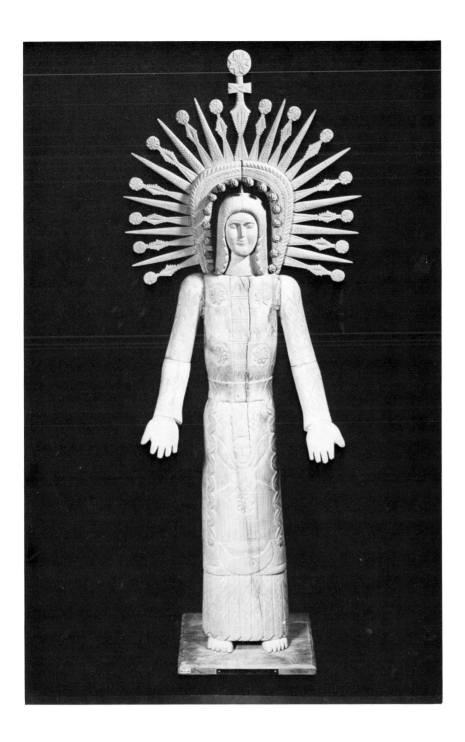

Plate 43. Our Lady of Light by José Dolores López (1 m. or 3.3 ft. in height). This image is one of the works by López purchased under the auspices of the Public Works of Art Project of the Federal Art Project. Taylor Museum Collection of the Colorado Springs Fine Arts Center: Permanent Loan from the U.S. Government; photograph courtesy of the Colorado Springs Fine Arts Center.

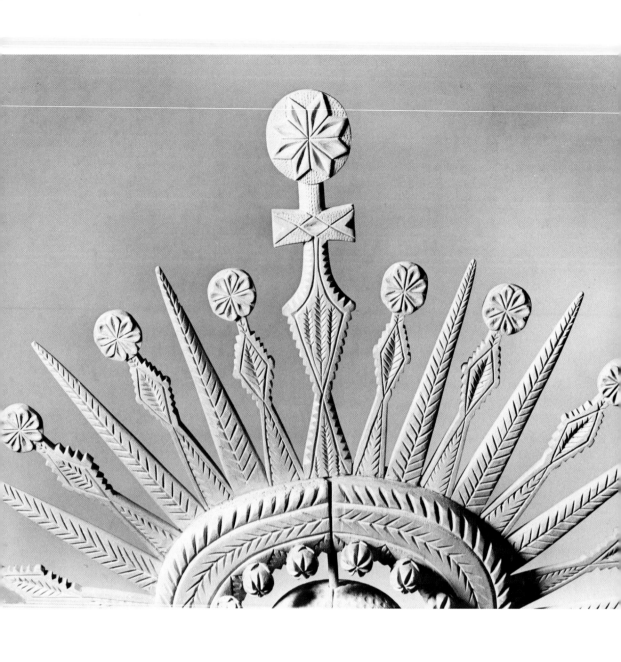

Plate 44. Detail of Halo from López's *Our Lady of Light* (Plate 43).

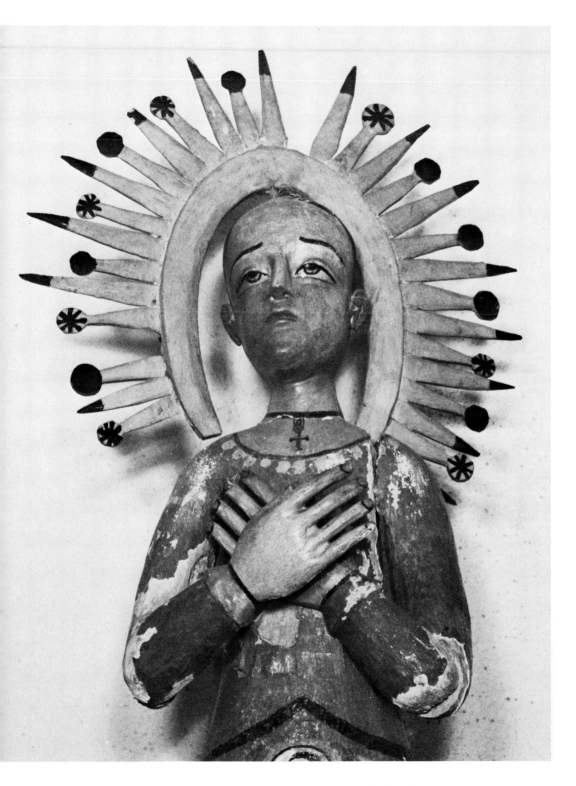

Plate 45. Polychromed Image by José Rafael Aragón, Detail of Halo.

leisurely winter months, and his farming duties lessened considerably when he handed over his lands to his four married sons.

José Dolores' career was cut short by an accident that he suffered while returning from Santa Fe about 1933. His stay in the hospital was paid for by one of his most avid patrons, the well-known newspaperman-politician Senator Bronson Cutting. López's convalescence restricted his range of activities for the remainder of his life. Although he continued to work occasionally on screen door frames, he was largely unable to attend to the rest of his carving. Shortly before his death, some of his Santa Fe friends visited him, and they did their best to assist López and the family. They bought many of his remaining carvings, and they gave the family a check to cover the funeral expenses.

José Dolores López died on May 17, 1937.[19] The importance of his role in the community was signified by his burial within the churchyard, just to the right of the chapel door. López's grave was marked by the cross that he had carved for himself early in his career, probably in 1917 (Brown, Briggs, and Weigle 1978:203–4). This cross was an intricately painted and carved matrix of intersecting smaller crosses, stars, squares, and the like (see Plate 46). Its destruction after 1945 resulted in its replacement with a cement marker (Boyd 1969:23). José Dolores is still remembered by older residents of Córdova, however, and a prayer is made for the welfare of his soul every year during the darkness of the Maitines and Tinieblas ceremonies of Holy Week. As his memory has lingered among community residents, his legacy has continued to influence the development of the contemporary carving art in Córdova. The next chapter considers the wood-carving industry that José Dolores López left behind.

Plate 46

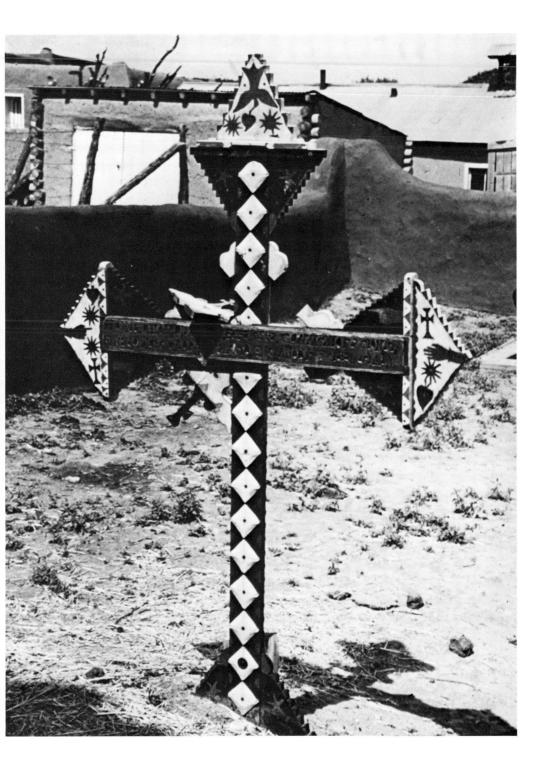

Plate 46. José Dolores López's Carved and Painted Cross As It Stood in the Cemetery of the Córdova Chapel. Photograph courtesy of the Taylor Museum Photographic Archives, Colorado Springs Fine Arts Center.

4.

The Expansion of the Industry

After the preceding outline of the motivation of the Santa Fe patrons for their participation in the "revival," it is only fitting to consider the Hispano motives as well. About the time that José Dolores López began carving (1917), Córdovans and other Hispanos were witnessing rapid changes in the world around them. This was especially evident with regard to the source of subsistence for the rural population. Access to farming and grazing lands had formed an important element of personal, familial, and community identity, and the reputation accorded a man and his family was based largely on the manner in which these resources were exploited. The life of the *ranchero* or farmer/rancher was an important cultural ideal, and the independence of working the land, working for oneself, was highly valued.

Nevertheless, the American conquest of 1846 and the coming of the railroads in 1879–1880 signaled a surge in commercial interests in the Territory of New Mexico. A prime element of this commercialization was the transfer of land from subsistence uses to commercial exploitation, especially large-scale cattle and sheep ranching. Such transfers were fueled by the imposition of Anglo-American land tenure principles onto Hispanic juridical procedures and local practices (cf. Van Ness 1976a). The appropriation of Córdova's land base and the response of its people to the situation are described below.

Livelihood was traditionally split between agricultural exploitation of the limited irrigated plots in the Quemado Valley and beyond, and the grazing of livestock, mainly goats and sheep, in the uplands surrounding the community and extending as far as the Truchas Peaks. This usufruct was not confirmed to the Córdovans by the Court of Private Land Claims, however, and it reverted to the public domain. On January 11, 1892, these lands became part of the Pecos River Forest Reserve (a copy of the presidential proclamation is on file in the office of the forest supervisor, Santa Fe National Forest). The rights of residents to graze their livestock on the uplands does not appear to have been restricted during either of these tenures. By an executive order dated April 6, 1915, however, the Pecos and Jemez National Forests were merged into one unit, known and administered as the Santa Fe National Forest. The secretary of agriculture was given the authority to manage the range resources on lands administered by the Forest Service under the Organic Act of June 4, 1897 (Forest Service 1970:iii). A series of changes in grazing regulations deprived Córdovans of nearly all of the subsistence that they formerly derived from the grazing of livestock. The Forest Service's reasons for this action involved the erosive dangers of overgrazing, which did indeed pose a threat in some areas. A limited number of grazing permits were issued, and subsistence goatherding was excluded in favor of cattle production. Furthermore, commercial operators gained control over large numbers of permits (Harper, Córdova, and Oberg 1943:63). In short, Forest Service policies resulted in the loss by Córdovans and other Hispanos of nearly all the subsistence they formerly derived from the grazing of livestock.

Since Córdovans had never been able to subsist entirely on garden produce, this undermining of their subsistence base forced them to depend on outside employment. This phenomenon was not wholly new; Córdovans had engaged in outside employment even during the Spanish colonial era. After 1915, however, Córdovans had to sell their labor to an unprecedented degree and to work for employers of a different cultural background. This situation, along with the transition from a predominantly barter to a predominantly cash economy and the replacement of locally produced goods with mass-produced goods, created a growing need for cash income.

Córdovans resorted to a number of types of migratory wage labor in coping with this situation. The building of railroads and the expansion of mining and other nonagricultural enterprises in the area, the harvesting of sugar beets, onions, potatoes, and other crops during the Colorado harvest, and the sheep camps of Colorado, Utah, Wyoming, Montana, and New Mexico all provided opportunities for outside work (Siegel 1959:38; Soil Conservation Service 1937a:2; Harper, Córdova, and Oberg 1943:77). It has been estimated that prior to the depression, 7,000 to 10,000 workers from the villages of the middle Río Grande Valley, the land drained by the Río Grande between Elephant Butte and the New Mexico–Colorado line, left each year to engage in these types of migratory labor (1943:76–77). This pattern resulted in a large dichotomy between the experience of persons of José Dolores López's generation and that of his children. His son George López, for example, began working in the sheep camps at the age of fifteen, in section gangs when he was eighteen, and subsequently at Colorado harvests. The younger López describes this difference:

> [My father] stayed at home. He never went out to work for another. He had his farmwork, and he had his farm plots, you see. His sons went out to work for others, but he stayed home and did the farmwork. I left for Chama when I was fifteen. I worked that summer, that's all. We didn't last very long working like that for others, you see, just for short periods of time. Because in the winter, a person stays at home and doesn't go out to work. When there was work a person went out, and when there was

none, he stayed here. Because in those times life was hard, very hard, because there was little work. The state was very poor. A person was here when there was no work. It was very hard on the people.[1]

Although Córdovans and other Hispanos had become highly dependent upon such employment, this source of income was sharply curtailed with the onset of the Great Depression. After the depression gained momentum, earnings from outside work were reduced by as much as 80 percent (Harper, Córdova, and Oberg 1943:77). Widespread starvation was prevented by the implementation of many federal work projects, but this was merely a stopgap solution.[2] The depression proved to be a bitter cup for rural Hispanos to swallow, as this constriction of outside employment made the residents even more painfully aware of the expropriation of land resources.

American artists in general were strongly affected by the depression. Accordingly, the Federal Art Project was organized as a part of the Works Progress Administration in 1935, and the New Mexico F.A.P. was launched in October of that year (Writers' Program 1940:169).[3] A number of Hispano artists were assisted by the Art Project, and, like other forms of outside "encouragement," this help influenced the development of Hispano art. The F.A.P. backing of Hispano artists assumed two primary forms. First, Brice Sewell directed a program of the state's Division of Trade and Industrial Education that fostered the creation of community vocational schools. Artisans were employed as instructors; students were trained in the techniques involved in production and marketing (Coan 1935; Mauzy 1935; Sewell 1935).[4] The Native Market provided an outlet for the students' products, and the two programs shared a similar set of goals (Nestor 1978:11–23). Second, the New Mexico F.A.P. directly subsidized the work of 206 artists between 1935 and 1939 under the direction of Vernon Hunter (Writers' Program 1940:169). The famed Taos wood carver Patrocinio Barela (1908–1964), for example, began carving in 1931, and by 1936 the Federal Art Project was providing his salary and exhibit-

Plate 47 ing his works nationally (Cassidy 1936:25; Crews 1968:9) (see Plate 47). The eight years that Barela was employed by the F.A.P. were highly influential in the course of his artistic development: "[The] W.P.A. years [were the] best time," he once said, since he was then able to devote more time to his carving (Crews et al. 1962:8). Margaret Berg (1965) wrote, "During this period he became more creative and broke away from the 'Santero' heritage . . ." (this trend is illustrated by the Barela carving

Plate 48 shown in Plate 48). The Lópezes were never employed by the F.A.P. Nevertheless, several of José Dolores' more ambitious pieces were purchased with Federal Art Project funds, and both his and George López's works were exhibited in traveling shows in the U.S. under the sponsorship of F.A.P. Director Holger Cahill. These exhibitions greatly increased the attention that such Hispano artists as José Dolores, George López, and Patrocinio Barela received from audiences outside New Mexico.[5]

A more permanent solution for this acute impoverishment followed the influx of population and capital into New Mexico during and after the

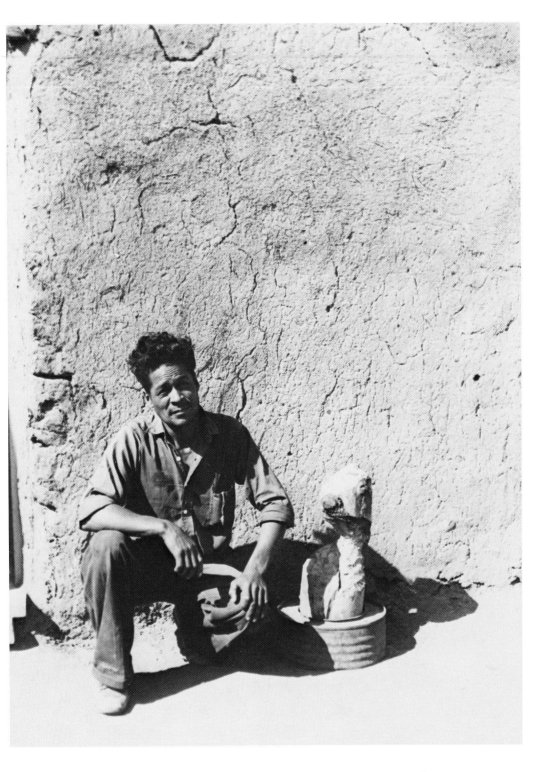

Plate 47. Patrocinio Barela, Taos Wood Carver, 1908–1964. Photograph courtesy of the Photographic Archives, Museum of New Mexico, Santa Fe.

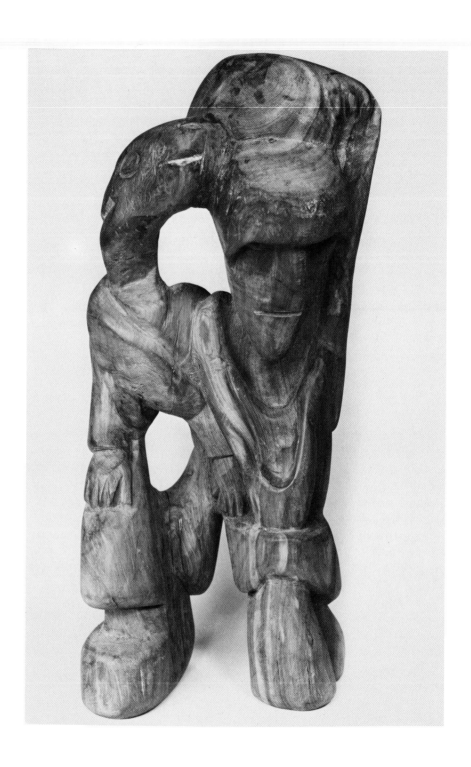

Plate 48. El Divino Pastor by Patrocinio Barela (43.5 cm. or 17.4 in. in height). On one side a man is represented, while the other portrays a man and an animal. In the collections of the International Folk Art Foundation in the Museum of International Folk Art, Santa Fe.

war. Much of this growth was associated with the federal installations in Albuquerque and Los Alamos. The Los Alamos facility and the service industries that grew in its shadow provided opportunities for daily wage labor, a new source of cash income for residents of the area. The participation of Córdovans in the national economy was further enhanced by improved accessibility to the community. Before 1946, the road to Córdova was little more than a trail, and daily travel to Santa Fe or Los Alamos was impossible. In that year, however, the road that traverses the plain above Córdova was graded and maintained with gravel, and in 1953 it was paved.[6]

In short, Córdovans were confronted with a conflict between the need to leave their community to obtain cash income and their desire to work their own land and to remain independent. Wood carving provided one means of dealing with this difficult situation. The sale of carvings became a compromise between two ways of life. On the one hand, sales of carvings helped provide a few Córdovans with necessary cash. By relying on his agricultural produce and the few head of cattle that he kept after 1915, José Dolores López was able to exist without having to leave the community in search of employment. Remaining in the community throughout the year enabled residents to participate in both life crises and community rituals, thus supporting important elements of Hispano culture. On the other hand, however, setting up a wood-carving shop resulted in the singling out of its proprietors for prolonged and unusual contact with the outside world. Furthermore, Córdovans who did not carve often reacted with distaste to the carvers' intercourse with outsiders, believing the artists to have encouraged the intrusion of members of a society that had appropriated Hispano lands in order to grow rich. The difficulty of the situation was compounded by the fact that the carvers sold images of the saints, objects of great importance in Hispano Catholicism, to Anglo-Protestants. The complex way in which the contemporary wood-carving industry interacted with other cultural and historical forces of the time appears to have largely determined the course of its evolution during the next half-century.

José Dolores López married Candelaria Trujillo in 1893, and they had seven children. Nicudemos was the oldest, born in 1894, and he was followed by Rafael in 1897, George in 1900, Ricardo in 1902, and María Liria in 1910. The couple's other two sons, Epitacio and Alfredo, died in childhood. Candelaria died in 1912, and López wed Demetra Romero the following year.[7] His second marriage was childless. López involved his children in the management of the household at an early age, and he brought them into the carving industry as well. His daughter, Liria, who stayed on the hearth with her father, began carving quite early. George took up the craft in 1925, his younger brother Ricardo did so in 1927, and the oldest son, Nicudemos, followed in 1930.

Although two of López's children became more highly acclaimed for their carving than the others, differences in innate artistic talent do not appear to have been responsible. Rather, two general social and economic factors affecting Córdova and other regional communities seem to have been much more influential in determining the development of the local carving industry.

The first factor, and the one that seems to account for Liria's greater success in the early years, is the growing importance of migratory wage labor in Córdova during the first half of this century. While Liria was hardly the only one of José Dolores' children with an interest in wood carving, her greater proximity to López provided her with more time to observe her father's carving and to try her hand at the art. She accompanied her father on fiesta selling trips, and here, as well as at home, she became acquainted with López's patrons. The boys, however, were away a good part of the year, and they were much less involved in the industry.

Plate 49
By the time of the elder López's death, Liria had become a competent producer of small trees, birds, mice, pigs, and boxes (see Plate 49). In her words, "I did everything except the images." Furthermore, she had gained some recognition by outside patrons of Córdovan carving. Speaking of George, Ricardo, and Liria, Brown writes: "Of the three, the daughter excelled in the work, and in time her work developed individual characteristics as eagerly sought as those of her teacher" (Brown, Briggs, and Weigle 1978:206).

José Dolores' death altered his children's participation in the industry. Liria left Córdova before long, and she never went back to her carving after moving to Santa Fe. These two events opened up the seller's market for Córdovan carvings considerably. José Dolores had ranked above his sons in terms of production and public recognition earlier; no other Córdovan gained such pre-eminence for several decades. George and his wife Silvianita responded first to the opportunity, but Ricardo and wife Benita were not far behind. Similarly, the monetary value of José Dolores' works increased greatly following his death.

George's early work is quite interesting in many respects. First of all, his repertoire was greatest at this time. He produced a number of images similar to those being made at the time by his father, and he experimented with such items as lazy susans and screen door frames. Furthermore, it is clear that when he had the time to carve he devoted considerable care to each figure. George's early carving was stylistically so close to that of his father that in some cases only minute differences permit one to distinguish between them. For example, compare *The Flight into Egypt* by José Dolores López (Plate 42) with a carving of the same subject by George
Plate 50
López (Plate 50).

Although José Dolores' work may exhibit greater finesse, George's image shows greater elaboration. Note, for instance, the flowering staff and carpenter's tool box on George's *Flight*. George's figures dwarf the donkey to a greater extent than do those of his father, and the bodies are more massive. *The Tree of Life* by George López in the collection of the Taylor Museum is quite similar to José Dolores' *Tree of Life* in the same collection. It is clear that the prototypes that George utilized in his earlier carvings were provided by his father's work. Only a small reduction in the

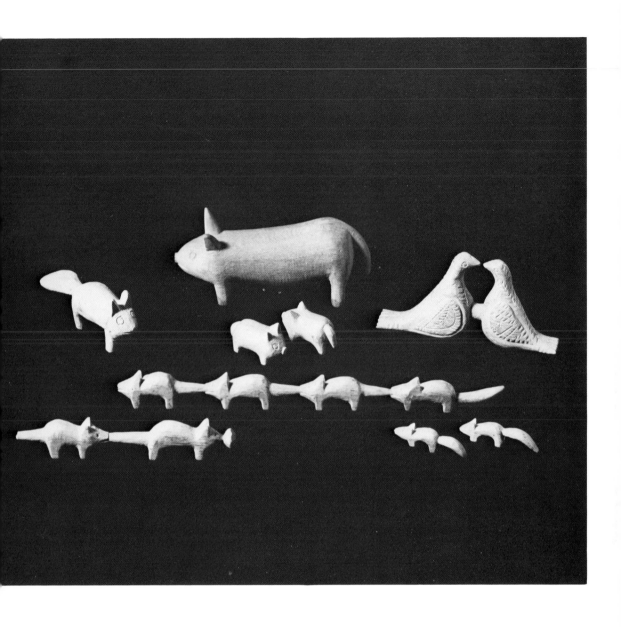

Plate 49. Small Bird and Animal Figures by Liria López (de García) (maximum length 3.75 cm. or 1.5 in.). Taylor Museum Collection of the Colorado Springs Fine Arts Center: Gift of Alice Bemis Taylor; photograph courtesy of the Colorado Springs Fine Arts Center.

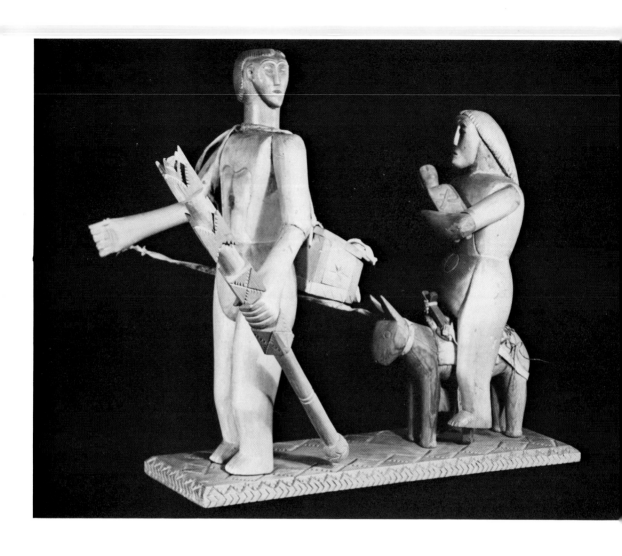

Plate 50. The Flight into Egypt by George López (base 41 x 12 cm. or 16.4 x 4.8 in.,
Joseph 36 cm. or 14.4 in., Virgin 31 cm. or 12.4 in.; made prior to 1941). In the
collections of the Spanish Colonial Arts Society, Inc., in the Museum of International Folk Art, Santa Fe.

amount of chip-carving on the trunk of George López's renditions of Our Lady of Solitude along with a slight modification in the anatomical proportions permit one to distinguish them from the prototypes by José Dolores. (The elder López's image is illustrated in Plate 51; George's is shown in Plate 52.)

Plate 51
Plate 52

A second factor that affected the success of José Dolores López's children in the carving industry was the availability of daily wage labor at Los Alamos. Like his brothers Rafael and Ricardo, George López was employed at Los Alamos. He first worked on the road to Los Alamos in the early 1940s, and later in the city itself. There he performed a variety of tasks, including work on the community water system and on construction jobs. At this time the wood-carving industry occupied the same economic niche that it had in José Dolores' day: sales had never provided an adequate income by themselves but had supplemented diverse occupational pursuits. Prior to World War II, carving earnings had augmented migratory wage labor and agricultural and pastoral income. Subsequently, carvings boosted the low wages secured by Córdova's primarily unskilled labor force. George López has aptly summarized the situation as follows:

> There was none of this carving before. I began carving after my father died in '37. I made a few small things before, but I never carved steadily. Because when we were [working] in Los Alamos I didn't carve. A person came back tired from there. Well in those times he [i.e., José Dolores López] stayed here and did the farmwork and one [i.e., his sons] went out for periods [to work]. Because that was what life was like before. And when I left work at Los Alamos I had farmwork to do here.

López later explained that he was speaking of his pursuit of carving as a primary vocation at these times; his work before 1937 and during the Los Alamos years was, more precisely, sporadic. George López's carving during this intermediate period of daily wage labor differed from other phases of his work in terms of style as well as in the rate of production. The preceding quotation illustrates the fact that George could devote little time and energy to carving during his years of daily wage labor. Accordingly, he developed a greatly simplified style during this period. Although his figures were still carved with a reasonable amount of care, the filigree surface ornamentation was reduced to occasional marginal designs (i.e., those accentuating the border between parts of a carving). Plate 53 shows one of the best examples of George López's intermediate style, a St. Isidore that he carved in 1949.

Plate 53

Apart from the fact that George López carved images at this time and his brothers did not, there appears to have been little difference in terms of style and quantity of production between the carving of George, Rafael, and Ricardo López. Following 1952, however, this situation changed radically. Nicudemos had moved to Truchas and was pursuing his calling as a carpenter there. His participation in the carving industry was apparently negligible at this time. Ricardo and Rafael continued to carve during

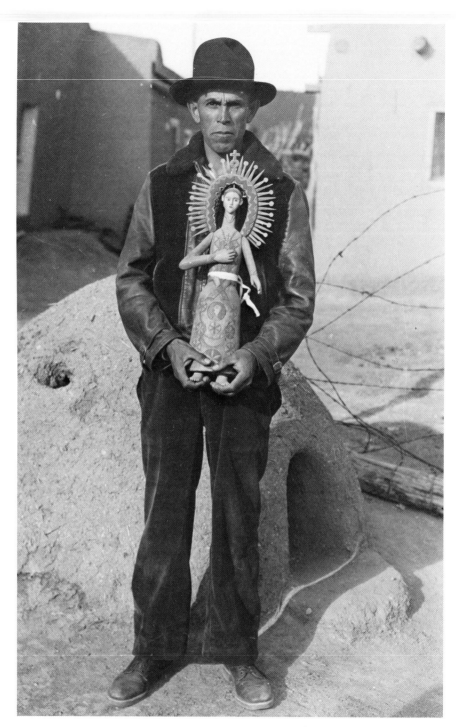

Plate 51. George López Holding a Representation of Our Lady of Solitude. Since this photograph was taken during the tenure of the Federal Art Project (1935–1939), the image is believed to have been carved by José Dolores López. Courtesy of the Photographic Archives of the Museum of New Mexico, Santa Fe; photograph by T. Harmon Parkhurst.

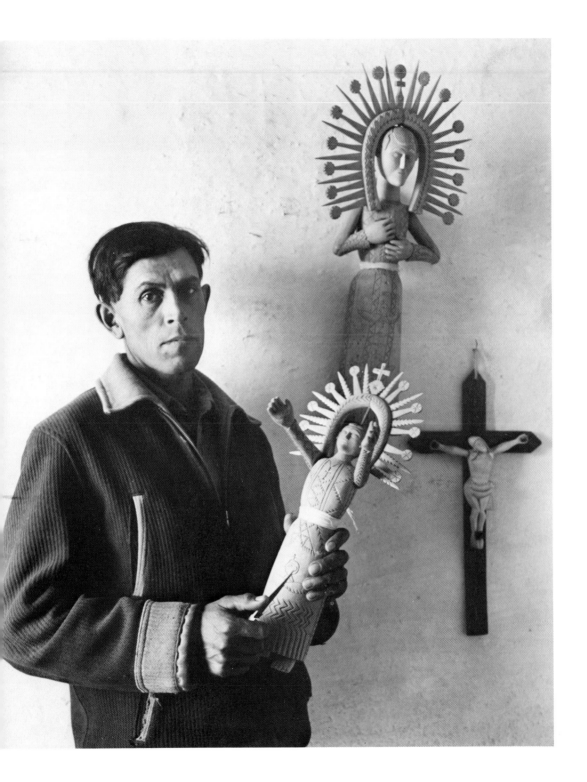

Plate 52. George López Shown with Several of His Images of Our Lady of Solitude, during the 1940s. Photograph by Laura Gilpin.

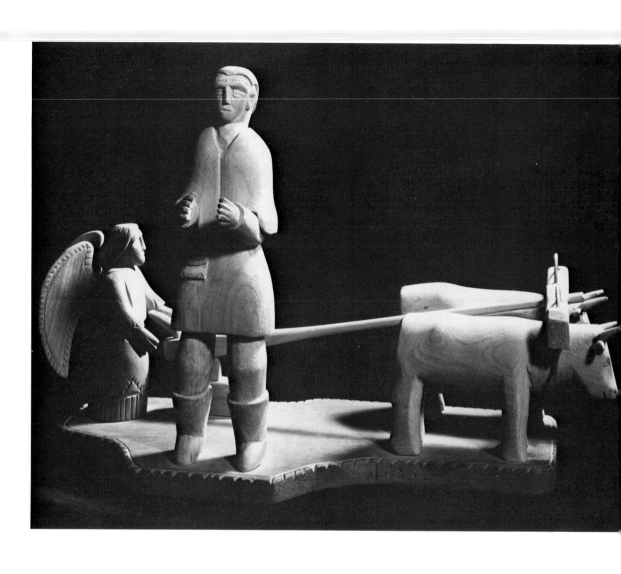

Plate 53. George López's First Image of St. Isidore, 1949 (St. Isidore 27.5 cm. or 11 in. in height, angel 13.8 cm. or 5.5 in. high, base 35.8 x 18.8 cm or 14.3 x 7.5 in.). From a private collection.

their employment at Los Alamos, however, and their wives Benita and Precídez were active as well. In 1952 George López quit his work at Los Alamos, and carving became his principal occupation. Although he continued to supplement this income by providing some meat and garden produce for his table, agriculture and husbandry had become a sideline for George, as it had for most Córdovans by this time. This event marked the first time that a village carver had relied upon his or her production of contemporary carvings as a primary source of income. It appears that one of the main reasons why George López effected this transition while his brothers did not related to the fact that he and Silvianita were childless. George's apparent inheritance of his father's entrepreneurial proclivities is perhaps of equal significance. Not surprisingly, George's new orientation to carving produced divers repercussions within the industry.

First, as George López's time was no longer split between wage labor and carving, he could greet his customers in person and pencil his signature onto the bottom of his works. This more direct and personal mode of interaction appears to have enhanced the ability of the Córdovan carvers to compete with larger tourist-oriented markets in Santa Fe and elsewhere.

Second, López was then able to devote a great deal of time to the preparation of a large inventory for sale at fiestas, and he was also able to be present on such occasions to sell his works personally. In short, George gained more and more recognition for his carving. Ricardo and Rafael continued working at Los Alamos until retirement age, however, and their work was sold under their wives' names. Benita and Precídez were on hand to greet visitors, and it seemed only natural to use their signatures on the bottom of carvings and on signs leading tourists to their shops. Ricardo López summarizes the situation in these terms: "I was out working when my carvings gained a reputation, so now no one knows me. If I was to tell someone who came here that these carvings were mine they would laugh at me."

George López consolidated his carving success by moving in 1963 from the central plaza to an isolated homestead in the valley (termed a *rancho*). This location increased his pre-eminence among Córdovan carvers for three reasons. First, many tourists hesitate to visit shops on the plaza for fear of damaging their vehicles on the uneven dirt roads or of being trapped in the narrow streets. López's new house was, however, just a short distance beyond the paved road from the highway, and his land yielded plenty of room for parking. Second, most tourists arrive in Córdova from the Chimayó side, and his shop is the first approached from that direction. Finally, unlike the old house with its limited space in a small back room, López's new location provided him with abundant space in which to display his works. In short, this move placed George and Silvianita in a more advantageous position than that of the other carvers. Although the others countered by placing signs on the main road before López's house, they were unable to offset his advantage.

All in all, George López had become Córdova's leading wood carver by

1960. Although he never quite dominated the community's carving industry as his father had, patrons of the genre had come to recognize him as the best, and many visitors did not even know that there were any other carvers in Córdova. His pre-eminence was especially crucial at this time because the early 1960s witnessed the saturation of the market for Córdovan wood carvings. This saturation had two aspects.

First, the demand for such work had become relatively stable by the 1960s. Many customers lived in the Southwest, and they constituted an established clientele of particular carvers. Furthermore, the vast majority of tourists came in seasonal waves without great variation in number from year to year. Merchandizing opportunities through middlemen, which will be discussed in the next chapter, had assumed patterns that endure to the present.

Second, saturation was evident in the fact that the supply was, on the average, greater than the demand. While the effect of López's full-time devotion to carving was substantial, it appears that the supply of carvings was greater primarily due to increases in the number of carvers in the families of José Dolores' sons and to the entrance of other families into the industry. Indeed, by the 1960s the ranks of Córdovan carvers had swelled to include many additional persons.

Juan Sánchez appears to have been the first Córdovan carver who was unrelated to the López family. Little is known about him—few villagers remember him, and he left no descendants in the community. Oral history characterizes him as a Mexican immigrant who lived in Córdova for a few years "some time around World War II." Other evidence suggests that his involvement in Córdova was occasioned by a W.P.A. assignment to the task of copying traditional images, and that he engaged in this pursuit elsewhere as well.

Sánchez's artistic goal was clearly to reproduce his models as closely as possible rather than to develop a distinct style of his own. His image of St. *Plate 54* Peter (Plate 54), for example, is a detailed copy of a polychromed *bulto* in the Córdova chapel, probably by José Rafael Aragón. Sánchez imitated the nineteenth-century work in both carving and painting stages, and he obviously spent a good deal of time on the piece. Nevertheless, the expressiveness of Aragón's work was not captured by Sánchez due to his inability to match Aragón richer colors, more skilled brushstrokes, and more delicate contours. Some variation in the quality of different works by Sánchez is also evident.

José Mondragón and his wife Alice joined the ranks of Córdovan carvers around 1959. According to Coke (1965:124), Mondragón "began his career as a wood carver after an accident which prevented him from continuing his activities as a farmer." The couple's entry into the industry is particularly notable for two reasons: they were the first Córdovans not related to the Lópezes to set up their own wood-carving shop, and although the Mondragóns live in the Plaza de los Trujillos section of Córdova, they run a shop on State Route 4 in Chimayó. The location has lessened the degree to which the carvers who have shops in Córdova consider the Mondra-

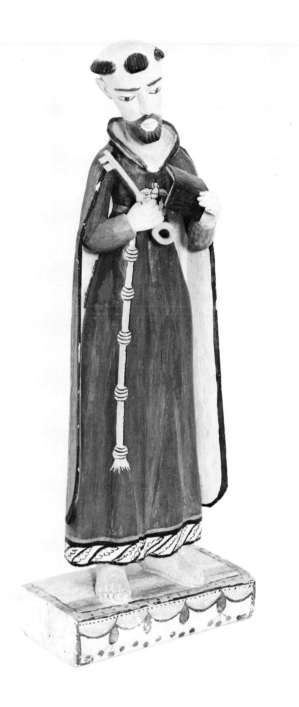

Plate 54. Copy of a Nineteenth-Century *Bulto* of St. Peter, Carved and Painted by
Juan Sánchez (102.5 cm. or 41 in. in height). This figure is a nearly exact copy of a
work by José Rafael Aragón. Taylor Museum Collection of the Colorado Springs
Fine Arts Center: Permanent Loan from the U.S. Government; photograph
courtesy of the Colorado Springs Fine Arts Center.

góns to be competitors. This attitude reflects a conceptual distinction more than an economic fact, however, since most of the Mondragóns' regular customers visit the Córdovan carvers as well, and the Mondragóns frequent the same Santa Fe craft fairs.[8]

Having their shop away from home does, however, create one difficulty for the Mondragóns—the time that they spend in Chimayó is primarily confined to the daylight hours of the summer, and they miss the customers who come at other times. They have tried to solve this problem by leaving a sign in the window to inform the tourists that a neighbor will open the shop for them. The neighbor in turn receives a commission.

The Mondragóns' work is quite similar to that of the Lópezes in basic technique. The Mondragóns' pieces are unpainted, most carving is done with pocketknives, and filigree designs are used for surface ornamentation. Unlike José Dolores, however, the Mondragóns never attempted to cover a figure with filigree. The simplicity of their figures is only interrupted by an occasional rosette or similar design (see Plate 55).

Plate 55

Two aspects of the Mondragóns' work are perhaps the most notable: its craftsmanship and its variety. They are highly competent craftsmen, and their carvings are technically refined and precise. In addition, their repertoire is quite extensive. José Mondragón produces most of the images that George López does—St. Peter, St. Isidore, St. Joseph, St. Rafael, and the Death cart—but he also carves a number of representations of Christ that George does not, such as Christ carrying the cross and the Sacred Heart of Jesus. The Mondragóns produce some of the more unusual wooden rosaries and straw-inlaid crosses, and their use of pulverized juniper in inlay is more extensive than that of the other carvers.

Within the last decade, a man from Chimayó, Apolonio Martínez, began carving in a style not unlike that of the Córdovan carvers. Born in 1889, Martínez was a carpenter until his retirement around 1964. Both he and his wife were weavers, and they turned to craft production as a mode of livelihood at that time. Shortly after leaving his first trade, Martínez began carving images and other figures. Some pictures of the saints provided his original prototypes. Apolonio's output was quite high at first, but his pace had slackened considerably by the time of his wife's death in 1973. Encouraged by such students of saint carving as E. Boyd and Richard Ahlborn, Martínez was successful in a number of craft competitions. He was a warm person with musical as well as visual artistic talent, and his death in 1976 was mourned by many. One of his grandsons who lives in Córdova has begun carving as well.

Córdovan carvers did not consider Martínez to be among their number, and his exclusion from this group is also suggested by stylistic differences. Martínez's intent was far more naturalistic than that of the Córdovan carvers, and this effect was reinforced by the lack of filigree designs for surface ornamentation. The Córdovan carvers thus consider his style distinct. As is evident in Plate 56, Apolonio often used multi-toned aspen, and the rougher texture of his carvings resulted from a more restrained use of sandpaper. Martínez's repertoire was also extensive; among his

Plate 56

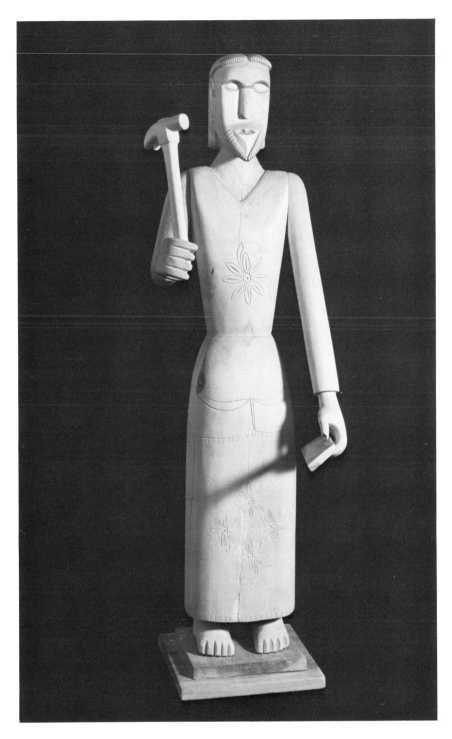

Plate 55. St. Joseph by José Mondragón (1.10 m. or 3.7. ft. in height). Note the exactness of the chip-carving and its relative sparsity. Taylor Museum Collection of the Colorado Springs Fine Arts Center; photograph courtesy of the Colorado Springs Fine Arts Center.

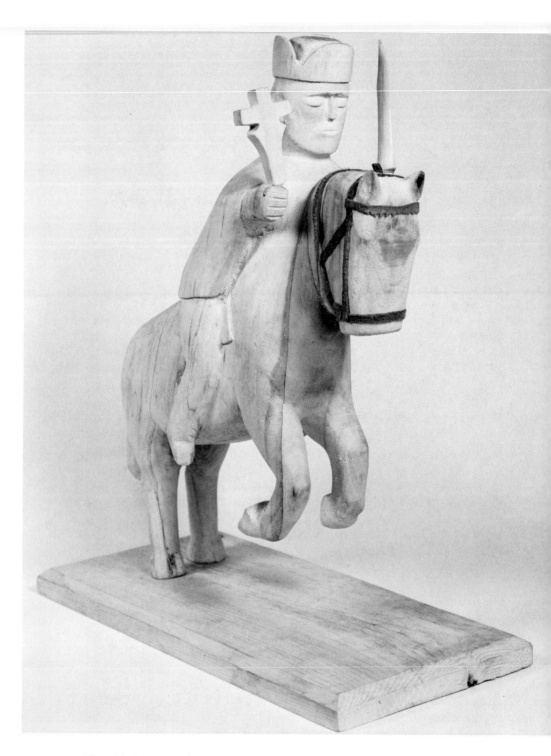

Plate 56. St. James the Major by Apolonio Martínez, 1975 (34 cm. or 13.6 in. in
height). The artist's technique relies more on the emergence of features from a
smooth surface than on elaborate chip-carving. In the collections of the Spanish
Colonial Arts Society, Inc., in the Museum of International Folk Art, Santa Fe.

subjects were the Flight into Egypt (see Plate 57), Adam and Eve in the Garden, a nativity scene, the Holy Family, the crucified Christ, St. Francis, St. Anthony, and St. James the Major. He also made a number of unusual pieces, and these included an old man and a small copy of a loom.

Nicudemos López, the eldest son of José Dolores, illustrates a common pattern among Córdovan carvers. Even a brief exposure to wood carving or a period of intermittent work will often be followed by a revival of personal interest after a lapse of many years. Nicudemos had begun carving in 1930, and he participated in his father's enterprise at that time. Following his father's death, however, Nicudemos turned to carpentry and worked for many years at this trade in the community of Truchas. After his retirement, Nicudemos took up several crafts in search of supplemental income. In the 1960s, he turned once again to wood carving, and produced a number of images in the succeeding several years. His repertoire included Michael the Archangel and the Dragon, Adam and Eve in the Garden, crucifixes, and St. George. His innovation of the latter figure as a carving subject was based upon a painting of the same subject illustrated in a small book of devotions to the saints. His output was limited, and the roughness of the surface of his carvings may be a reflection of his age. As Plates 58 and 59 show, filigree chip-carving also graces his figures, but Nicudemos' treatment of these designs is sparser than José Dolores', and his cuts are shallower. Nicudemos abandoned wood carving upon joining the iconoclastic pentecostals of the Assembly of God church. He also feared that the work was detrimental to his eyesight.

Nicudemos' younger brother Rafael began carving late in life. While Rafael never produced images, he and his wife Precídez carved trees and animals for sale until they died in 1968. Their position in the industry is illustrative of the pattern that emerged with the advent of daily wage labor. Rafael worked at Los Alamos until his retirement in 1965, and sales from carvings served to supplement his wages. Consequently, Precídez gained outside recognition as a carver, and it was her name that was used on the bottom of carvings and on signs directing tourists to their house on the plaza.

Rafael and Precídez were assisted in their work by their daughter Gloria (see Plate 60). After marrying Herminio Córdova in 1961 and working for a while as a domestic, Gloria began carving occasionally and sold her works out of Uncle George's shop. In May 1973, however, she began selling carvings from her own front room, and she set up a number of signs in order to bring tourists to her home. She also taught her husband to carve (Tucson Museum of Art n.d.:29). Herminio works in Los Alamos, but he devotes a great deal of his spare time to carving. True to the pattern associated with wage labor, he does most of the work on the images while Gloria is responsible for trees, birds, necklaces, crosses, animals, and detail work on the *bultos*. It is Gloria, however, who has received most of the recognition for their work. In the intervening years their clientele has grown considerably, and Herminio's and Gloria's images have taken first prizes in the 1975 and 1976 Spanish Markets. Their eldest child, Evelyn,

Plate 57

Plate 58
Plate 59

Plate 60

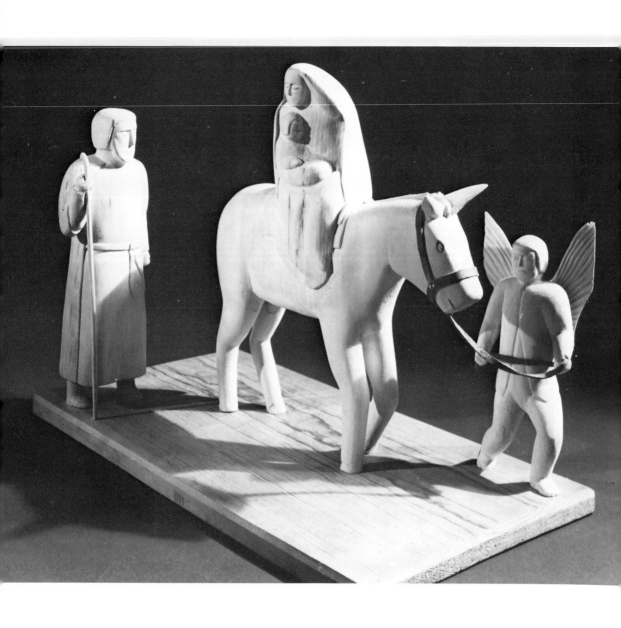

Plate 57. The Flight into Egypt by Apolonio Martínez (height 36 cm. or 14 in.; length and width, 51.2 x 28.2 cm. or 20 x 11 in.). Martínez's intent seems to be strongly naturalistic in this set. Courtesy of the Museum of History and Technology, Smithsonian Institution, Washington, D.C.

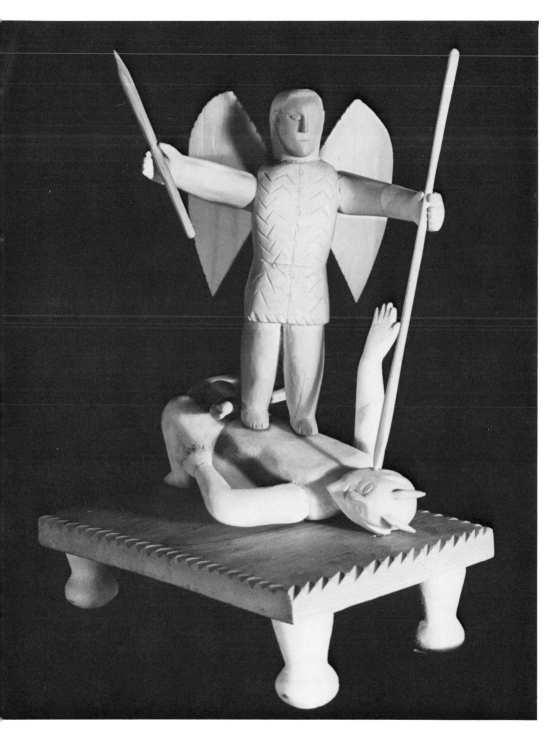

Plate 58. *Michael the Archangel and the Dragon* by Nicudemos López (total
height 31 cm. or 12.4 in., base 21 x 15 cm. or 8.4 x 6 in.). López left the surface of
his carvings quite rough, creating a blurred effect. In the collections of the
School of American Research in the Museum of International Folk Art, Santa Fe.

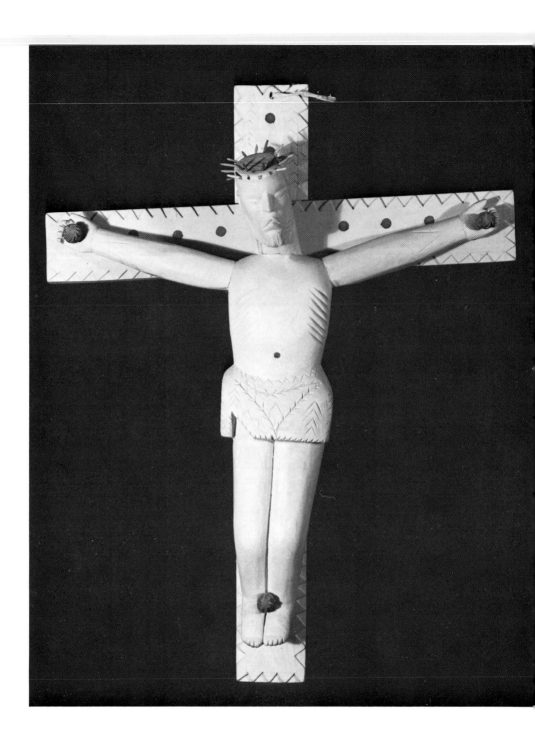

Plate 59. Crucifix by Nicudemos López, 1956 (cross 40 x 50 cm. or 16 x 20 in., Christ 39 cm. or 15.6 in. high). The diffuse whiteness of the wood is offset in this image by bits of berried juniper and inlay juniper sawdust. In the collections of the Museum of International Folk Art, a unit of the Museum of New Mexico, Santa Fe.

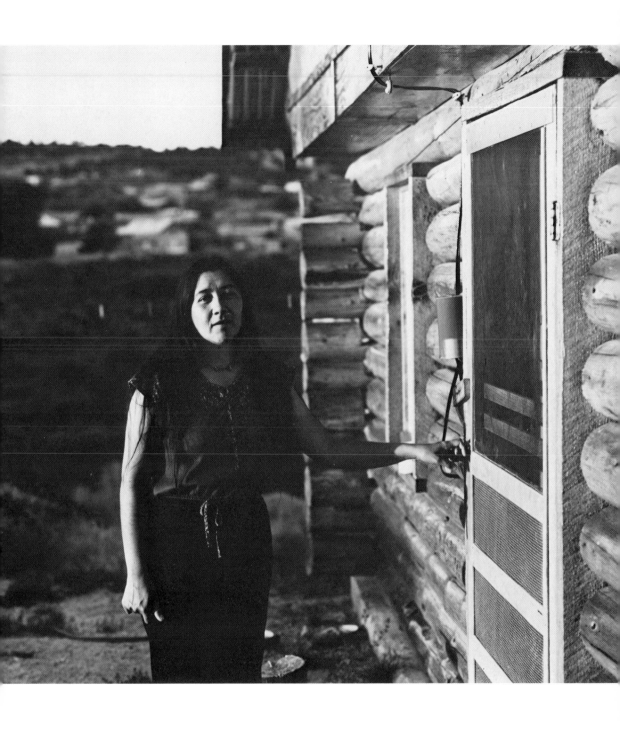

Plate 60. Gloria López Córdova outside Her Log Cabin Workshop in Córdova, 1977.

now regularly produces miniature trees and birds, and the younger children, Gary and Rafaelito, have begun to carve.

The success that Gloria and Herminio have enjoyed in the marketing of their images seems to be largely based upon the illusion of movement produced by their carvings. While George López's images tend to be squarer and more massive, Herminio uses such features as curved wings, protruding foreheads, and smaller waistlines to lend a greater angularity *Plate 61* to his figures (see Plate 61). The expressiveness of the forms is further accentuated by Gloria's liberal ornamentation with filigree designs, and the chip-carving is more deeply incised than that of most other carvers.

Herminio's nephew Sammy Córdova, a distant relative of the Lópezes, had been carving for a number of years prior to the opening of Gloria's shop. Having received encouragement and some instruction from George López, Sammy had built up a substantial clientele by the time he graduated from high school. Although special orders continued to be sold through his grandfather's home in Córdova, Sammy had never set up signs to beckon the tourists. He produced a limited repertoire of images of the *Plate 62* saints and a few non-traditional subjects such as deer (see Plate 62). His meager carving income proved insufficient, however, especially after he was married in December 1975. His subsequent employment outside Córdova undermined his participation in the carving industry. In 1978, however, he set up his own workshop just off the plaza and devoted himself full-time to carving.

Federico Córdova and Lina Ortiz de Córdova, Sammy's grandparents, assisted him for many years in the sanding and the sale of his carvings. A photograph of José Dolores López's *Animal Musicians* (refer back to Plate 26), published in an article on the Córdova carvers in 1974 (Briggs 1974a:44), inspired Lina to carve on her own, and she first marketed her *Plate 63* version of López's work at the 1976 Spanish Market (see Plate 63). The bird and animal on the center pole of López's piece have been replaced with a single animal on Lina's, and the variety of the instruments and the number of the musicians have been reduced in Lina's carving.

George's younger brother Ricardo has also been carving for some decades, although his work is known under the name of his wife, Benita Reino. Ricardo began carving the larger images in 1927, but he neglected this work in the post–World War II period because "it is wrong to sell the saints to the tourists."[9] Unlike Nicudemos, he remains a devout Catholic. Ricardo and Benita later concentrated on the production of small trees, birds, and animals. They are quite imaginative and have innovated a number of features in carvings of this genre. Curved branches often grace trees, and piglets nurse from the sow in neat rows. Perhaps their most striking innovation was the placement of a small figure of the Holy Child of Atocha on the base of a *coronita* or circular willow branch *Plate 64* punctuated with curved leaves (Plate 64). Benita and Ricardo have mastered the art of carving these intricate figures, and their repertoire of such pieces is possibly the largest. Other members of their family have helped with the work, and their married daughter Nora Cerrano became the

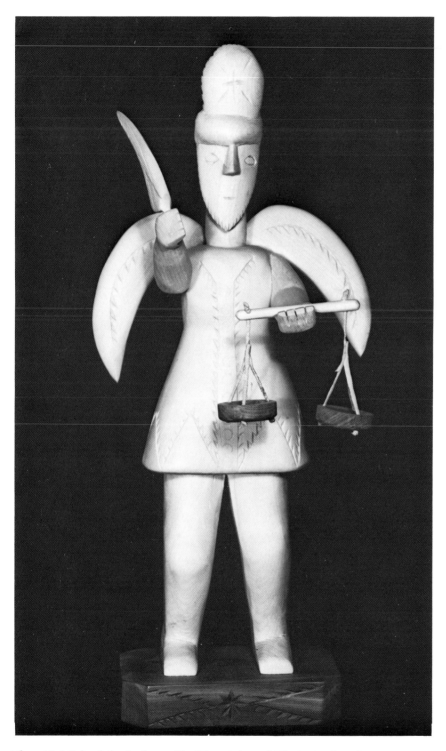

Plate 61. Michael the Archangel by Herminio and Gloria Córdova (37 cm. or 14.8 in. in height). In the collections of the Museum of International Folk Art, a unit of the Museum of New Mexico, Santa Fe.

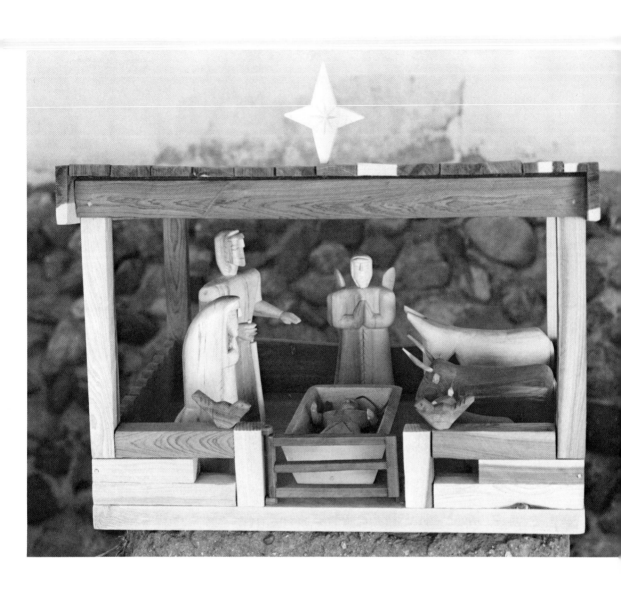

Plate 62. Manger Scene by Sammy Córdova, 1978 (stable approximately 40 cm. or 16 in. in height). This set differs from the work of other carvers in that all the pieces are glued in place. In the Museum Foundation Shop of the Palace of the Governors, a unit of the Museum of New Mexico, Santa Fe.

110 *Beginnings*

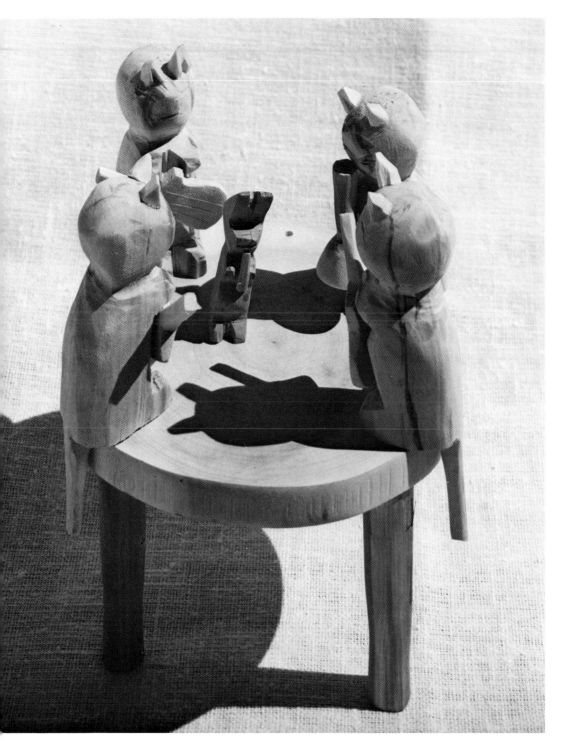

Plate 63. A Copy of José Dolores López's *The Animal Musicians* by Lina Ortiz de Córdova, 1978 (total height 25 cm. or 10 in.). In the Museum Foundation Shop of the Palace of the Governors, a unit of the Museum of New Mexico, Santa Fe.

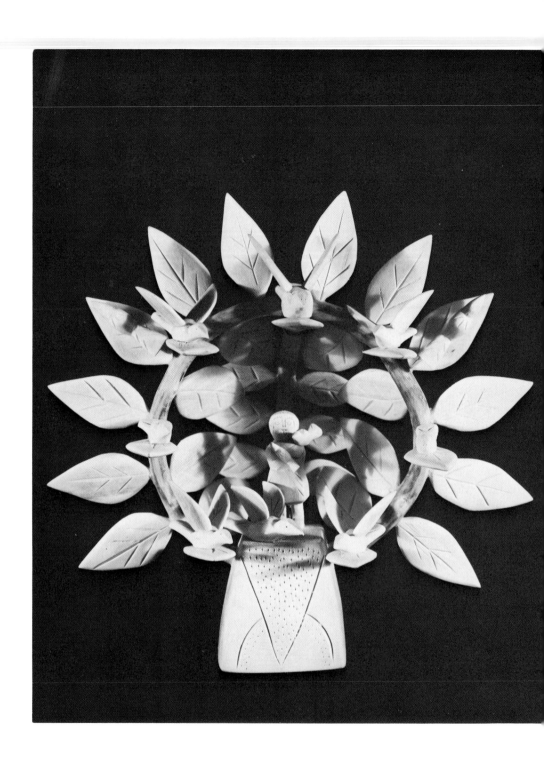

Plate 64. A *Cuevita* or *Coronita* with the Holy Child of Atocha by Benita and Ricardo López, 1972 (carving 22 cm. or 8.8 in. in height, figure 5.5 cm. or 2.2 in. in height). In the collections of the Spanish Colonial Arts Society, Inc., in the Museum of International Folk Art, Santa Fe.

recognized carver in the family following Benita's contraction of a debilitating illness. In June 1977, Córdova mourned the death of Benita López, a kindly and respected neighbor and relative.

Ricardo's and Benita's son Eurgencio carved occasionally during the last couple of decades, but only recently did he go into business for himself. A sign leads prospective customers into his driveway, and he sells a few carvings from his living room. His location at the far end of the Quemado Valley keeps such sales to a minimum, however. Most of his limited business is transacted during the Santa Fe Fiesta, Spanish Markets, and fairs, as well as through other village shops. Eurgencio is a competent carver of graceful images of St. Francis and birds, crosses, and trees. A roadrunner with a yucca plant set in the same base is one of his delightful innovations. His wife, Orlinda, is new to the production and marketing of carvings, but she is devoting increasing amounts of time to the pursuit, and some of her children are learning to carve as well. Eurgencio López's work is illustrated in Plate 65.

Plate 65

Although George's sister Liria has not carved for many years, the art is not dead in her family. Her son, Eluid L. Martínez, was born in Córdova but left with his mother for Santa Fe at the age of one. Spending summers with Uncle George and Aunt Silvianita, Eluid became acquainted with the art form that his grandfather had innovated. Following his marriage and graduation from engineering school, he went to work for the state engineer. Nevertheless, his interest in contemporary Hispano wood carving manifested itself in two ways.

First, he began carving in 1970 or 1971, and before long he had exhibited his images at the Spanish Market, the Pasadena Art Museum, and elsewhere. Martínez's *bultos* are carefully planned and executed, and his rounded curves and his utilization of multi-toned aspen enhance the expressiveness of his figures (see Plate 66). His images are often quite enterprising, in both size and attention to detail. Unlike his relatives in Córdova, Martínez carves a limited number of items for sale at higher prices to connoisseurs. Some of his figures of Death have received a coat of gesso, and he has polychromed a small image of St. Anthony.

Plate 66

Second, he is quite interested in maintaining a record of the family's artistic tradition and in conveying the nature of his heritage to others. This desire has inspired him to collect examples of the family's carvings and to write a short book on the art. This publication has been primarily illustrated with his own images (1978). Although his mother no longer participates in the industry that her father created, Eluid convinced her to incise filigree designs on one of his carvings. The results show that she has hardly lost her talent (see Plate 67).

Plate 67

Although George and Silvianita had considerable experience in the industry at the time when the Córdovan wood-carving market was becoming saturated, this period marked significant changes in their style. As stated above, the images that George carved during the time he was employed at Los Alamos were generally less intricate than his early work, especially in the application of chip-carving. Although the scarcity of

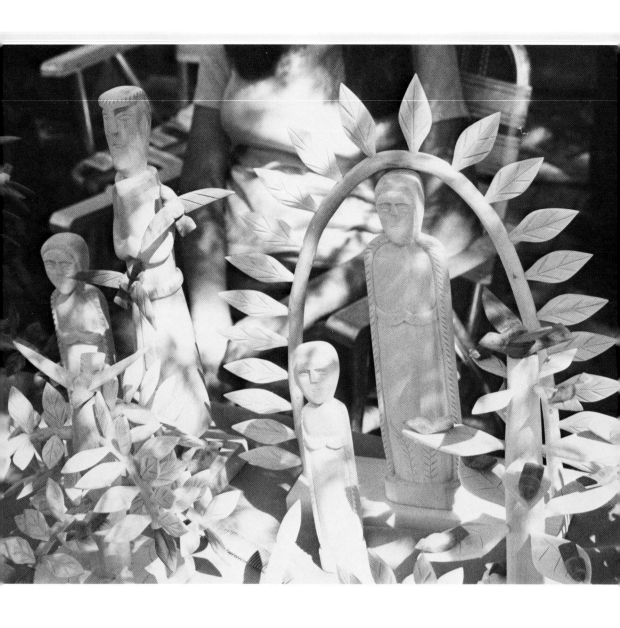

Plate 65. Several of Eurgencio López's Images at the 1976 Santa Fe Fiesta. López's slender figures, *coronitas*, and composite carvings are visible in this detail of the table he and his wife, Orlinda, used at the fiesta.

114   *Beginnings*

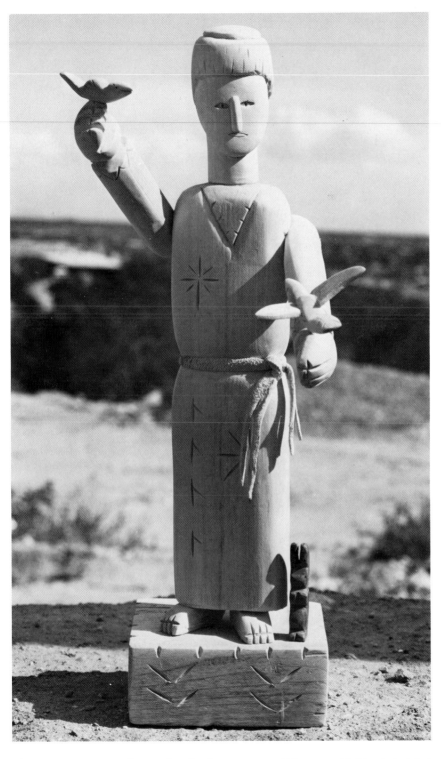

Plate 66. St. Francis of Assisi by Eluid L. Martínez (33 cm. or 13.6 in. in height). From a private collection.

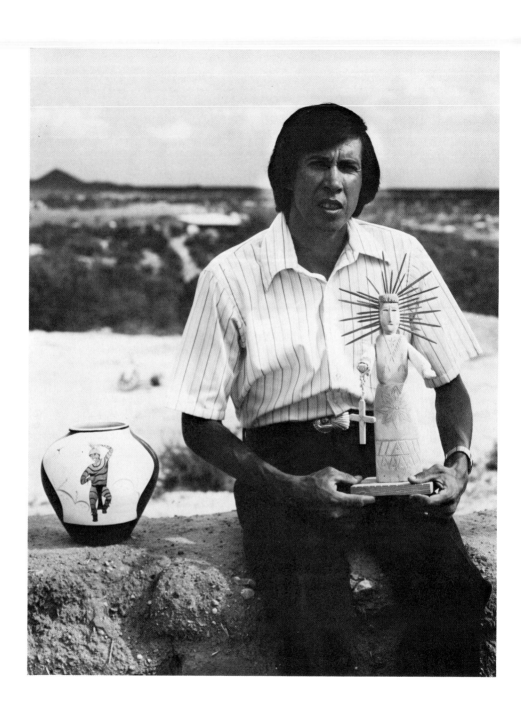

Plate 67. Eluid L. Martínez with His Image of Our Lady of Light. This image bears the same title as a work by his grandfather, José Dolores López. The pottery vessel was made by a friend.

dated examples from that period precludes a detailed characterization of his style immediately after the time of his wage labor, figures such as Gabriel the Archangel depicted in Plate 68 indicate that he returned to his earlier style. The image of St. Gabriel was produced shortly after López retired from work in Los Alamos in 1952 and is notable for the amount of chip-carving, the width of the incisions on the leaf patterns, and the doweled and nailed joints. Nevertheless, López does not appear to have continued the production of many of the more complicated scenes introduced by his father.

Plate 68

A number of important stylistic changes were evident in López's carving, however, in the years after 1952, when he devoted himself to carving full-time. One of the first changes consisted of a limited experimentation within the medium. Most strikingly, E. Boyd reported (1972: Personal communication) that she bought George López's one and only carving in stone. George had also tried his hand at carving antler while he was working the sheep camps of Wyoming. In addition, he produced a number of pieces in wood that vary considerably from his usual style during this period, with the St. Francis illustrated in Plate 69 and the angel photographed by Adams (1976:iv) providing good examples of this deviation. The articulation of St. Francis' beard, feet, robe, and facial features forms a departure from López's usual style, as does the roundness of the image. Although in this case a number of characteristics permit the identification of the piece as López's, such apparent anomalies in an individual's style often reflect the sale of another carver's work under the name of the more established carver.

Plate 69

Second, George López's *bultos* started to become less ambitious in execution than his treatment of the same subjects had been in previous years. With regard to a recent crèche, for example, it is initially apparent that the three kings, who were included by José Dolores, have been omitted (compare Plates 40 and 70). In addition, the number, the complexity, and the chip-carving elaboration of the human figures and the stable have greatly diminished in George López's piece. Similarly, the Garden of Eden with three elements has been generally replaced by a simpler version containing only one or two pieces. The difficulty involved in adding hands and arms has also been circumvented on many images of the Virgin and St. Francis by folding the hands as if the subject were praying.

Plate 70

Third, one of the most important changes took place in the chip-carving designs. While the surface ornamentation of López's images made soon after his wage labor employment was not entirely unlike his work in the late 1920s and in the 1930s (see Plates 71 and 72), the execution of such filigree designs decreased steadily after that point. The incisions became shallower and less precise, and the chip-carved surface ornamentation became less integrated with the overall plastic design. The two modes of artistic discourse ceased to interrelate so closely, thus decreasing the aesthetic impact of the carvings on the observer. This period is well represented by the St. Isidore pictured in Plate 73. This work is

Plate 71
Plate 72

Plate 73

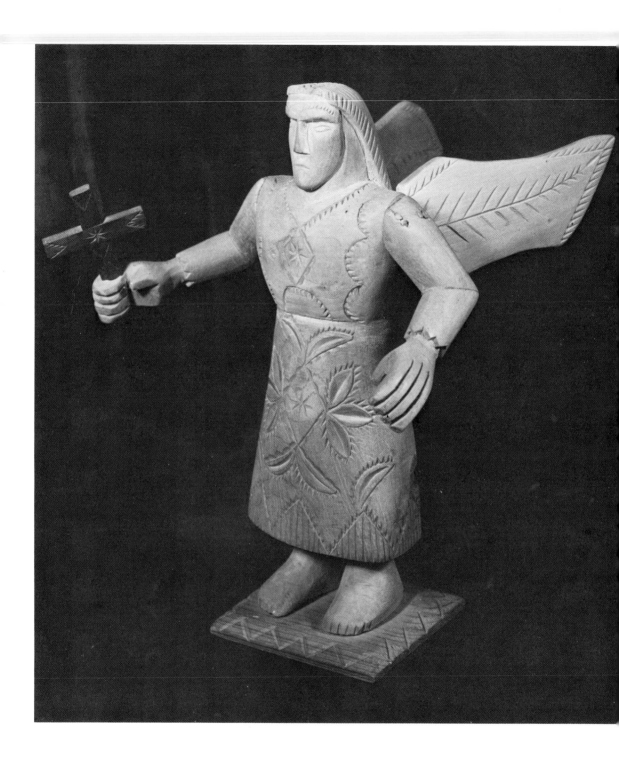

Plate 68. Gabriel the Archangel by George López (26.9 cm. or 10.7 in. in height). From a private collection.

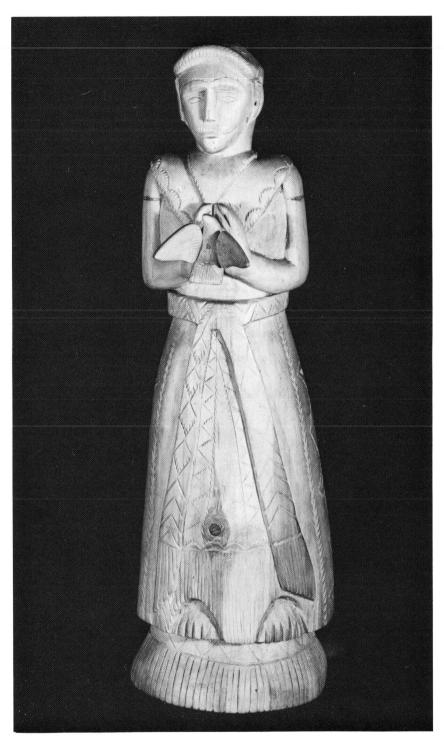

Plate 69. An Unusual Image of St. Francis of Assisi by George López (51.5 cm. or 20.6 in. in height). In the collections of the School of American Research in the Museum of International Folk Art, Santa Fe.

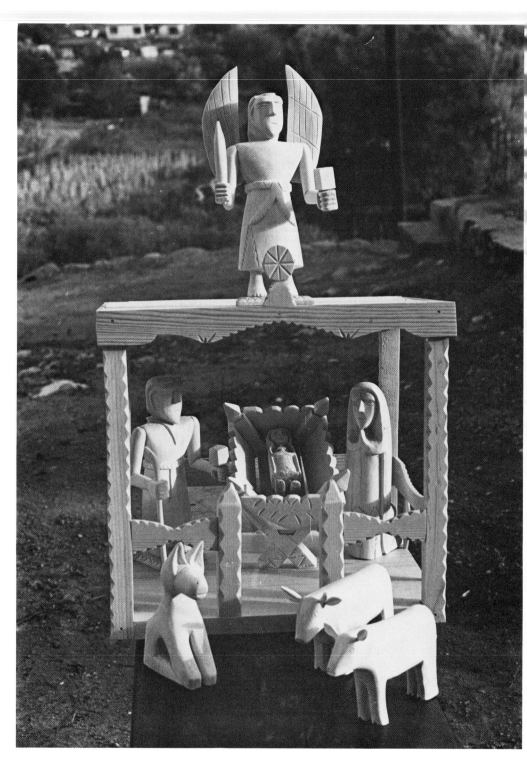

Plate 70. Crèche by George López, 1974 (stable 33.8 cm. or 13.5 in. in height, 36.3 cm. or 14.5 in. wide, 30 cm. or 12 in. deep). From a private collection.

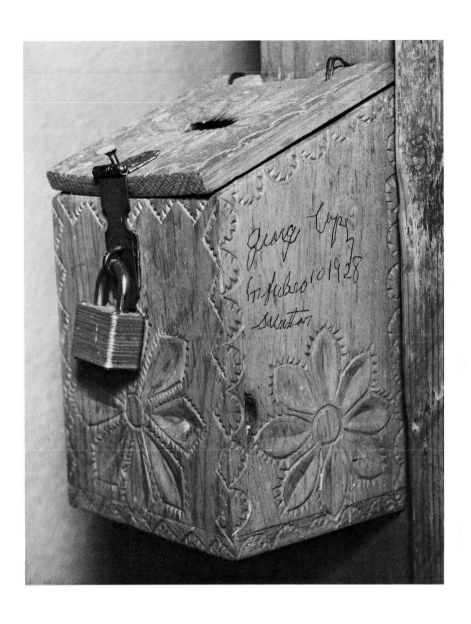

Plate 71. Offertory Box by George López, 1928 (total height 22 cm. or 8.8 in., width 15 cm. or 6 in., depth 11.3 cm. or 4.5 in.). This box was carved for use in the Córdova chapel. Note the width of the incisions in the floral designs. From a private collection.

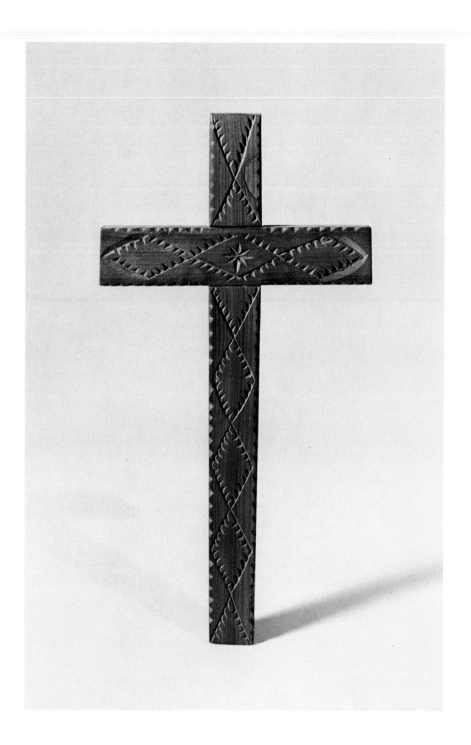

Plate 72. Carved Cross by George López (20 cm. or 8 in. in height). An example of his earlier work, this small cross of berried juniper is, like the small birds and animals, the sort of carving that tourists frequently purchase as souvenirs. Taylor Museum Collection of the Colorado Springs Fine Arts Center; photograph courtesy of the Colorado Springs Fine Arts Center.

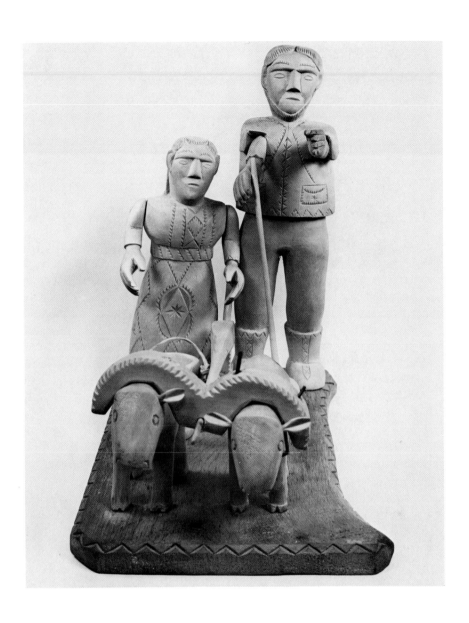

Plate 73. St. Isidore (Right) *with the Angel Who Plowed His Fields* by George López, 1957 (base 41 x 24 cm. or 16.4 x 9.6 in., saint 37 cm. or 14.8 in. in height). In the collections of the Museum of International Folk Art, a unit of the Museum of New Mexico, Santa Fe.

graced with more chip-carving than López's first St. Isidore (Plate 53). The balance, precision, and the finesse of the latter piece are, however, lacking in the former piece as in much of his recent work.

Further changes are apparent in the chip-carving. The frequent occurrence of the wide indentations, such as those on the Gabriel the Archangel in Plate 68, were gradually replaced by narrower cuts. The old indentations were partially retained on the carved crosses sold in the López shop, however. The amount of chip-carving that embellished images also decreased substantially. Unlike early attempts to cover figures, recent works have largely rejected multiple curved designs in favor of single straight lines (see Plate 74). This tendency is most apparent from a comparison of López's St. Peter with his father's (see Plates 36, 38, and 74). George López's work differs in its shallower chip-carving, stockier figure, and decreased elaboration of the inscription. Most importantly, the expressiveness of José Dolores' image is greatly enhanced by the illusion that the saint is actually reading the Bible. This effect is not conveyed by his son's image.

Plate 74

This period thus witnessed the constriction of George López's repertoire in terms of a concentration on a smaller number of regularly carved pieces and in terms of the detail with which he executed his pieces. Nevertheless, this constriction was partially offset by his innovation of several figures in recent decades. López has devised two Virgins, Our Lady of Guadalupe (Plate 75) and la Conquistadora, a representation of Our Lady of the Rosary. In addition, he created versions of St. Pascal Baylon, the "patron saint of the kitchen" (see Plate 76) and St. Rafael (Plate 77).

Plate 75

Plate 76
Plate 77

George and Silvianita López are not the only carvers in their workshop. The couple adopted Savinita, the eldest daughter of George's brother Ricardo, and raised her from infancy. Having learned how to carve as a child, she occasionally pursued this work following her marriage to Cristóbal (Junior) Ortiz. Junior learned to carve shortly thereafter, and he describes his entry into the industry:

> One day I was just fooling around making the head for a Muerte. When I was finished, my aunt [Silvianita López] said, "Why don't you just go ahead and make the rest of the Muerte?" So I asked [George López] for assistance and for the loan of some books. When I had finished it, my aunt asked me how much I wanted for it. I said that I would be lucky to get $25 for it. In about a week, my aunt came to me and told me that she had sold it for $125. That was just after I got married, and in those days that was a lot of money. That was when I realized that there was money in this business.

Many other carvers have articulated their initial experience in the carving industry quite similarly. Like so many Córdovan carvers, Junior and Savinita utilize income from wood carving to supplement their wages. Savinita has worked as a cook and domestic in Los Alamos homes, usually two to three days per week. Junior has been engaged in various construction jobs, but he now serves as the head janitor of the Whiterock

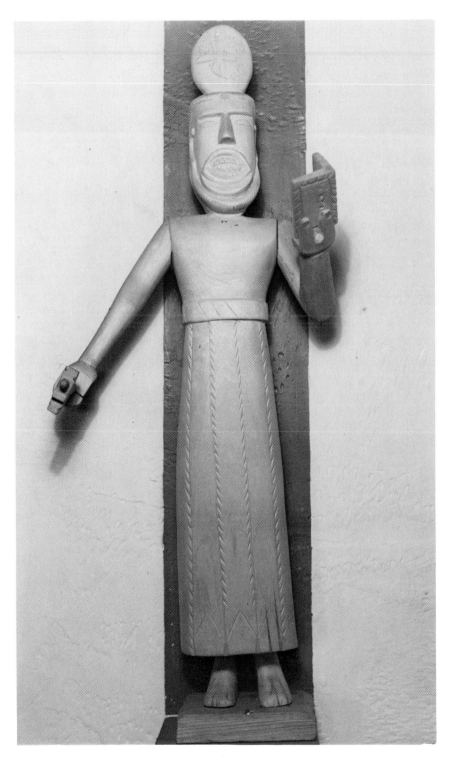

Plate 74. St. Peter by George López (approximately 60 cm. or 24 in. in height). In the Chapel of the Fountain Valley Day School, Colorado Springs.

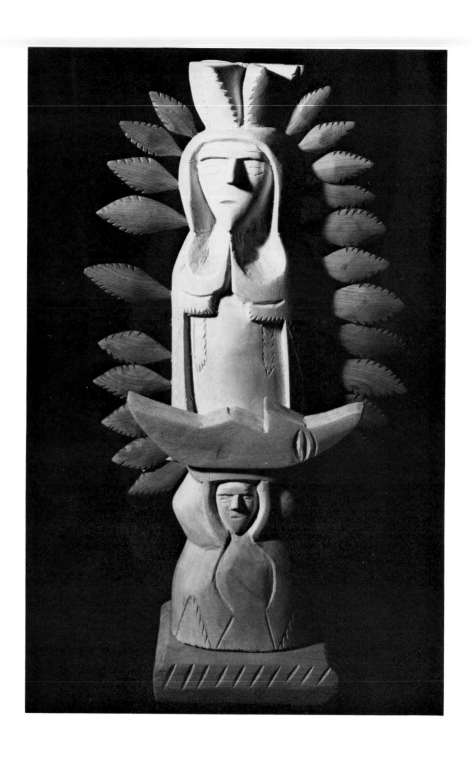

Plate 75. Our Lady of Guadalupe by George López, 1972 (33 cm. or 13.2 in. in height). The rays of light which surround the virgin are represented by inserts of berried juniper. Note the stoutness of the figure and the roughness of the surface. From a private collection.

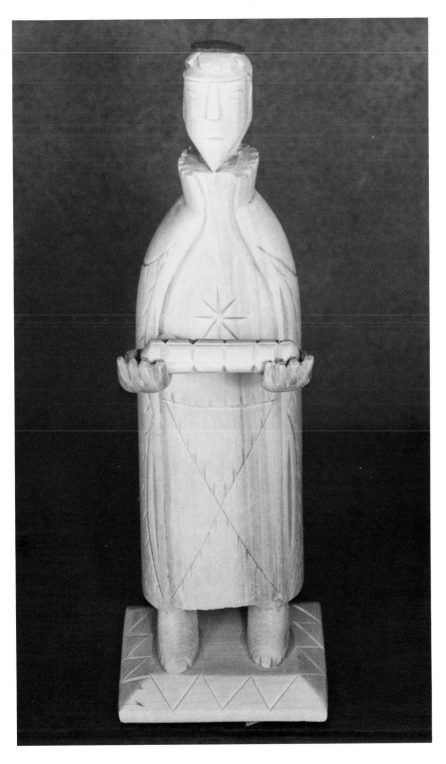

Plate 76. St. Pascal Baylon, the Patron Saint of the Kitchen by George López (33.8 cm. or 13.5 in. in height). From a private collection.

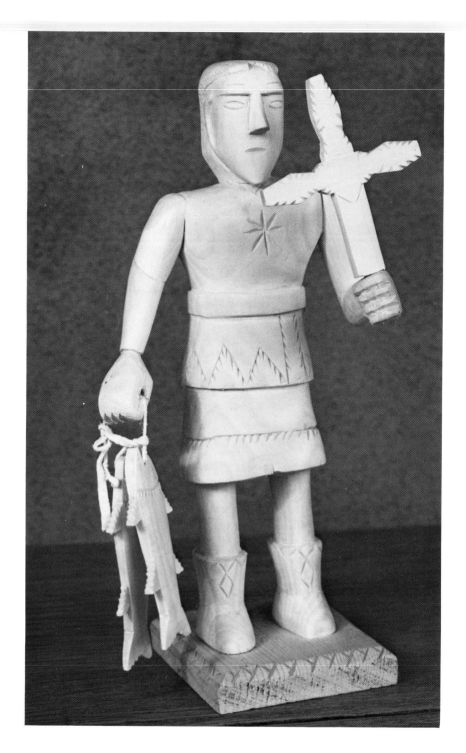

Plate 77. Rafael the Archangel by George López (29. 4 cm. or 11.8 in. in height). In the Bible, Rafael instructed Tobias to heal his father's blindness with the ashes of burned fish. Lopez sometimes provides Rafael with wings. From a private collection.

Elementary School near Los Alamos. In addition to wood carving, the Ortizes keep a garden and a few animals.

Participation in "George López and Ortiz's Wood Carving Shop" is not, however, limited to these four members. Savinita and Junior have five children—Alex, Lawrence, Elvis, Orlene, and Amy—and all of them began carving while they were in elementary school. The sons have been carving images for years, and they are now quite proficient. Their younger sister Orlene concentrates on small Christmas trees, while Amy, the youngest, is still learning. They have also experimented with the medium; Alex produced a figure of the old miner with his burrow and tried his hand at making *retablos*. His work is influenced by training he received in high school art classes. Now that the three boys are out of high school, wage labor reduces the time they may spend carving.

George, Silvianita, and the Ortizes consider themselves to be part of the same workshop, and this perception of a shared identity has led them to value consistency of style in their carving. Indeed, they are surprisingly successful in the accomplishment of this goal. They share a common set of prototypes, and the features of their works are very similar (see Chapter 6 for further discussion). Individual differences are more apparent, however, in two facets of their carving.

Stylistic idiosyncrasies often allow one to distinguish works by the different carvers in the workshop. These variations appear particularly consistent in the treatment of hands, feet, and heads. Plate 78, for example, illustrates an image of St. Peter by Elvis Ortiz. This image, which Ortiz produced in 1974, can be distinguished from George López's work by its slimmer head and neck, more deeply incised chip-carving, and the sharper edges on the belt, hem of the robe, and the toes (refer back to Plate 74 for a corresponding example of George López's work). Elvis's heads are much more elongated than his Uncle George's, and the right hand and Bible are also dissimilar. Lawrence Ortiz's distinctive style is especially apparent in his use of curvilinear forms and lines (see Plate 79). Proportion of body to head differs on his figures from that on carvings made by his Uncle George.

Plate 78

Plate 79

Limited specialization has taken place within the workshop, and many of the members tend to concentrate on one or more figures. While such preferences are hardly absolute, Lawrence and Elvis produce most of the large images (two to five feet tall), especially the images of St. Francis and St. Peter. In addition, they carve many large scenes of the Tree of Life. Savinita and Junior Ortiz concentrate on images of St. Francis and St. Pascal Baylon that are eight to ten inches tall. Silvianita López produces the full range of smaller trees, animals, and birds, and much of her time is spent in assisting the other carvers in their work and in replacing diminished inventories of the smaller items. George López is probably the most versatile carver in the shop. Much of his time is spent in filling orders for medium-sized images.

As the preceding discussion suggests, the mere enumeration of the main carving families in Córdova is no simple task, and other individuals

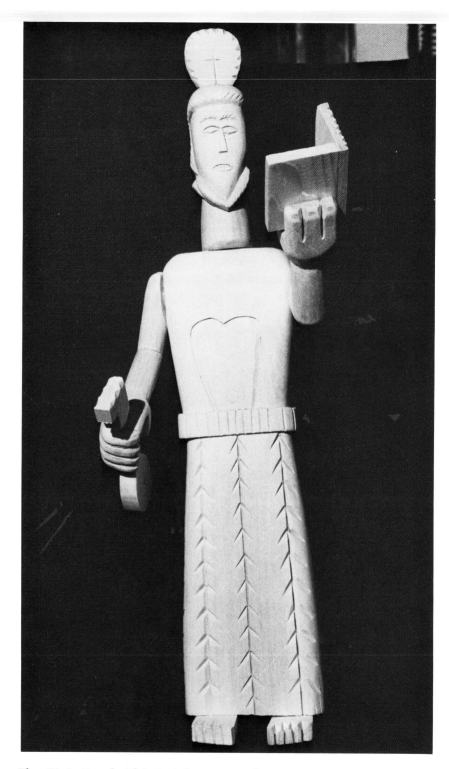

Plate 78. St. Peter by Elvis Ortiz (approximately 65 cm. or 26 in. in height). From a private collection.

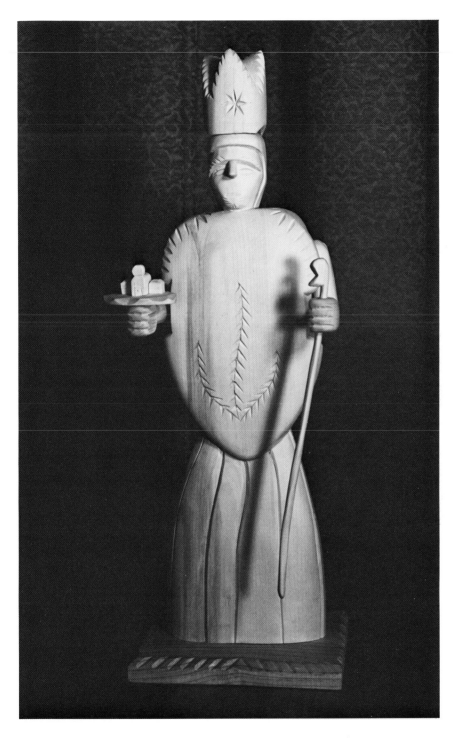

Plate 79. St. Patrick by Lawrence Ortiz (approximately 45 cm. or 18 in. in height). Lawrence's first image of St. Patrick was produced for a special order for which the patron provided a graphic prototype, but it has become part of his repertoire. From a private collection.

outside these families occasionally carve in order to supplement their incomes. Although the established carving families keep fairly informed about each other's work, they are not able to name all of the part-time carvers in their community.

Indeed, the orientation of persons who are recognized as carvers and those who are not to their work is quite distinct. While this difference is partially accounted for by economic factors, the distinct attitudes of the two groups reflect a fundamental principle in the social organization of wood carvers in Córdova. Furthermore, aspects of social organization are evident in the marketing practices utilized in the industry, as the next chapter shows.

Part II

The Contemporary Period

5.

The Marketing of Contemporary Wood Carvings

Picture once again the visitor to Córdova's wood-carving shops. Most potential customers have seen or at least heard about the industry beforehand, but some are drawn to the carvers' homes by the many

Plate 80 hand-painted signs (see Plate 80). These begin back on the highway about a mile before the community, while the road to the main plaza is dotted with signs bearing directions to the various artists' houses. George and Silvianita López's driveway, for example, boasts a large advertisement—"George López and Ortiz's Wood Carving Shop, Visitors Welcome"—and

Plate 81 a similar sign adorns the front of the López house (Plate 81).

As soon as an unfamiliar car turns off the road, George López, whose seat in the kitchen commands a view of the driveway, rises from his chair and heads for the door. He quickly opens the door to the room that contains the carvings and emerges from the house. López calls an invitation to the customers from the porch. Each is greeted with "Come in, how are you?" and a handshake, and López holds the door while the patrons pass into the living room. By this time Silvianita López has entered the

Plate 82 room and has removed the tablecloth covering the carvings (see Plate 82).[1]

As the patrons enter the room, Silvianita greets them from behind the table. Their attention is quickly drawn to her husband, however. His command of English is much greater than that of his wife,[2] and he usually queries tourists as to their place of origin, whether they like New Mexico, and so forth. Many customers disregard George's questions in order to move closer to the table and examine the carvings. It is not uncommon, however, for the men to converse with George in the center of the room while Silvianita shows the carvings to the women.

Once a customer concentrates on a particular piece or begins to pick it up, Silvianita López, who follows this part of the intercourse closely, responds quickly. She uses syntactically Spanish phrases containing English nouns descriptive of the carving: "*Esta es un* San Francis. *Es* cotton-

Plate 83 wood *y* cedar. *Esta es un* Christmas tree" (see Plate 83). She does not understand any request for information beyond the labels or prices of carvings, and George or a member of the Ortiz family must come to the rescue.

Meanwhile, George alternates between helping Silvianita display the carvings and conversing with his clients. As the visit progresses, however, he almost invariably exhibits various forms of recognition that he has received for his work. First, however, he points to a portrait of his father.[3] George explains, "She name is José Dolores López. She was my father and a great carver!" He may also refer to a set of postcards from Expo '67 in Montreal, where he gave a carving exhibition. He displays materials relating to the honorary doctorate conferred upon him in 1971 by the University of Colorado and, frequently, magazine or newspaper articles, mainly Horwitz (1975:98–101), Briggs (1974a), and Briggs (1974c). Even regular customers are shown these documents on every visit.

Although the majority of the Lópezes' customers do not leave without buying at least one carving, most customers buy small secular objects such as birds, animals, or Christmas trees. Once they have made a selection, patrons immediately check the bottom of the carving to be sure that George has signed it. Silvianita pencils the price of each item on a stationery pad, but she often requires assistance from the Ortiz family in totaling more than two figures. The role of the Ortizes is quite subsidiary, however, and they do not usually become involved with customers. Silvianita then places all purchases in paper bags and receives payments in checks or cash.

Once a transaction has been completed or a decision made to refrain from purchasing anything, most visitors leave without much ado. Few visits deviate significantly in duration from the usual ten to fifteen minutes, although this uniformity is not induced by any signals from the Lópezes. Silvianita López calls out "Thank you, goodbye" and smiles at the customers from her position behind the table. Patrons often return the thanks. Most visitors reach the door before George, but he usually follows them outside. His actions at this point largely reflect the intensity of the preceding interaction. If the customers were not rushed in their conversation with the Lópezes, then George López will often accompany them to their car, conversing with them on the way, and he will then direct them out of the driveway. If the visitors have been quite hurried, George generally calls goodbye from the porch and observes their departure.

Once the patrons have left, the Lópezes return to their previous activities. Silvianita replaces the tablecloth over the carvings and returns to the kitchen. Although most visits engender little comment, unusual features of the interaction sometimes receive mention. Women traveling alone or people in a great hurry contrast sharply with Hispano expectations, and the Lópezes often remark uncritically on such deviations. Finally, the total amount gained from the sale of a piece carved by one of the Ortizes will be transferred to the carver as soon as possible.

The evolution of this mode of interaction has greatly enhanced the success of the Lópezes' carving enterprise, and the central features of

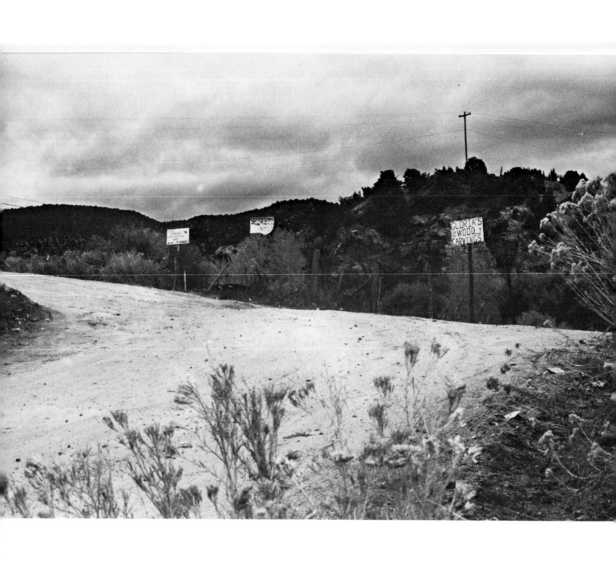

Plate 80. Group of Signs for Wood-Carving Shops at a Crossroads below the Córdova Plaza, 1978.

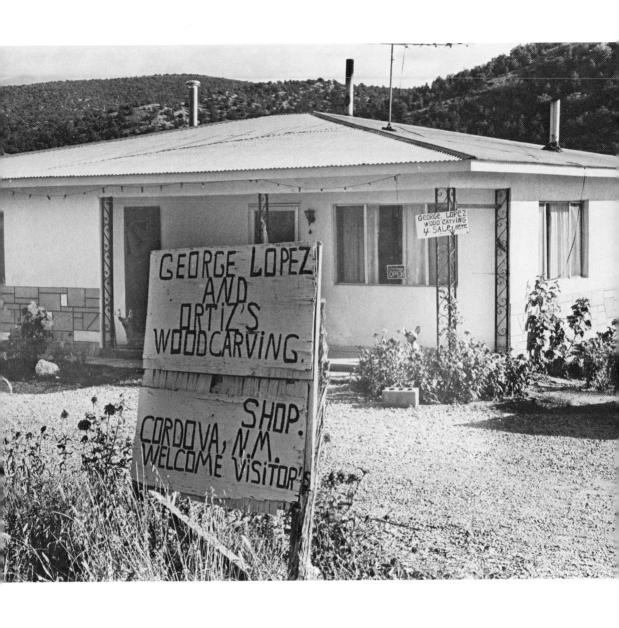

Plate 81. The House of George and Silvianita López in Córdova's Rito Quemado Valley. Both of these signs and one at the top of the driveway direct patrons to the Lópezes' house.

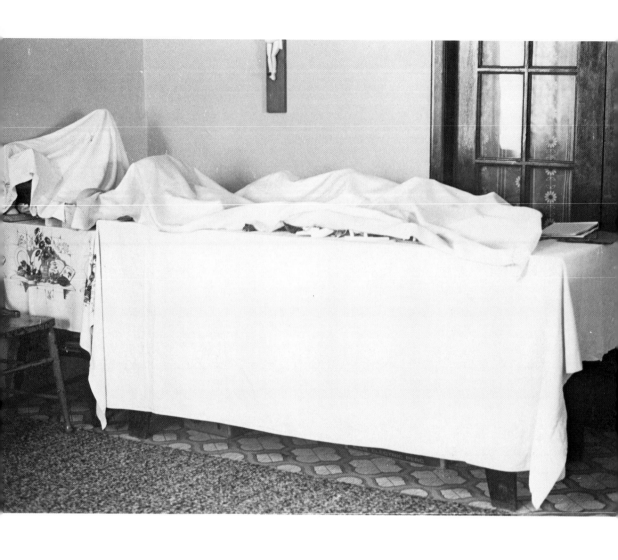

Plate 82. The Lópezes' "Table" or Counter. This photograph, taken in 1974, shows the carvings with their usual cloth cover.

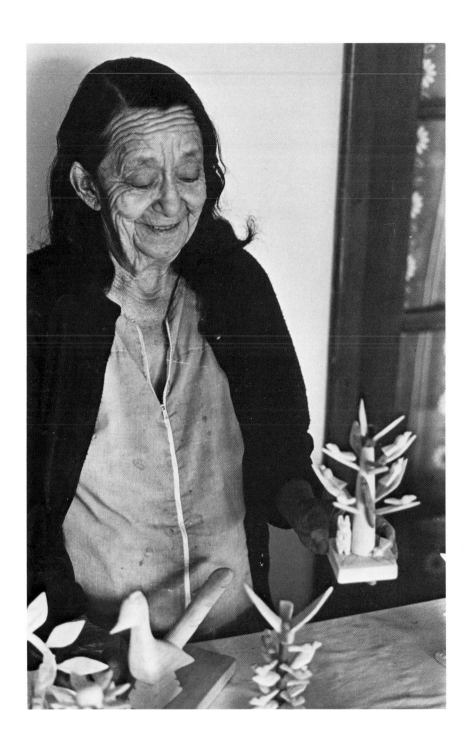

Plate 83. Silvianita López Shows a Carving to Customers from Her Position behind the "Table."

these visits thus warrant further examination. After a brief analysis of the interaction, the conceptual organization of the encounter between carver and visitor will be sketched from the viewpoints of each group.

This pattern of events can be profitably studied as a performance standardized by the Lópezes in order to cope with the frequent entry of strangers into their home. It is a highly regular sequence of events, and the same set of phrases is used with nearly every customer. This standardization is encouraged by the Lópezes' lack of familiarity with English. Silvianita López knows only a few words of English, and although George is much more competent in the language, he is far from fluent. Nevertheless, by responding to the visitors' every word, and always with a smile and a nod, George and Silvianita minimize conversational strain and often create the impression that both are fluent in English.

Silvianita is quick to reinforce a customer's interest in a carving and in this way she encourages sales, but the Lópezes never give any kind of sales talk. Although most of their customers differ from them culturally and socially, the Lópezes manage to control the interaction in such a way that a similar performance gives each visitor the feeling that hospitality has been extended to him or her personally. The Lópezes work as a team in executing the performance. George receives recognition for the couple's work. Nevertheless, Silvianita's role is equally important in making the encounter a success. Her constant smile and amiable chuckle are often remembered. Nor is the hospitality insincere; it is very much a part of Hispano culture. It is, however, expressed in a very specialized manner and creates a fairly predictable effect. This is the basis of much of George's success, because tourists much prefer entering an Hispano's home and listening to the artist describe the carvings to purchasing them in an impersonal curio shop.

Second, recognition of a name plays a very important part in the interaction of carver and customer. The carvers have discovered the importance of impressing their names upon patrons, and they utilize road signs, place their signature on the bases of carvings, and display publicity they have received to accomplish this goal. Name recognition is of great importance to their customers. Nearly all customers insist that their purchases be signed, and several carvers have reported incidents in which out-of-state visitors refused to accept their special orders when the works had not been signed and the artist was unavailable. Some patrons, in fact, speak of owning "a George López." It is not unusual for a regular customer to treat the introduction of a friend to López as a significant event.

The Lópezes are quite cognizant of the importance of name recognition. In discussing the problem, George and Silvianita, along with most of the other carvers, explain that they are merely responding to their customers' concern with names. George has said:

> We can sell the carvings if I sign them on the bottom with my name. The people want to buy things which have my name on them. If I don't sign them, we can't sell them. I don't know why the business is like

that, but I must do it. It's the same with this magazine which we sell here [Briggs 1974a]. I have to sign it before they'll buy it. Perhaps this is because they now know me, and this is why they come. But they will stop coming if we die.

Since nearly all the traditional image makers preferred anonymity, the concern with names probably originated with the Anglo-Americans. Nevertheless, George's signature on an offertory box he made for the local chapel in 1928, which would not traditionally have been signed, indicates that the concept was transmitted both successfully and rapidly to the Córdovan carvers (refer back to Plate 71).

A third feature affecting the character of encounters between carver and customer is the seasonal distribution of sales. The frequency with which tourists arrive at the Lópezes' house differs at various times of the year, and the same is true for the other carvers. January to April, for example, is the wood carvers' slow period. Very few customers arrive; nevertheless, Silvianita and George make sure that they are around the house in case someone should stop. Most of their working time during the winter is devoted to building a large inventory in anticipation of the peak summer season. Beginning in May, however, business begins to increase as more out-of-state tourists travel through the region.

The period between the middle of June and the first week in September is hectic. At times carloads of visitors arrive almost continuously, and the Lópezes often find little time to carve. These frequent interruptions are at times disconcerting. The rate at which carvings are sold from the Lópezes' table during this period exceeds the rate at which they are replaced to such an extent that by the end of the summer the tables are nearly bare. The carvers consider themselves to be disappointing their customers in such situations, and they usually try to extricate themselves from these predicaments by placing carvings by other artists on their tables. The Lópezes, for example, count more heavily on help from the Ortizes during the summer months. Most of the other carvers do not approach the success enjoyed by the Lópezes, and their inventories are not so heavily depleted.

Labor Day weekend constitutes an apex, and business slows down considerably after it has passed. The volume of sales during the rest of the month closely resembles that of May, while the slowdown continues into October. A number of orders for Christmas gifts come in during the fall, and this keeps the volume of business somewhat higher than during the winter. The slackened pace of the winter season allows the Lópezes to build their inventory, however, and to catch up on unfilled orders from the summer.

Although this seasonal pattern exhibits a surprising degree of consistency, sales of Córdovan carvings are subject to variation between years. Visitors to the Córdovan shops can be classified into two groups according to place of origin. New Mexico residents do not have as far to travel, and they tend to return more frequently than do tourists from other states. The non-resident group constitutes a subset of New Mexico's tourist industry, and its patronage fluctuates as tourist business does generally. For example, the period during and following the Arab oil embargo showed a decrease in sales, and the non-resident patrons were largely responsible for this drop.

A basic similarity is evident in the views the carvers take of Córdovan marketing practices and of the organization of wood carving in general. This rapprochment is provided by a central symbol, the "table" (*mesa*), and the significance of the "table" can be represented on three levels.

First, on the physical plane, a "table" serves as the carvers' counter. They frequently stand behind it when waiting on customers, and all but *Plate 84* the largest carvings are exhibited on top of it (see Plate 84). Paper bags and other sales accessories are usually stored beneath it. Its location further serves to orient carver-patron interactions spatially. This spatial orientation is especially significant in that many Anglo-Americans expect the carvers' signs to lead them to an impersonal shop, and the anomalous situation of walking into a stranger's living room is partially resolved by the presence of a counter-like entity.

Second, the "table" is associated with a number of social aspects of the marketing of Córdovan wood carvings. Carvers believe that an artist has not really set up a table until at least one sign is placed along a road where tourists are likely to pass by. Normally, at least one sign giving directions to the shop will be placed on the main road into Córdova, and one or more signs on the carver's house or the gate leading to the house will identify the shop. Besides giving directions, these signs set the stage in two ways for potential encounters between carver and tourists.

First, the array of signs that greet the visitor contains many phrases such as "visitors welcome," "wood carvings for sale here," or the more unusual *visite* (visit). These expressions assist tourists in changing their perception of the carver's home from that of a private and noncommercial space to a place where total strangers can do business without regard for the privacy of the carver or the carver's family. José Dolores López's initialed screen door appears to have fulfilled this function as well. In this regard, the function of the signs is quite similar to that of the "tables." In recent years a number of the carvers have taken to the placement of a printed "come in, we're open" card in the shop window. The notion that this placard serves to depersonalize a private home and not to indicate a carver's business hours is supported by the fact that the "sorry, we're closed" side is never exposed.[4]

The Lópezes are not reluctant to interrupt a meal in order to wait on customers. The sight of food on the table prevents most Anglo-Americans from envisioning the shop as a public and commercial space, however, and they frequently depart without seeing the carvings. Silvianita therefore covers the dishes with a table cloth, because, as she explains, "If the people see that we are eating they will go away, saying 'go on and eat; we don't want to disturb you.'" This and other features of the interaction suggest that the Lópezes are at least intuitively aware of the difficulty

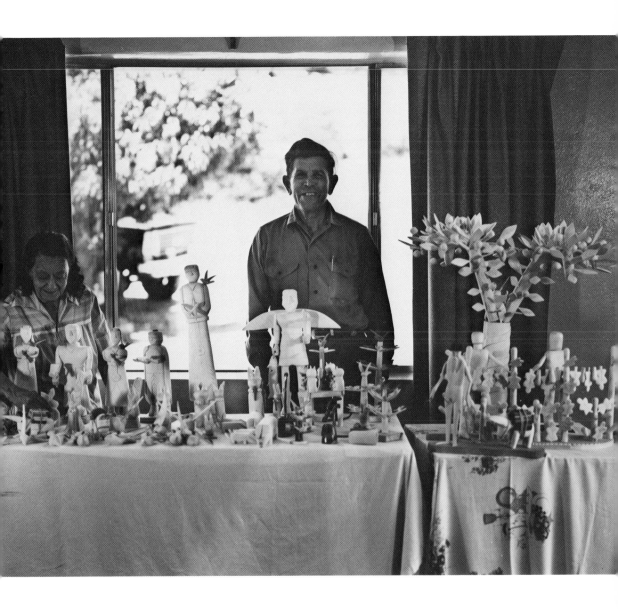

Plate 84. George and Silvianita López and Their "Table," 1977. The Lópezes occasionally change the location of their "table," and at this time it was in their living room.

experienced by their customers in making the transition from a private space to a public one, and that the Lópezes do not themselves perceive incongruity in the two functions of their house. This situation results from differing concepts of privacy in Hispano and Anglo-American cultures.

A second feature of the signs, the inclusion of the name of the carver associated with the "table," appears on all of the signs, and it reflects the carvers' heightened interest in becoming recognized by the outside world for their work. This concern appears to have been heightened by the saturation of the market for Córdovan carvings in the early 1960s and by George López's move to the *rancho* in 1965 (refer back to Map 2). López's location assured that his shop would be the first to be passed by tourists on their way into Córdova, and the placement of other carvers' signs closer to the highway represented their attempt to offset this advantage. The use of proper names does not merely relate to the carver's desire to attract potential customers to one shop rather than others; it may also serve to increase the carver's chances of being specifically remembered following a visit.

A third aspect of the "table" symbol is its identity as a cultural category. At the present time more than thirty persons in Córdova engage at least occasionally in wood carving. Nevertheless, only a limited number of these individuals are considered by the established artists to be direct competitors. The criterion involved in this distinction is termed "keeping a table." Once a carver has set up a "table," which also entails the display of signs, he is considered to have entered into the ranks of those who sell carvings to outsiders. Prior to setting up a table, most carvers sell their products from the shops of other carvers. Almost without exception, the credit for such works, which is symbolized by the signature of the artist on the bottom of the carving, accrues to the keeper of the "table" rather than to the producer. After a carver has set up a separate "table," however, he or she begins to receive recognition for his or her work, and others may sell from the new "table."

The importance of "keeping a table" appears to have been influenced by recent developments in the economics of wood-carving sales. Following the saturation of the market for Córdovan carvings in the early 1960s, the emergence of a new competitor, symbolized by setting up a table, was seen by the established carvers as a further division of the same pie. The belief that new competitors reduced sales among the existing carvers increased competiton between the established carvers.

Córdovan carvers explained much of the competition as selfishness on the part of the other carvers. Members of the group of recognized carvers frequently expressed the belief that all the carvers should share their customers, especially among José Dolores' sons and their spouses (*los de la familia*). When speaking with patrons, the carvers maintained that they did in fact share customers, although hostilities between carvers were common knowledge among Córdovans. Friends and relatives were told a different story, however. In every case the respondent claimed to be the victim, contending that other carvers never returned the favor of sending over customers and that competitors had even tried to steal business on a number of occasions.

Such a high degree of competitiveness between recognized carvers reflects their unusual symbiosis with the outside world. This range of concerns is characteristic exclusively of carvers with tables—Córdovans who play no role in the industry are not envious of the publicity received by the prominent carvers. Persons with tables are nevertheless quite jealous of their competitors' sales, awards, and publicity, and of the size and eminence of their clientele. Although Anglo-Americans are hardly responsible for this situation, the obsession of Applegate and his friends with competition does appear to have grown among the Hispano artists, as indeed these patrons hoped it would.

The central concept of the "table" plays a major role in determining the manner in which carvers relate to their work, and it has a significant impact on their overall lifestyle. First, keeping a table requires a person charged with the responsibility of opening the shop to be constantly nearby, waiting on customers and guarding against theft. The unpredictability of patrons' arrivals, along with Hispano concepts of time and privacy, does not dictate the restriction of sales to specific hours. The Córdovans respond to the unpredictability of patrons' arrivals by keeping someone on hand to tend the shop at all times. Most families with tables leave one member always at home and frequently refuse invitations that would necessitate leaving the shop unattended.

Second, "keeping a table" dictates another major difference between carvers with tables and carvers without them. While the second group will often cease carving for substantial periods of time, this fluctuation is not possible for the former. Persons who keep tables deem it necessary to replenish depleted inventories quickly. The high volume of sales during the summer frequently induces them to devote increasing amounts of time to their carving and, as noted above, to place other carvers' works on their tables if necessary.

Finally, the decision to "keep a table" singles out a particular household for a persistent and unusually direct set of encounters with the outside (and especially Anglo-American) society. The Córdovans who work in Los Alamos also interact frequently with Anglo-Americans, but such contact is maintained with a limited number of individuals and at a substantial distance from the Córdovans' home ground.

Aspects of the Córdovans' interpretations of interactions of carvers and patrons that relate less directly to marketing practices will be taken up in later chapters. I will now complement the Hispano view of this set of events with a sketch of the carvers' visitors and of the nature of these customers' participation in the industry.

Data on the patrons were accumulated through informal interviews with customers at the wood-carving shops, at the Santa Fe Fiesta and Spanish Market, and elsewhere. In addition, I attempted to overcome the difficulties of interviewing the patrons during their trips to the carvers' homes by distributing 300 copies of a questionnaire and cover letter to George López, Nora López and her mother Benita, Gloria L. Córdova, and José Mondragón (see Appendix 1). These carvers agreed to cooperate by handing out one copy of both documents to each customer.

Of course, the number of returned questionnaires does not accurately reflect the number of customers who visited the carvers during the period of the questionnaire study (July–December 1976). Similarly, the idiosyncrasies involved in distribution of the questionnaires by the carvers and in completion and mailing by the customers would not permit an assertion that a highly accurate profile of the clientele was obtained. The results do, however, provide valuable information on the customers' backgrounds and on their perceptions of the carvers. The following discussion focuses on customers' characteristics and preferences; a detailed listing of the responses is contained in Appendix 2.[5]

In essence, the patrons of the Córdovan wood carvers during the 1970s bear a strong resemblance to the customers of the late 1920s and early 1930s. This similarity is apparent in their backgrounds as well as in the manner in which they perceive the carvers and their work. The carvers' clientele continues to consist primarily of Anglo-Protestant men and women. A few exceptions were noted—two respondents bore Spanish surnames, and six indicated that they were Catholics. Most important, however, was the finding that customers for carvings continue to be "outsiders"; the residents of Córdova and similar communities do not patronize their neighbors. All but eleven of the respondents resided outside New Mexico, and these eleven came from Albuquerque, Santa Fe, and Los Alamos. Like patrons forty and fifty years ago, customers in the 1970s are still drawn from the middle and upper middle class.

The bases for attraction to Córdovan carvings also appear to be similar. The "uniqueness" or "simplicity" of the carvings constituted a major theme in both promotions of and reactions to Hispano work of the early, "revival" period. Similarly, patrons of the 1970s demonstrate continued concern with a perceived departure of the carvings from mass-produced products of mainstream America. The word "primitive," for example, appeared quite frequently in the completed questionnaires, and most responses to a query regarding overall impressions contained the terms "simple," "crude," "interesting," or "unique." The following responses convey this impression most clearly: "very beautiful, simple portrayals of life and animals"; "unique, primitive, charming"; "quaint, lively, and unique"; "charming, primitive"; "very original, different from anything I have seen."

There is perhaps more to this concept of primitiveness than meets the eye. Hispano communities in northern New Mexico are commonly stereotyped as "primitive," "remote," "backward," "quaint," "simple," and the like. Even communities that contain nearly 1,000 residents are generally referred to as "mountain villages" or simply "villages," and this geographic classification connotes a wealth of cultural stereotypes. Indeed, nearly all of the pejorative traits ascribed to Appalachian "hill-billies" are commonly used by Anglo-Americans in New Mexico to describe the "mountain villagers." Interestingly, the "traditional," "fami-lial," and "violent" components of this stereotype of Hispano society are believed to be especially characteristic of Córdova and Truchas.

The relevance of this image for the carver-patron relationship is twofold. First, the belief that Hispano villages are "exotic" and "unique" partially induces tourists and New Mexico residents to drive through the area. In this regard, the opportunity to visit the wood carvers' shops provides the passers-by with an invitation to enter this "foreign world." Several respondents indicated on the questionnaires that the "primitive-ness" and "simplicity" of the carvers and their communities prompted the newcomers' decision to visit. Second, the fact that the patrons de-scribe the carvings, the carvers, and their communities in nearly identical terms is no accident. The appeal of the carvings to outsiders derives partially from the images' perceived encapsulation of the characteristics of the carvers and their society. At the risk of oversimplification, one might say that the birds, trees, and animals evoke the closeness to nature associated with Hispano "villages," while the saints depict the purported spirituality—or even paganism or superstitiousness—of the Hispanos. The function of the carvings in this regard is, however, rather paradoxical. These beliefs are of course informed by the cultural concerns of the Anglo-Americans themselves; furthermore, as was noted in Chapter 3, the present form of the art was partially molded by the Anglo-Americans.

In short, the "mountain village" image of Hispano society intrigued the carving patrons and brought them to the artists' homes in Córdova. Paradoxically, however, not all of the customers respond in the same manner to the perceived "primitiveness" of the carvings. In fact, a bifur-cation appeared in the responses to nearly all of the questions regarding customer preferences. This dichotomy does not exactly define two types of customers; more precisely, it suggests two ideal types from which the customers themselves diverge in varying degrees.

On the one hand, a substantial number of the respondents felt that the "primitive" or "simple" quality of the carvings diminished the artistic merit of the work so substantially as to render the industry a process of "craft" or "curio" production. This attitude corresponded in many cases to a preference for smaller carvings such as birds, animals, and trees rather than images of the saints (see Plate 85). Although several of the respond- *Plate 85* ents were repelled by the images, most found them "interesting" yet sufficiently foreign to render them unappealing as house furnishings. As one respondent remarked in a comparison of the larger carvings with the smaller, he was "intrigued by images but less attracted" by them. These individuals tended to associate the "simplicity" of the carvings with a lack of technical virtuosity, describing them as "crude," and were more likely to judge the figures on their approximation of "natural" models than as artistic expressions. I have seen a number of such customers tell

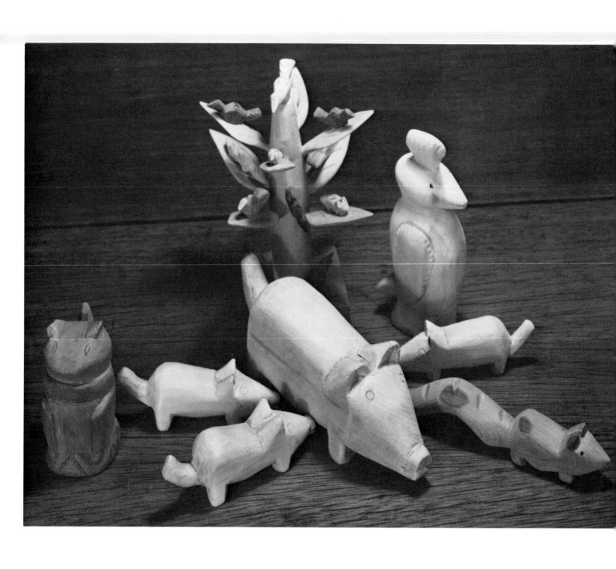

Plate 85. Small Bird, Animals, and a Tree by George and Silvianita López, 1970s (tree 16.3 cm. or 6.5 in. in height). From a private collection.

the Lópezes that their work was priced above its value, and the four respondents who found the prices excessive appeared to perceive the art in this manner.

On the other hand, another group of customers treated the production of Córdovan wood carvings as a mode of artistic expression rather than as a handicraft industry. These persons had usually learned of the carvers through publications or museum exhibitions, and they generally knew more about the history of the Córdovan carvers. Unattracted by mass-produced curios, they valued the "primitiveness" of the art, which enhanced their feeling for its uniqueness and originality. The "primitive" or "simple" quality of the unpainted carvings was considered to be aesthetically desirable, and it was said to make the carvings seem "strong," "sturdy," and "earth-like." Furthermore, "simplicity" has apparently retained its Victorian association with antiquity; a number of patrons noted that the "simplicity" and "primitiveness" of the unpainted wood gave the carvings the appearance of antiques. Interestingly, a number of images by José Mondragón that had been smoke-damaged in a fire in 1978 were snatched up by patrons because they looked "more antiqued" (see Plate 86). Patrons who viewed the Córdovan carvings as art were more likely to *Plate 86* deem prices conservative. Their judgment also prompted them to utilize canons of artistic creativity rather than approximation to natural models in considering aesthetic merit. These customers were much more impressed by ambitious Córdovan works such as images and were far more likely to buy them than were the curio seekers. This group also exhibited a greater awareness of Southwestern ethnic or folk art in general, and many of their comments sought to place the carvers' products within this larger context. Many customers with this orientation have purchased Southwestern weavings, baskets, katchina dolls, and even traditional images of the saints, and these items are frequently displayed in their homes along with Córdovan carvings (see Plate 87). *Plate 87*

The presence of two distinct orientations among the carvers' patrons should come as no surprise. Several Indian societies in the Southwest responded to the completion of the transcontinental railroads in the 1880s and 1890s by producing souvenirs for sale to the arriving hordes of tourists (Spicer 1962:558). Many of these buyers were unconcerned with adherence to traditional techniques or the quality of craftsmanship but desired small, easily transportable, and "exotic" mementos. A different set of Indian craft industries arose slightly later; fostered by rich connoisseurs, virtuosos and "name" artists produced fewer and finer objects for sale at higher prices. These wealthy patrons developed individual relationships with artists and established new marketing outlets such as the fiesta and the Indian Fair to promote sales (Brody 1971; 1976; Kent 1976; Spicer 1962).

Santa Fe artists and writers were involved in the latter movement, and there was much overlap in membership between the patrons of Hispano and Indian arts. Austin, Applegate, and others who visited López in Córdova constituted his early patrons associated with the fine arts, while

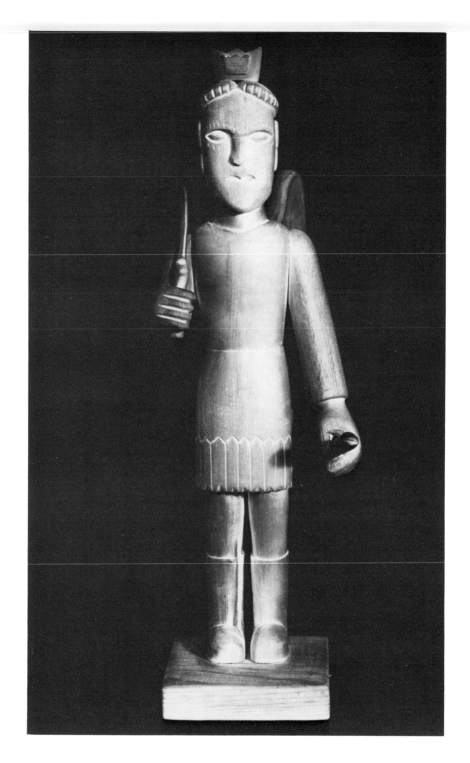

Plate 86. Smoke-Damaged Image of Michael the Archangel by José Mondragón, 1978 (36 cm. or 14.4 in. in height). Collections of the International Folk Art Foundation in the Museum of International Folk Art, Santa Fe.

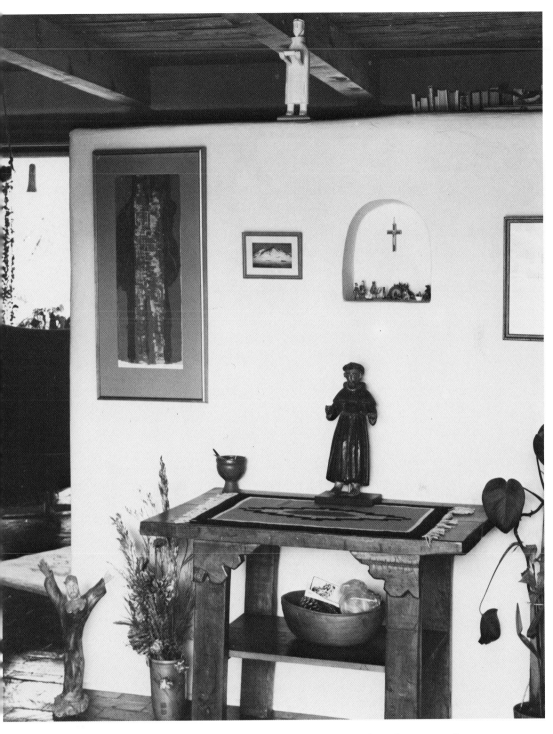

Plate 87. The Front Hall of a Carving Patron, Showing Display of Images. This private collection of carvings includes the display of a San Pascual by George López (top), a traditional polychromed image (center), and a work by Ben Ortega (lower left). This collection also includes Anglo-American and Indian art.

The Marketing of Carvings 151

López's wares were purchased by the curio seekers during his visits to Santa Fe. An increase in the number of Anglo-Americans in the area and improvements in transportation in the early postwar period brought the latter group to the carvers' doors, however, and the carvers satisfied them with a stream of smaller and more rapidly produced carvings. The market for Southwestern ethnic arts was becoming increasingly specialized, however, and the Córdovans' relationship with the tourists further alienated them from the upper echelons of the connoisseur market (see Brody 1976:76).

The carvers' clientele continues to include a few individuals who remain as dedicated to the study and encouragement of their work as were Austin and Applegate. Nevertheless, the more knowledgeable patrons of the Córdovan artists seem to represent a category that falls between the curio seekers and the elite connoisseurs of the pottery of María Martínez and Two Grey Hills rugs. Indeed, the elaborate images executed by José Dolores López's descendants have never received the prices commanded by internationally recognized Indian artists.

Córdovan wood carvings are not marketed solely in the community, however. Additional sales are generally made through shops, museums, annual Spanish markets, and the Santa Fe Fiesta. Beginning with the shops, a number of dealers in Southwestern arts and crafts are regular customers of the carvers. Many make annual buying trips, and such persons will frequently purchase a number of carvings from one carver for resale. Special orders, either for mailing or to be picked up, are frequent, and these occasionally include several dozen items. At times, particular carvers may depend upon a single shop for the majority of their sales. Cidelia Pacheco de López, for example, does not keep her own table, but she has served as the primary Córdovan supplier for Ortega's Weaving Shop in Chimayó. The Córdovan wood carvings are generally surrounded in these shops by other carvings as well as by weavings, pottery, jewelery, and the like. Hispano furniture and *retablos* are sometimes exhibited as *Plate 88* well, and Plate 88 illustrates the diversity of such displays.

The Córdovan carvers have exhibited and sold their work through museums since the 1930s, and a variety of arrangements are made with such institutions. Museum personnel will often arrange for the completion of a particular work or works in advance, although it is not unusual for a curator to select from a carver's current inventory. Examples are sometimes borrowed for exhibition alone and are then returned, while some institutions buy the works outright or will sell the works to patrons at the end of the show. Museum gift shops often sell Córdovan carvings, as shops at the Museum of International Folk Art and the Fine Arts Museum in Santa Fe, the Museum of Albuquerque and the Maxwell Museum in Albuquerque, and the Colorado Springs Fine Arts Center have done through the years.

Córdovan wood carvings are marketed through these outlets in two distinct manners. Tourist-oriented shops tend to concentrate on the smaller, secular carvings (birds, animals, *coronitas*, and small trees).

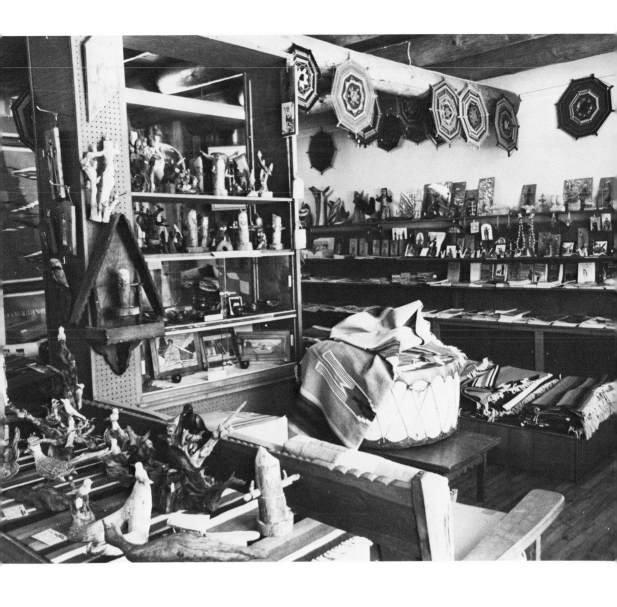

Plate 88. A Display of Wood Carvings in Ortega's Weaving Shop, Chimayó, New Mexico, 1977.

Museums, on the other hand, usually request more ambitious works, such as large trees, medium and large images of the saints, Death carts, and the like. Moreover, Córdovan carvings tend to be categorized in different ways in the two situations. Both the staff and the patrons of tourist-oriented shops generally regard the carvings as curios, and prices tend to reflect this view. Pieces on display in museums tend to be categorized as art or at least crafts, especially if they are presented in the context of a formal exhibition. If exhibition items are offered for sale, the prices tend to be much higher.

The Spanish Market of the Spanish Colonial Arts Society similarly provides the carvers and other Hispano artists with a chance to display and sell their works under the *portal* of the Palace of the Governors in Santa Fe. Reinstated in 1965 (Alan Vedder 1972: Personal communication), the Spanish Market takes place each year on the last Saturday and Sunday of July. The number of tourists in the area has roughly peaked at that time, and many artists sell a great deal of their inventory during the weekend. The society also awards cash prizes and ribbons for the best work in a number of categories, including painting, tinwork, embroidery, and weaving. Córdovans frequently take first prizes in carving. The standards of the judges and organizers bear a strong resemblance to those of former officers of the society; they accept only "traditional" Hispano work and applaud quality and originality in craftsmanship. Regional museums often send curators to search for examples of contemporary Hispano art to add to their collections. The concept of the "table" plays an important role in the interaction between Córdovan carvers and their patrons here as well, and the tables with their multifarious accouter-
Plate 89   ments separate the artists from the throng (see Plate 89).

The annual fiesta in Santa Fe continues to provide another marketing outlet for the carvers. The apical importance that it held for José Dolores López's work has diminished considerably, however, and only a few Córdovans generally attend each year.[6] This effect appears to have resulted partially from the absence of special events relating to carving, such as the Spanish Market and fair at the fiesta in the 1920s. The Spanish Colonial Arts Society no longer organizes the participation of the His-pano artists in the September event, and the fiesta finds the carvers in various locations around the plaza. They are often engulfed in a sea of
Plate 90   people and objects (see Plate 90). The carvers watch their tables for the two or three days of the fiesta, and in previous years sales at the fiesta constituted a large portion of annual carving income.[7] Nevertheless, not all of the time is devoted to business. A number of family members usually come, and slow periods allow visitation with friends and relatives
Plate 91   who reside in Santa Fe (see Plate 91). A few of the carvers have befriended Anglo-American patrons who live in Santa Fe, and the fiesta provides the carvers with an opportunity to socialize with them as well. A few of the Córdova carvers used to attend the state fair in Albuquerque, but their participation there has been affected, as it has at the Santa Fe Fiesta, by concerns with the size and at times with the unruliness of the crowds.

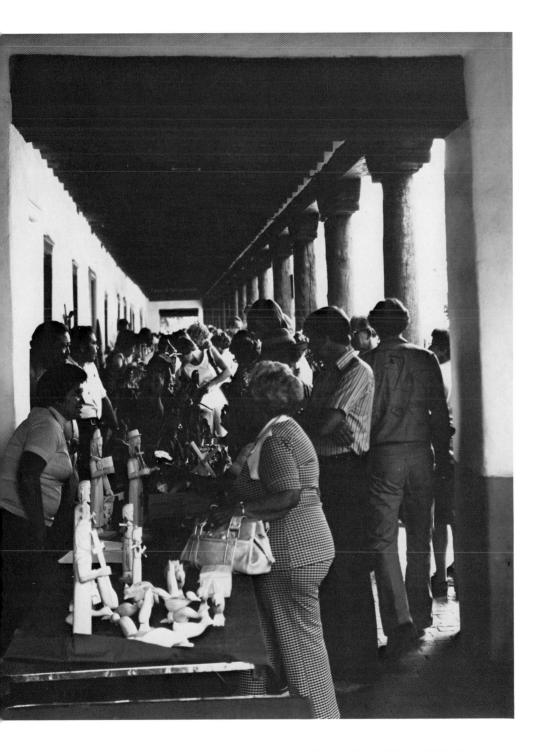

Plate 89. The Hispano Artists Greet Customers from behind Their "Tables" under the *Portal* of the Palace of the Governors at the 1977 Spanish Market of the Spanish Colonial Arts Society.

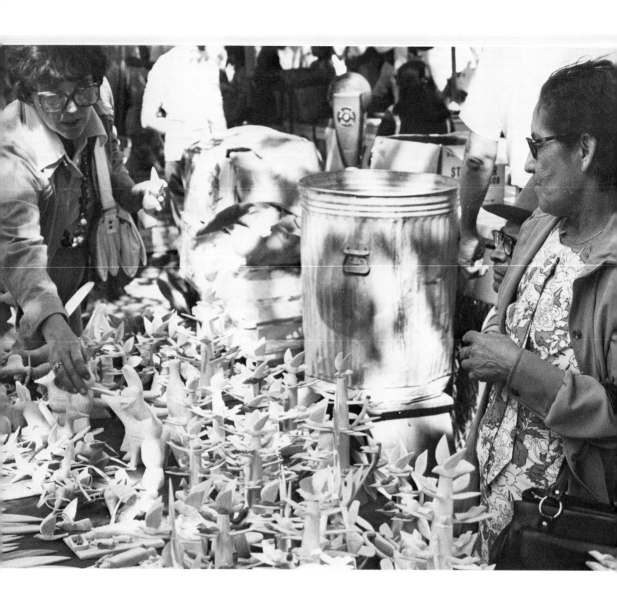

Plate 90. The Late Benita López Waits on a Customer at the 1976 Santa Fe Fiesta. The carvings on her table illustrate Benita's and Ricardo's specialization in small birds, animals, trees, and the like.

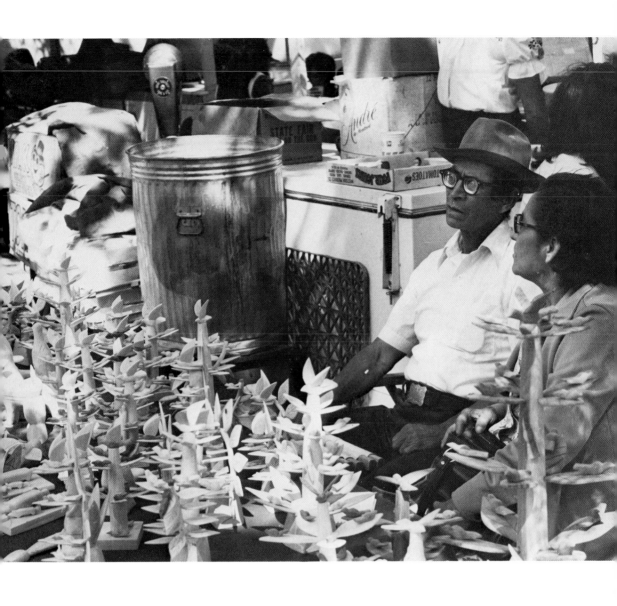

Plate 91. Benita López Converses with a Relative at the 1976 Santa Fe Fiesta.

The Marketing of Carvings   157

In conclusion, the pricing practices of Córdovan carvers bear mentioning. The amount asked for a given item is based upon the size and complexity of the item and upon the amount of detailed work (especially filigree) that it contains. Surprisingly, Córdovan works increased little in price between the time of the initial sales by José Dolores López and the early 1970s, although prices rose slightly between 1975 and 1977.[8] This stability is in large measure due to the Córdovans' belief that their customers would simply cease buying carvings if the price were to rise substantially. At the present time they do not, however, lower their prices in response to declines in the demand for their work as did José Dolores López and Celso Gallegos. A ten-inch Gabriel the Archangel purchased from George López in the 1950s went for $15.95; the same carving was sold in 1974 for $18.00 or $20.00, and it would bring $30.00 to $35.00 today.

Table 1. Inventory of Carvings Available for Sale
in López-Ortiz Shop, October 13, 1974

Item Description	Size	Artist	Original Price	Shop Price
Muerte (Death cart)	20″	Lawrence Ortiz	$ 95.00	$130.00
Saint Peter	40″	″		350.00
Our Lady of the Conquest	30″	″	185.00	250.00
Saint Joseph	25″	George López	85.00	112.00
Muerte (Death cart)	40″	Lawrence Ortiz	350.00	550.00
Crucifix	25″	Cristóbal Ortiz	85.00	112.00
Crosses (Aspen)	6″	Lópezes	2.75	5.00
Crosses (Aspen)	10″	″	8.00	12.00
Crosses (Cedar)	6″	″		5.50
Saint Christopher	15″	George López	55.00	75.00
Tree of Life	7″	Lópezes	8.50	10.00
Donkey	5″	″	7.00	9.00
Crown (with birds)	7″	″	10.50	15.00
Doves	large	″	10.00	16.00
Doves	medium	″		7.50
Doves	small	″		6.00
Yucca (Plant)	6″	Eurgencio López	4.75	8.00
Roadrunners	medium	Lópezes	8.00	12.00
Roadrunners with yucca	10″	Eurgencio López		35.00
Christmas tree	25″	Lópezes	45.00	60.00
Saint Gabriel with cup	20″	George López	75.00	95.00
David and Goliath	20″	Lawrence Ortiz	60.00	80.00

A most unusual situation occurs in the sale of carvings to commercial shops. Most businesses take 20 percent to 30 percent off the carvers' retail prices as a wholesale discount. The carvers believe, however, that they should receive at least their retail price for carvings. Therefore "wholesale" prices are raised sufficiently so that the carvers' retail price remains after the discount is subtracted from the wholesale price. If a piece must be mailed, then prices are also raised to compensate for shipping costs and the risk of loss or breakage en route.

Table 1 lists a set of carvings with the artist, height of figure, the price if the carvings are sold in the López home, and an adjusted price (for sale to shops where both 25 percent commission and shipping costs would have to be paid by the family) given for each item. By way of comparison, an eleven-inch Rafael the Archangel by George López sold for $40.00 in 1976, while a thirteen-inch St. Francis brought $45.00 and a version of Adam and Eve in the Garden (with ten-inch figures and a twenty-four-inch tree) went for $150.00.

Future changes in both pricing and marketing practices, as well as patterns of interaction between carvers and patrons in general, would seem to depend largely upon whether or not Córdovan carvings come to be defined as objects of art or as curios. If the carvers continue to sell their works to both the curio seekers and the patrons of the arts, the prices cannot rise drastically or the quality diminish greatly without alienating one of the two groups. Contemporary Hispano carvers who live outside of Córdova, such as Eluid Martínez (Santa Fe) and Horacio Valdez (near Dixon) have removed their work from the curio market entirely. They produce a smaller number of more ambitious works at considerably higher prices for collectors and museums. It is possible that the Córdovan carvers will follow suit, but the continual entry of part-time and relatively unskilled artists into the local market suggests that such a movement is hardly just around the corner.

6.

The Technology of Contemporary Wood Carving in Córdova

This chapter addresses itself specifically to the concepts, tools, and techniques utilized in the production of unpainted wood carvings by George and Silvianita López. Occasional references are made to other contemporary carvers in Córdova, but the scope of the inquiry was limited mainly to one couple in order to present an in-depth picture of one set of methods of production. Although most carvers differ slightly in technique, the description that follows is largely representative of all Córdovan carvers who do not utilize power tools in their work. This sketch of the process by which carvings are produced will be followed by an analysis of the relationship between carving technology and the symbolism associated with the transmission of the requisite techniques.

The data from which this chapter is drawn were collected for the most part early in the field study. On 9 September 1972, I began carving under the guidance of George López. As with other Córdovan carvers, this was not a formal apprenticeship, but a highly informal relationship in which the novice watched a carver work for a period of time (in my case, three weeks) and was then provided with a piece of wood, a knife, and occasional suggestions when help was sought. By 26 October 1972, the end of the first substantial field stay, I had carved several figures (including two large *bultos*). The fact that I had learned to carve was important to the family, and family members have told my friends that the purpose of my working with the Lópezes was to learn the carving trade. In addition to bringing me closer to the Lópezes and Ortizes, my carving gave me a new understanding of the technical processes involved in production.

The carving process begins with the acquisition of materials. Each carver has access to an inventory of tools, a few specific to the carving industry but most included in the carpenter's repertoire. These will be described as they are used in the production process. Glue (usually Elmer's) and sandpaper must also be on hand. No artist can work without a medium, so carvers or their relatives make one or more trips onto national forest lands to obtain native woods.

1. Contemporary carvers utilize aspen, berried juniper, willow, and pine. The quantities of pine required are small, and lumber is generally obtained from the sawmill in Hernández (just northwest of Española). One truckload of scrap cost $3.00 in 1974, and this quantity is more than sufficient for a year. Aspen, juniper, and willow are all cut by the carvers. George used to cut his own wood, but as he once proudly proclaimed to a visitor, "I don't have to cut my own wood any more. Now they bring it to me."

Junior Ortiz is charged with providing the family with wood for carving, and he generally accomplishes this task during his yearly vacation. In order to obtain the aspen he must travel to Española to obtain a permit to cut green wood in the Santa Fe National Forest. The going rate was one dollar per cord of wood in 1974; the permit was good for ninety days, and Junior and other recognized carvers were given priority in permit issuance in the area due to their dependence on the local aspen.

Even after the permit has been secured, cutting the aspen is no easy job. The green logs are heavy, so two or three pickup trucks are often needed to haul the cut wood to Córdova. The day on which aspen is to be cut must be preceded by several days of dry weather to insure the passability of roads. The wood must be cut during late spring or early summer, as the bark sticks to the wood and cannot be peeled if logs are cut before about May 15 or after July 13. Finally, the quality of the aspen varies, depending on location. All aspen is cut near Borrego Mesa, south and east of Córdova, but the percentage of wood suitable for carving in each tree is only sufficient in certain locations. Trees are selected for height and diameter, but examination of the exterior reveals little information about the quality of the wood. Trees are felled, cut into six- or eight-foot sections, and the wood is inspected for a number of qualities. The wood must be alive and solid throughout, the grain must be relatively straight, and the number of knots should be minimal. Two or three full-sized logs are sufficient for a year, and Junior and his sons fell trees with a power saw until a sufficient quantity of good wood has been obtained. Branches are razed, and the green wood is hauled to Córdova (see Plate 92). *Plate 92*

A similar process is involved in the acquisition of berried juniper. This wood is cut in the Carson National Forest near Ojo Sarco (north and east of Córdova on the High Road to Taos), and a separate permit must be obtained at the ranger station near Peñasco. The small amount of willow used is simply cut along the banks of the Rito Quemado.

2. Once home, Junior and his sons peel the bark off the aspen and juniper logs, cut them into lengths of between four and six feet, and split most of the blocks lengthwise to facilitate drying. The wood is then placed outside in the sun or between the earthen ceiling and the tin roof of Junior's adobe house for drying. Since green wood is poor for carving, wood must be cut far in advance of use to allow for partial drying (see Plate 93). *Plate 93*

3. An individual carving is begun when the artist looks for a piece of wood of suitable size and quality for the object he has in mind. Aspen is used for the main parts of an image, but berried juniper is often used for

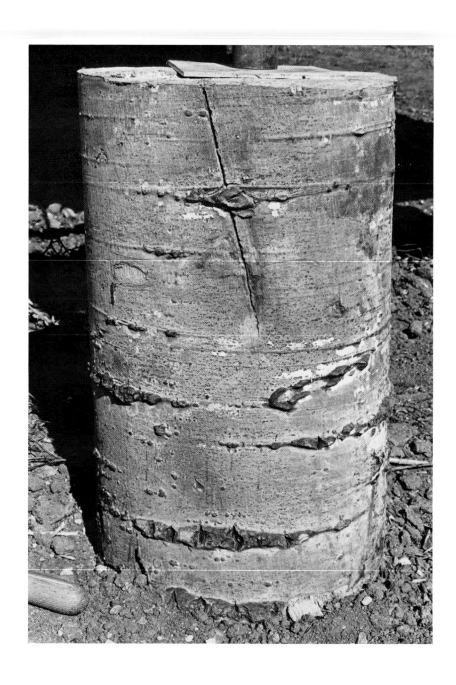

Plate 92. Section of Unpeeled Aspen Log.

162　　*The Contemporary Period*

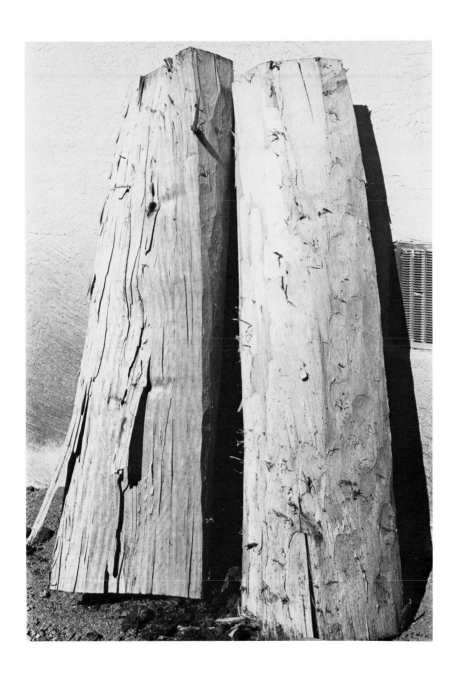

Plate 93. Peeled and Quartered Aspen Drying in the Sun.

The Technology of Carving 163

ornaments such as birds and drops of blood, and many customers prefer the two-toned effect. Once a block is selected, it is sawed to a height between one-half and one-quarter inch greater than the final height desired.

4. The next step is to cut the block to fit the general size of the image. Here a hatchet and/or large kitchen knife is used to obtain the proper dimensions by tapering the block and initiating major indentations. Once this step is completed, the wood will be round or rectangular in shape and will have assumed the approximate height and width of the finished figure.

5. The next step determines the basic form of the finished piece. The carvers say that this is the most important phase in the carving process, and it is termed "making the cuts." This expression has two referents. First, "making the cuts" refers to notching the block with a saw (see Figure 1). This "cut" is then widened with a knife, and it defines the exact location and depth of structural units. In its second sense, "making the cuts" refers to the entirety of the technological processes that underlie the production of a particular saint. "Knowing the cuts"—possessing a knowledge of the requisite technological or structural principles—is deemed essential. The fundamental question of how this information is transmitted will be taken up below. Cuts are made at such places as the neck, shoulders, waist, legs, and shoes.

This process is circumvented when mechanized tools such as band and jig saws are used. While carvers without power tools often pencil the location of the cuts onto the block, carvers with power tools will generally draw the entire outline of the figure. Once this has been done, the lines are traced out with the band or jig saw, leaving a block that is flat on top and bottom with rounded edges. Mechanization thus forms a departure in two ways from the technique previously used in Córdovan carving. First, the cuts need not be made, and a familiarity with the location is no longer necessary. Secondly, mechanization often results in a decrease in the level of technical excellence of the carving—curves are frequently rounded and lack the angular quality characteristic of the Córdovan style. Close attention is not paid to the grain of the wood, and the piece's overall aesthetic appeal is thereby diminished. If the process of mechanization largely displaces the notching, it will be interesting to note the effect of such a technological change on the importance of the concept of "making the cuts."

6. Once the structural units have been determined, the next phase entails the removal of wood down to a limit imposed by the extension that prominent features will assume. This process consumes much of the time spent on a piece. It is generally accomplished with a pocketknife alone, but a variety of other tools may be used by the more adroit. George López uses a wood rasp and/or small hand plane on larger pieces, especially those with a skirt or robe.

At this stage a mastery of the medium is most important. When obtaining the rough shape of the figure and "making the cuts," a good

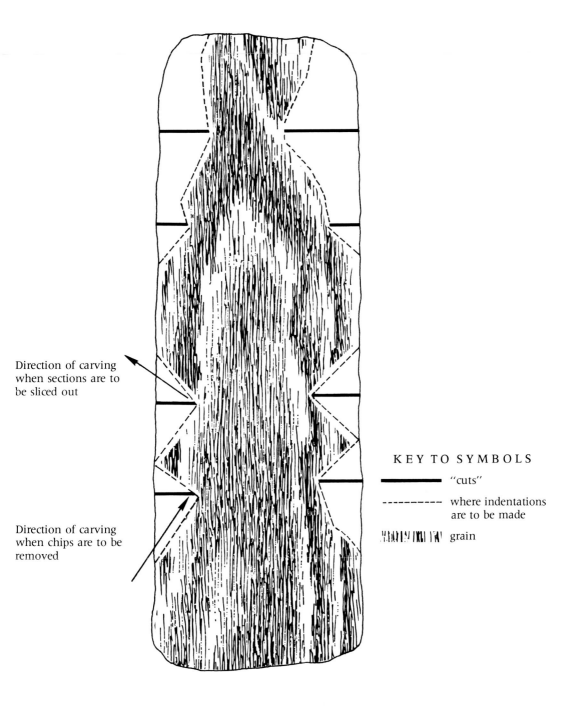

Direction of carving
when sections are to
be sliced out

Direction of carving
when chips are to be
removed

KEY TO SYMBOLS

━━━━━━ "cuts"

---------- where indentations
are to be made

〄〴〴〴〴〴〴〴 grain

Figure 1. Location of "Cuts" in the Production of an Image of Our Lady of Guadalupe by George López.

The Technology of Carving　165

carver plans his or her work so that the cuts are perpendicular to the grain of the wood and the grain runs parallel to the length of the piece. By cutting in this way, the carver can keep close control over the amount of wood that he or she removes with each slice of the knife. If the grain runs across the length of the piece, then the work is extremely slow and the chances of inadvertently splitting off a chunk of wood and ruining the piece are much greater. As shown in Figure 1, indentations are made by slicing across the grain in the direction of the center of the block. Aspen is a soft wood that splits easily, so that a chunk of wood will split along the grain if the wood is cut from the inside out across the grain. This technique can be utilized to remove larger sections of wood along the grain if the grain runs parallel to the length of the figure. It does, however, require a higher degree of skill in the medium. The economy of carving and the quality of finished products are thus related to the ability of the carver to control the grain of the wood.

7. The next step in the production of an image is the articulation of the features of the particular saint. This is accomplished with the pocketknife, but occasionally a chisel is brought into play. The feet of the image must be separated and formed, any belt or tie strings must be left in low relief while the rest of the robe or dress is incised, and head, neck, and shoulders should assume their basic shapes. In addition, the carver must plan the joints at which arms or other accessories are to be attached, shaped to fit the other parts, and smoothed.

Here again, planning and experience in carving the images of the saints are important, for if enough wood has not been left for the prominent features, the block must be discarded or a caricature will result. Most novice carvers lose pieces at this stage; most frequently they plan for the bulk and not the features, thus leaving insufficient wood for incision. Similarly, they may break off a protruding feature by carving against the grain away from the center of the figure. Once the features are separated from the rest of the carving, the point of the knife is used to incise a line around each feature, and excess wood is cleaned to that point. The final result of the work in this stage is a set of sharp lines that emphasize structural units.

8. Next comes the carving of additional pieces to be added to the main block. The head and feet are generally carved out of the same block; the remaining items include the base, arms and hands, wings, leaves, crosses, birds, and any of a variety of accessories. Each saint, however, must be carved with certain attributes in order for it to be recognized as a specific representation. St. Francis carried a skull as he was rendered by the traditional image makers, but contemporary versions include the cord around his habit, birds, and sometimes a cross. No Our Lady of Guadalupe is complete without crown, halo, quarter moon, and the impression of a face on her robe. Some attributes have been lost and others gained over the years.[1] There are variations on some of the basic accessories; George carves hands clenched as a block-like fist, extended with the fingers shallowly incised, or—on smaller images—folded across the chest in

one-piece construction. Accessories are frequently produced for several carvings at the same time.

9. The parts are then fitted together. Ends are carved and sanded until the fit is good, with small chips filling unwanted cracks, and many pieces receive a small depression at the joint so that an excess of glue can be applied (see Plate 94). Leaves are carved to a point, and a punch or a drill is used to provide a matching hole in the body of the figure. The ends of arms and wings are often carved to a point and similarly doweled. Once the parts are matched they are generally removed for final preparation.

Plate 94

10. Now the pieces are sanded. Unwanted indentations are smoothed with a coarse grit paper, leaving the entire surface area even but rough. A smooth finish is attained by the use of a medium grit paper followed by a fine grit paper. The final surface is so smooth that on a well-carved piece only the chip-carving remains to demonstrate clearly that the work was in fact carved. This separates the Córdovan wood-carving style from many modern Western sculptures, as the texture in many works in the Western tradition is designed to reflect materials and techniques to a greater extent ("the medium is the message") (see Plate 95).

Plate 95

11. The next-to-last process is termed *laboreando la cosa*, the engraving of the chip-carving and incised designs that José Dolores López was said to have adopted from his work in filigree jewelry. Such designs are usually carved on the base or platform of the piece as well as on the figure. The term *laboreando* also refers to incision of the eyes, mouth, eyebrows, and ears, which brings the carving to life. George López makes the images, and Silvianita rarely assists him with the gross work on *bultos*. Nevertheless, she performs nearly all of the *laboreando*. The filigree work is perhaps the most technically demanding phase of carving production. She accomplishes the chip-carving with a well-sharpened penknife. A line is notched on one side, a parallel incision is made, and the chip is removed. The depth of the incision is determined by the pressure placed on the blade and the width of the chip by the angle of entry. When the knife is held nearly perpendicular to the surface of the carving, the incision is very thin. A thin line generally connects shorter, wider indentions and frequently serves as a marginal pattern to emphasize the structure of the piece. The gouges given the Lópezes by admirers (see Plate 96) are not used on chip-carving. They are generally reserved for making small round incisions or holes, especially those filled with glue in order to reinforce a joint. These gouges are also used in carving the eyes.

Plate 96

12. As a final step, the pieces are glued together. Elmer's glue is used on all parts, and a small clamp may be used to insure a good bond. Gluing may be followed by additional sandings of bulges at the joints. Once the joints are dry, George López signs the carving in pencil on the bottom, and his wife places it on the table for sale. Small items generally receive only his name, larger carvings are also inscribed "Córdova, N.M.," and an occasional piece is given the date and title of the figure. The price is added if the carving is for the "table."[2]

Now that a discussion of the basic techniques is complete, a few ideas

The Technology of Carving   167

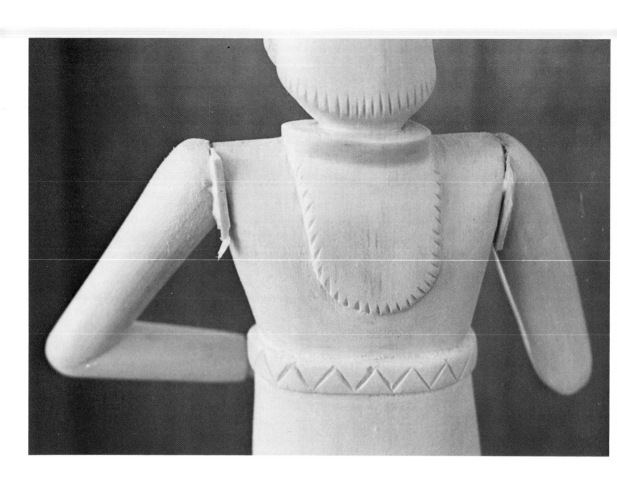

Plate 94. The Back of an Unfinished Image of St. Francis of Assisi by George López. Aspen chips have been glued into the cracks between the arms and the torso. Once dry, the joint will be carved and sanded smooth. Note the one-piece construction of head and torso.

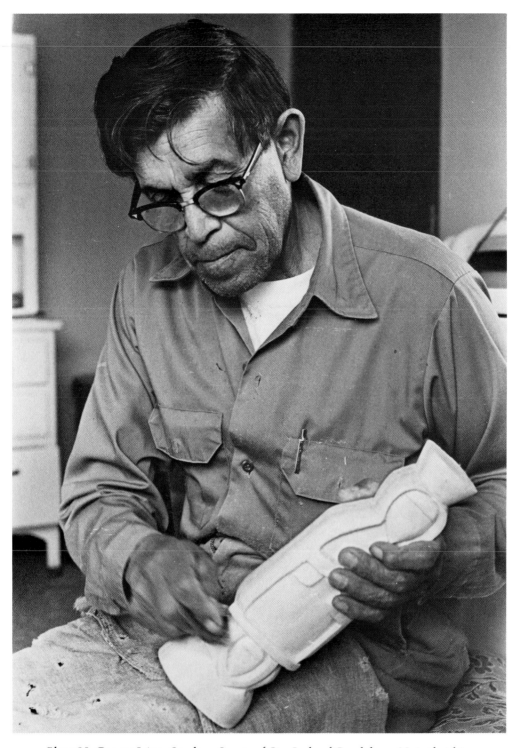

Plate 95. George López Sands an Image of Our Lady of Guadalupe. Note that his legs, covered with heavy cloth, act as a vise; the intensity of his concentration on the piece is also noteworthy.

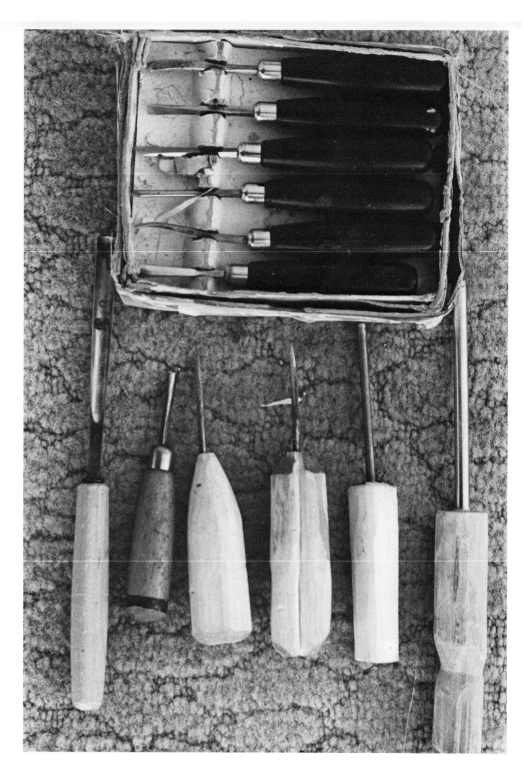

Plate 96. The Lópezes' Gouges. Most of the gouges on the right were fitted with handles by the Lópezes.

regarding variations in technique and other aspects of the production of images may be considered before we examine the production of other carvings. First, Geroge López discovered a new technique of facial construction in the 1960s. Formerly he had carved the nose on figures as he had all the protruding features—by rounding the block to the tip of the nose and then removing the wood surrounding it. He found that this method involved additional planning and work, however, since the nose often protruded more than the other features. Therefore, he carved flat noses on his images for many years. Eventually he began carving the face as a continuous rounded surface up to the forehead and gluing on a block that extended from the forehead halfway to the mouth and could be trimmed to leave a substantial nose. This method has its drawbacks too, however: the face is often circular and the block flat, so a small crack is left. Furthermore, George seems to have become so proud of his discovery that in recent years his noses have been disproportionately large (see Plate 97).

Plate 97

Knowledge of the spatial relations involved in carving is important if one wishes to understand the production process (see Plate 98). First, George López carves in his kitchen. He sits next to the window, where he can watch horses entering the alfalfa, customers turning into his driveway, and even cars passing on the road above. Next to him is a multishelved metal table on which he keeps the carvings on which work has begun as well as his sandpaper, glue, and most of his tools. A small cardboard box or two to his left contain small and medium-sized blocks of wood. Additional tools, particularly spare pocketknives, are kept in the cupboard next to the sink behind him. Finally, the wood shavings are collected before each meal and at the end of the day and are piled into the firewood box in the opposite corner.

Plate 98

López sits on an average-sized wooden chair as he does his work. He utilizes no table; all carving is done on his lap, while chopping and hammering are performed on the floor from a sitting position. A piece of cloth is spread over his lap to keep sawdust off his clothes and to protect his pants and legs against any slips with knife or saw. George uses his legs as a vise to hold one end of the carving while the other rests on his chest or stomach or is held with the left hand. Carving strokes that involve substantial body movements are directed outward, but the direction of smaller strokes depends on the area being carved. López uses the broad part of the blade for all carving except for hollowing deep recesses, where the point plays a more important role.

Silvianita López usually sits just to the right of the kitchen table on a small wooden chair. She too works freehand most of the time, but her *laboreando* and the intricate work on small figures are often performed while she sits at the table. She pencils the shape of a leaf or bird on her small block, and her penciled designs sometimes guide her hand in the filigree work. Probably due to the intricacy of her work, Silvianita holds the piece much closer to her eyes than López does. The Ortiz children sit opposite George López when they carve with the Lópezes in their

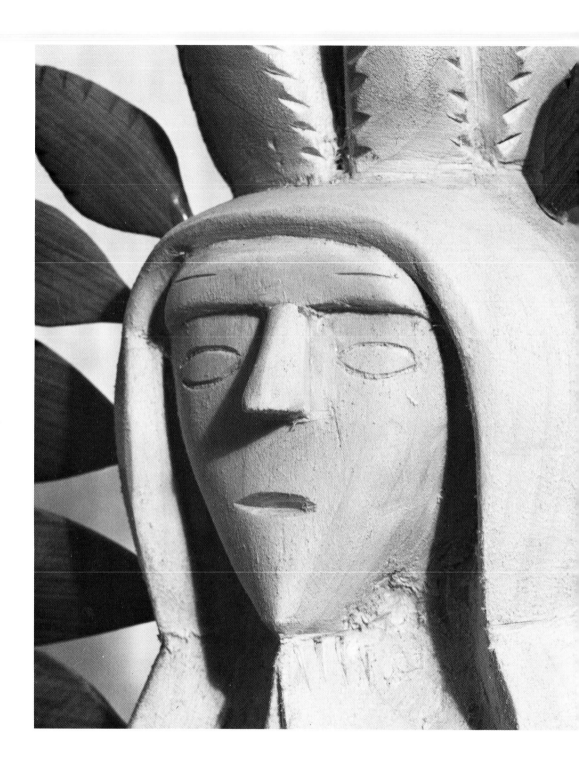

Plate 97. Detail of Head on Image of Our Lady of Guadalupe by George López. Note the size of the nose and the unevenness of the point at which it is attached to the face. The surface of this image is unusually rough for Córdovan carvings.

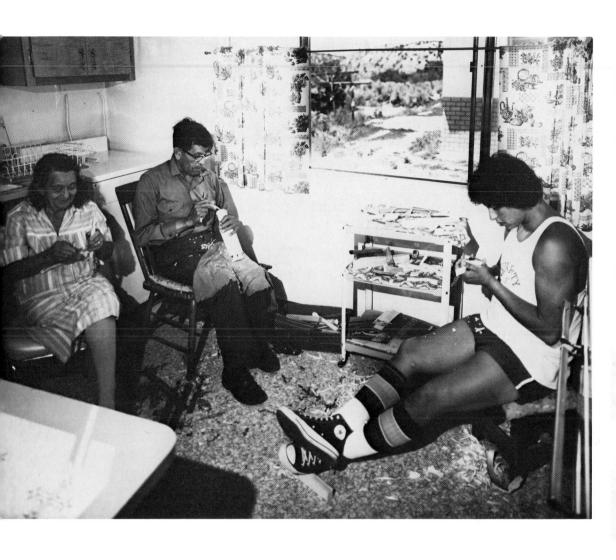

Plate 98. The Lópezes and Their Grandnephew Alex Ortiz at Work. The artists generally work in these locations in the kitchen, although Silvianita performs her *laboreando* at the table. Note the concentration of the carvers on their work.

kitchen; otherwise they use the back porch and garage, which their parents prefer.

Both George and Silvianita López give their full attention to their work. They watch each stroke; if they must answer a question or look up for any other reason, they will cease carving until they can again concentrate. This constant attention is the fatiguing element in carving and is cited by carvers as evidence that theirs is hard work. George's brother Nicudemos claims to have quit carving partly to avoid damaging his eyes. He maintains that George's two cataract operations show that carving ruins one's eyes, for one must stare intently at a highly reflective surface constantly while carving. The Lópezes do not even listen to the radio while carving, although some of the other carvers do so frequently.

Plate 99

Various tools and aids are used in addition to those mentioned above. (See Plate 99 for an inventory of tools used by the Lópezes.) A large kitchen knife is often used in step 4 to cut along the grain to shape the length of the block to fit more closely the image to be carved. The knife is positioned over the place where the split will be made and is then struck by a hammer, so that the knife acts as a wedge. This process can save much time in later shaping of the figure, but here again it is necessary to have a straight grain running parallel to the length of the figure.

Plate 100

In the carving trade it is highly important to keep the knives well sharpened. This is especially true for López and his family. Other carvers pride themselves on the use of more expensive pocketknives; the Lópezes, however, use Japanese knives that cost as little as $1.50 (see Plate 100). Although these knives may not last as long as more expensive models, they can be given an edge that is just as sharp. The edge is lost quickly, however, so George must sharpen his knife after every hour or two of use. He is an expert at this skill, and mastery of it requires much experience. The Lópezes first temper a new knife by inserting it in a boiled potato until it cools. Next, a coarse whetstone is used to put the initial edge on the blade. In contrast to many sharpening techniques, George López moves the blade circularly on the stone. Once he has obtained an edge, he uses a marble stone to refine it and to remove burrs. Still, as López explains, many sharpenings of a raw knife are necessary before a very good edge is obtained. A sharp knife is essential in carving, and putting a good edge on a blade is an art in itself.

A small hand drill is used with one-half or three-eighths inch bits for a variety of purposes. For example, a drill is used to hollow the clenched fist to hold a cross or other accessory. It is most extensively used, however, in hollowing out the skull of figures of Death. López occasionally uses a small square to produce right angles or as a straightedge. A pencil or pen is sometimes used "to get the cuts right." Here the rough outline of the figure and/or the positions of cuts are sketched on the uncut block. Silvianita López often marks a block in this manner, as George does on animal figures. After many years of carving, his skills of extrapolation are well refined. Although he carves some figures with his memory alone to guide him, on most images he either consults photographs of his work or

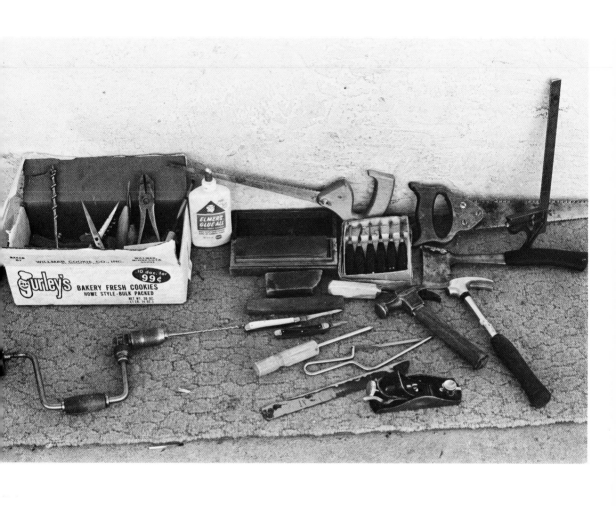

Plate 99. Inventory of the Lópezes' Tools, 1974.

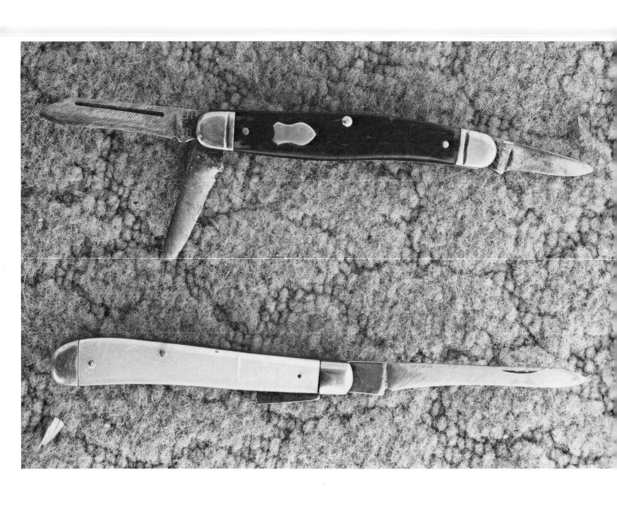

Plate 100. Knives of the Variety Commonly Used by the Lópezes.

The Contemporary Period

uses Breese and Boyd (1966) to refresh his memory with regard to attributes and proportions.

With a few exceptions, the production of carvings other than images follows the same set of techniques. Silvianita López produces most of the smaller carvings with occasional assistance from George. Most carvers will make as many as twenty examples of smaller items simultaneously in assembly-line fashion. In carving the smaller trees with animals and birds (labeled "Christmas trees" for the tourists and termed *arbolitos* among carvers), the artist makes the entire set of one part, such as leaves, at the same time. If Silvianita is working by herself, she will carve, sand, and decorate each set of parts separately, repeat the process for the remaining parts, and then glue the carvings together. Other persons frequently assist her in one of two ways. Either they work on leaves while she produces birds, or she carves each leaf, hands it to her helper for sanding, and then ornaments all leaves herself once they are sanded.

An interesting variation on the basic technique is presented by the production of the "little crowns" (refer back to Plate 64). First, long before a crown may be made, willow branches must be cut, peeled, wrapped around a cylindrical object such as a telephone pole or a coffee can, and allowed to dry (see Plate 101). Once dried and shaped willows are available, a base is carved out of aspen (rather than the usual pine board). This medium is selected because of the amount of carving that must go into the base; pine would take too much time and effort. Once the base is shaped, two holes are drilled into the sides, and the ends of the willow are fitted into the base. Since willow is brittle, several willows are often broken before a good fit is secured. Now two sets of leaves are carved and decorated, a larger group to be inserted in the willow in vertical position and a smaller set to be placed perpendicular to the first set. Birds are carved for each of the horizontal leaves and a rabbit or other figure for the top of the base. The number and placement of birds and animals varies among carvers. The distribution of aspen and cedar also varies, but many customers prefer the use of both types of wood on the crowns and trees. Once all the parts are readied, holes are made in the willow with a punch, ends are glued, and the pieces are fitted. Such joints are weak and break easily, so carvings are often returned years later to have parts reglued.

The time involved in production is difficult to determine. A number of smaller items are usually produced at the same time, as I have noted. This practice makes it difficult to estimate the time required for one piece, since it is not possible to follow an individual carving from rough-hewn block to finished product.[3] Images are often produced singly, however, so estimation of the time they require is easier. It takes the Lópezes about ten hours to complete phases 3 through 7 (trimming the block, carving, and articulation of main features) and about five or six hours to complete items 8 through 11 in the production of a St. Francis approximately twelve inches in height. A tree or crown ten inches in height would take approximately seven and one-half hours to carve if produced singly.

The amount of time that the Lópezes devote to their carving varies

Plate 101

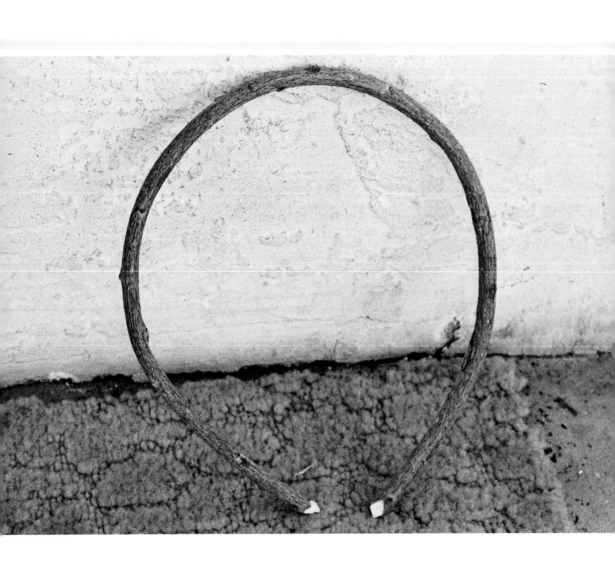

Plate 101. A Willow Shoot, Curved, Dried, and Ready for Use in Making a *Coronita*.

seasonally. Responsibilities unrelated to carving, such as gardening and duties relating to the ditch association, are fewest in the winter, and this is the carvers' most productive season. Also, few tourists visit after Christmas, and the number of interruptions is thus at a minimum. This seasonal variation characterized José Dolores López's work as well as that of George, Silvianita, and most carving artists who do not hold down other jobs.

The number of hours in each day that the Lópezes spend carving is greatly determined by social and other obligations to various Córdovans. George occasionally spends the entire day engaged in other activities, especially when a member of the family needs assistance or is experiencing a life crisis. George and Silvianita never carve on Sunday, a prohibition that José Dolores observed as well. Their working hours have varied greatly, however. Other carvers related that the Lópezes used to carve all day long and late into the night. Because there is hostility between established carvers, this report is difficult to assess. It is true, however, that in 1972 the Lópezes carved many more hours per day than in 1974. They say, "We don't carve much anymore, just for short periods of time. We get tired quickly." George's two cataract operations in 1972 and 1973 have restricted his carving somewhat. In 1974, the Lópezes still carved a good part of the time from early morning until seven or eight o'clock at night, although the number and duration of breaks they took had increased. By 1977 their level of production showed another substantial decrease. Silvianita spends less time carving than George, since she must cook and clean house as well.

As the reader may have noted from the preceding description of the technology of wood carving in Córdova, a central symbol dominates this aspect of the industry. Just as the "table" played a crucial role in the marketing phase, the "cuts" provide a sensitive indication of the social and conceptual organization of Córdovan carving. The importance of this concept emerges when one considers the process of transmission of the carving technology.

First of all, the artists differentiate between carvers who were taught the trade and "those who figured it out by themselves." The second category consists of persons who are not related to any carver and are not known to have spent much time with any carvers. On the other hand, the established carving families (with the exception of José and Alice Mondragón) are said to have "got the cuts as a family." Although this expression refers explicitly to the transmission of the knowledge regarding the manner of completing step number 5 for a substantial number of figures, it is sometimes used to refer to the stylistic characteristics of a particular family's work. This association is connected with the carvers' belief that it is primarily the cuts (i.e., the depth and location of sawed incisions) that produce stylistic differences.

Boyd (1974:470) is correct in noting that carving skills are not passed on through strict apprenticeships. The nature of such learning is much more informal. The Ortiz children, for example, watched their uncle and aunt for many years before picking up a knife. Later they began smoothing small carvings that had already been cut. Actual carving is usually begun by whittling on discarded scraps. Once a novice decides to attempt a particular carving, a small block of wood is selected by or given to the person. Once step 4 has been accomplished and the block is even and the grain runs parallel to the length of the figure, George López will generally assist by sketching the silhouette and making the cuts for the novice.

Most of the assistance offered is nonverbal; only a few general suggestions are made. "Carve with the grain of the wood. If you carve against it, you'll break off the legs." Help in the carving process itself is more frequent, and George often answers questions regarding technique by taking the figure in his hands and carving out the troublesome section. *Laboreando* (chip-carving and the articulation of features) is one aspect of carving that takes a steady and experienced hand, so at least the first pieces produced by the novice are *laboreadas* by Silvianita López. Although legs, ears, and the like are usually broken off during the first few attempts and such pieces must be discarded, the first completed carvings are often sold along with the work of experienced craftsmen.

Persons who receive such informal training in the carving art are generally considered to be part of the group of persons who work "under their teacher's table." Carvers never forget that a particular artist "got the cuts" from this carver or the other. Bonds formed between the novice and his or her tutor usually endure, and often lead to the sales of the novice's work from the senior's table, especially if the novice never sets up an independent table. It is of great importance to the younger carvers to be able to trace their artistic genealogy to those who have received more recognition. This lineage is believed by many, although implicitly in most cases, to enhance their status in the eyes of patrons. George López has not overlooked this possibility, for he is careful to show a picture of his father to each visitor and to add that José Dolores "was a great carver." He also identifies himself as descending from the nineteenth-century image-carving tradition, claiming to be "the fifth in the line of the old *santeros*," referring to the Aragóns and his grandfather.

This emphasis on the links through which carvers "get the cuts" and one's "artistic genealogy" suggests the importance of ties to past carvers as they may be important for the Córdovan artists' self-concept and the manner in which they present themselves to customers. Celso Gallegos told his Anglo-American patrons that his great-great-grandfather was a *santero*, a term that some contemporary image makers use in referring to themselves as well as their predecessors. Both Hispano artists and Anglo-American patrons have cited the nineteenth-century art in characterizing the resurgence of image carving in the present century, claiming that they are two phases of the same religious art. The salience of this belief leads, however, to perhaps the most difficult question encountered in connection with the art: to what extent are the two traditions actually related?

Part III

*The Symbolism
of the Image-Carving Art*

7.

The Search for Meaning

The question of the relationship between traditional and contemporary phases of the image-carving art in New Mexico might conceivably be addressed from divers points of view. I believe that one of the most important aspects is the meaning of the images—how the various symbols are conveyed, from which sources they are drawn, and what the carvers and their neighbors say about the images. How do the carvings function in the cultural milieu of their producers? The question demands an investigation of the features of the art that have changed and those that have remained more or less intact in their twentieth-century manifestations. Many aspects of the industry present themselves in the pursuit of this complex problem; the iconography of the images and their prototypes as well as their ethnotheologic status—how the statues are characterized as functioning in religious life—will receive primary attention.

Iconography forms a central feature of religious art, and the attributes that are portrayed long outlive the artists who utilize them in designating particular holy personages. Such visual symbols are complemented by a host of other means utilized by Hispanos in communicating information about the saints, the Virgin, and Christ. A rich body of legends, prayers, hymns, and rituals is used in the veneration of these holy personages. Older carvers such as George López command a substantial corpus of legends and hymns that deal with the lives and acts of the saints they portray in their carvings. The texts that I have collected from George López fit closely with those given me by other Córdovan informants; it appears that the image makers do not possess an esoteric knowledge of the subject. They have learned the hymns and legends more as members of their communities than as artistic specialists. The older carvers have also participated in a host of rituals that center on the holy personages they portray, and these experiences inform their work. An inventory of this material would necessitate more space than is available at present. One example might serve, however, to provide the reader with a glimpse of these other components of the world surrounding the saints in Hispano culture.

Many of the rituals that commemorated the feast days of the saints and those on other occasions involved the use of images; an example of such a ritual, the May 15 wake for St. Isidore, was provided in Chapter 1. Here St. Isidore was called upon to bless the fields and to protect the harvest from storms, floods, and pestilence. This theme is echoed in the *alabanza* (hymn) sung during the ceremony. George López's version runs as follows:[1]

San Isidro Labrador	St. Isidore the Farmer
San Isidro labrador	St. Isidore the farmer
patrón de los labradores	Patron of farmers
liberta nuestro sembrado	Deliver our fields
de langostas y temblores.	From locusts and earthquakes.
Por el gran merecimiento	Because of the great merit
con que te adoró el Señor	With which you worshiped the Lord
liberta nuestro sembrado	Deliver our fields
San Isidro labrador.	St. Isidore the farmer.
Por el sudor y trabajo	By the sweat and work
con que fuistes fatigado	With which you were fatigued
liberta nuestro sembrado	Deliver our fields
San Isidro labrador.	St. Isidore the farmer.
Porque estás comisionado	Because you are commissioned
por patrón de la labor	As the patron of farmwork
liberta nuestro sembrado	Deliver our fields
San Isidro labrador	St. Isidore the farmer.
Porque fuistes anunciado	Because you were called
de Dios por trabajador	By God as a worker
liberta nuestro sembrado	Deliver our fields
San Isidro labrador.	St. Isidore the farmer.
Del ladrón acostumbrado	Accustomed to thieves
y sin temor al Señor	And without fearing the Lord
liberta nuestro sembrado	Deliver our fields
San Isidro labrador.	St. Isidore the farmer.
En ti esperamos	We trust you to
llevar cosecha en unión	Bring good crops
por tu gran misericordia	By your great mercy
San Isidro labrador.	St. Isidore the farmer.
Adios mi santo glorioso	Farewell, my glorious saint
cortesano del Señor	Courtier of the Lord
hasta el año venidero	Until the coming year
San Isidro labrador.	St. Isidore the farmer.

López's repertoire of such hymns is quite extensive, and he is one of the best hymn singers in his community, although his voice has faded somewhat in recent years.

George López and other older Córdovans tell a legend explaining the manner in which St. Isidore gained such miraculous powers. It portrays St. Isidore as a devout resident of the area who finds himself temporarily at odds with God. The disasters with which St. Isidore is threatened in the following legend are, with one exception, the ills that he is called upon to avert in the ritual and hymn:

St. Isidore is very miraculous. He was first a Pope, then a bishop, and later a priest. When he got to this country, he put himself to tilling the earth. He was very manly [*muy hombrote*], a very good farmer, and he adored our Lord a great deal. One time it was Sunday, and his wife made him work. Once he was working, the Lord spoke to him, telling him that as it was Sunday he should not work. St. Isidore responded that he had to work. The voice then said that if St. Isidore didn't stop working, God would send hail. But St. Isidore said that he wasn't afraid of hail, that he was going to keep working. Then the voice spoke to him again, and said that if he didn't stop working, God was going to send him a plague of locusts. But St. Isidore was not afraid, and he kept on working. Then the same voice spoke to him again, saying that if he didn't leave his work, God would send him a bad neighbor. St. Isidore replied that this he couldn't stand, and so he left his work and went to mass. When he returned from mass his wife was not angry, because an angel had planted his fields. You see, he wasn't afraid of a storm or a plague of locusts, but he couldn't stand a bad neighbor. St. Isidore is very miraculous, because our Lord Jesus Christ loves him a great deal. Before, on the [feast] day of St. Isidore, all the people used to get together to take the saint's image around the fields so that he would see how things were and there would be a good harvest. And they used to raise everything in abundance back then. But now it's been about forty years since they've taken St. Isidore around like that, and now they hardly harvest anything. A few beans, a bit of *chile*, but this is nothing compared to what they used to get.

As the reader may recall from Plates 53 and 73, the legend informs the attributes used in images of St. Isidore. An angel plows the saint's field while St. Isidore clasps his hands in prayer. Other legends of the saints describe miracles performed on behalf of local residents.

The question remains, however, regarding the degree to which information on the iconography of the images has been altered in the industry's transition to its contemporary situation. One immediately apparent change is that a number of subjects have been introduced by patrons into the carvers' repertoire. Even the older carvers have little more informa-

Table 2. Traditional and Contemporary Iconography[1]

Saints	Traditional	José Dolores López		George López
Michael the Archangel	sword	sword[2]	sword[3]	sword
	crown	halo	crown	crown
	scales	scales	dagger	dagger
	wings	wings	wings	wings
	dragon	dragon	dragon	dragon
St. Joseph	staff		staff	staff
	beard		robe	robe

Saints	Traditional	José Dolores López	George López
	Christ child (crown)		(Christ child) hammer
St. Francis of Assisi	beard cross skull robe	——	3 birds (cross)
Rafael the Archangel	pilgrim's tunic staff gourd fish	——	cross fish
St. Isidore	oxen angel goad hat plow farmer's boots & jacket	——	oxen angel goad (hat) plow farmer's boots & jacket
St. Peter	key robe beard	key robe beard Bible dove crown	key robe beard Bible dove crown
St. Anthony of Padua	habit Christ child	habit Christ child	habit Christ child rosary cross
Our Lady of Guadalupe	crown rays or halo gown moon cherub	——	crown "rays of light" gown "angel" "angel's wings" moon
Our Lady of the Rosary	crown (Christ child) rosary	——	crown rosary
Gabriel the Archangel	monstrance wings (staff)	——	cross wings
St. Christopher	beard Christ child staff	——	beard Christ child staff

[1]The attributes listed for traditional period iconography are largely taken from Breese and Boyd (1966) and are not meant to constitute a definitive listing. The reader should also bear in mind that the use of color to define and create attributes was of great importance to the traditional image makers but plays no role (except through the occasional use of berried juniper) in the Lópezes' work.

[2]From an image contained in the Lepard Family Collection, on loan to the Museum of International Folk Art, Santa Fe (see Plate 37).

[3]From the image of St. Michael in the Taylor Museum of the Colorado Springs Fine Arts Center (see Plate 35).

tion on these holy personages than that provided by the prototype given them by the patron. Similarly, a number of the rituals, such as the wake for St. Isidore, have not been performed for several decades, and the younger carvers have not participated in them. Many of the younger artists are also less versed in the hymns and legends associated with the saints. This is not necessarily a sign that this knowledge is being lost, however, as only older persons are expected to be in substantial command of this information. Finally, a major change results from a difference in the cultural background of the patrons—Hispano patrons of the nineteenth century were much more aware of the legends, hymns, and rituals dealing with the saints than are twentieth-century Anglo-American customers.

The attributes used in the contemporary images have changed in some ways from those characteristic of nineteenth-century polychromed versions. A number of iconographic abbreviations have been noted, and a few innovations are present as well. An overall comparison of these attributes (see Table 2) shows that many of the attributes used in portraying and identifying the images from the two periods are, however, identical. The variations that do exist do not lead one to believe that a major departure from the iconography of the nineteenth-century imagery has taken place.

The use of prototypes in image production provides another means of assessing symbolic change. The traditional image makers utilized plastic prototypes in addition to such graphic sources as woodcuts, prints, lithographs, and chromolithographs (Lange 1974; Boyd 1974:80-81). The Lópezes draw upon three classes of prototypes, and the first two follow the eighteenth- and nineteenth-century pattern closely.

First, although plastic prototypes have been used by the Córdovan carvers since the days of José Dolores López, they form probably the least important source of inspiration. As I noted in Chapter 3, José Rafael Aragón's *Our Lady of the Seven Sorrows* served as one of the prototypes for José Dolores López's *Our Lady of Light*. A type of Virgin produced by both José Dolores and George López was called *Our Lady of Solitude;* Aragon's *Our Lady of Sorrows* is said to have served as its prototype as well.[2] Similarly, José Dolores López as sacristan was surely familiar with a polychromed *bulto* of St. Peter in the Córdova chapel.[3] Although López's St. Peter, unlike Aragón's, is graced with a crown, both feature a single key in the right hand and an open Bible in the left. Furthermore, Boyd (1974:471) notes that López executed his own versions of commercial Swiss toys.

Second, it appears that graphic prototypes have inspired the production of Córdovan images to a greater extent than have their plastic counterparts. As noted in Chapter 3, López's prototypes for the Garden of Eden figures were drawn from "an old book of French drawings which López displays with pride to his visitors" (Anonymous 1933:126). He also used an encyclopedia owned by a local schoolmaster in carving a set of swallows for a special order. José Dolores was not, however, alone in this practice. George López reports having carved a St. Jude from a print given him by a customer. Similarly, when Alex Ortiz replaced a traditional polychromed St. Cajetan that had been stolen from the Santuario of Chimayó, the priest gave him a postcard of the old image to aid him in his work (see Plates 102 and 103). His brother Lawrence produced a St. Patrick when a customer brought him an illustration, and it has become a regular part of his repertoire (refer back to Plate 79). Graphic prototypes were also used in Herminio's and Gloria Córdova's rendition of Our Lady of Monserrat. The extent of this phenomenon is suggested by Lange's claim that Puerto Rican patrons frequently brought a cheap print of a saint to an image maker in order to obtain a *bulto* of the same subject (1977: Personal communication).

Plate 102
Plate 103

The carvers do also work from graphic prototypes that they own, however. Nicudemos López, for example, used an illustration from "a small book of the saints" in producing a St. George, and he claimed that his father had used the copy as well. It is not uncommon for carvers to possess copies of books containing pictures and text regarding the saints, apparently, for Giffords (1977:23) reports that contemporary Mexican popular image makers also have such prototypes. Furthermore, Lawrence Ortiz was once observed with a snapshot of a traditional polychromed Our Lady of Guadalupe that he was using as a prototype for the production of a figure of the same subject. Interestingly, a Guadalupe recently completed by George López was standing in the next room, but it was not used as a prototype.

Finally, the Córdovan carvers utilize a class of prototypes with which their ancestors were never familiar. An extensive literature has grown up around the traditional images, and the contemporary carving industry has also received some attention. A number of writers have shared the fruits of their research with the Córdovan artists, and many of these publications contain drawings and photographs of both polychromed and unpainted images. These have served George López and others for years as handy references with regard to attributes and proportions for items in their own repertoires. López, for example, occasionally consults Breese and Boyd (1966) and other sources before attempting a less frequently carved image, and he uses a copy of Le Viness (1963) containing many photographs of his own *bultos* for the same reason. Several of the carvers have studied photographs of José Dolores López's work in recent years, and Lina Córdova began a revival of the production of López's *Animal Musicians* (see Plate 26) after receiving a copy of an article (Briggs 1974a) in which the piece was depicted (refer back to Plate 63). The significance of this class of prototypes lies in the fact that the artists' perception of the image-carving tradition has been influenced by outside appreciation of the work. I will return to this point below.

In the first chapter it was noted that images of the saints serve as mediators in relating such diverse aspects of Hispano social life as individual and society, man and God, formal iconography and local legend, legend and ritual, and the like, and it is significant that this role is symbolically represented or "encoded" in the production of each image.

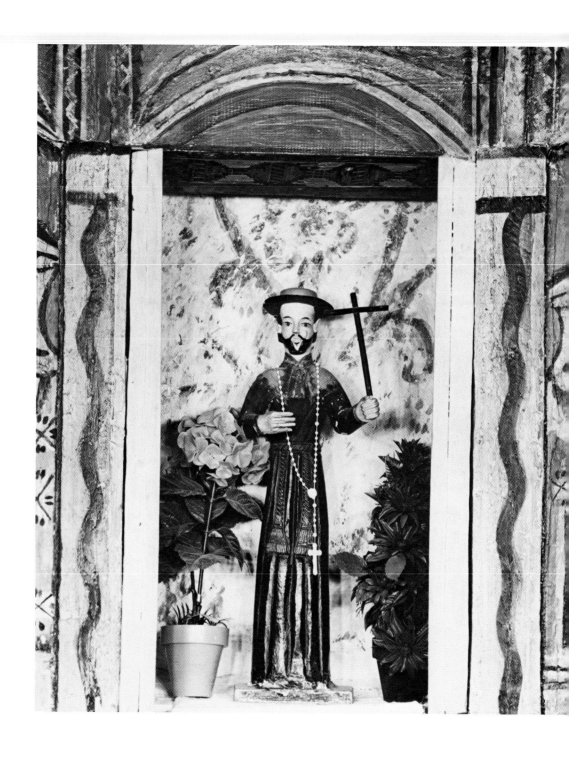

Plate 102. A Traditional Polychromed Image of St. Cajetan (total height approximately 60 cm. or 24 in.). This postcard depicts the *bulto* of St. Cajetan that was located in a niche of one of the side altar screens at the Santuario of Chimayó. From a private collection; photograph by John S. Candelario.

188   *The Symbolism of the Art*

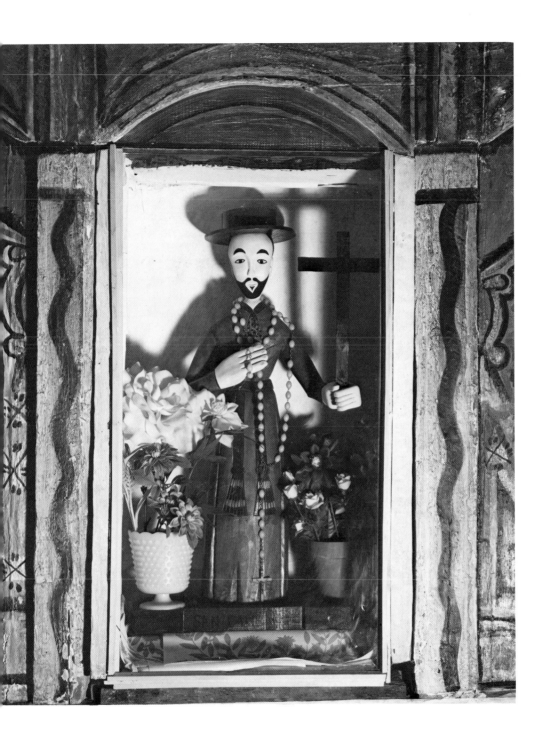

Plate 103. A Polychromed Image of St. Cajetan Produced by Alex Ortiz in 1977 (total height 68.8 cm or 27.5 in.). Ortiz's copy of the stolen nineteenth-century image was first blessed and then placed in the niche in the Santuario de Chimayó altar screen that its predecessor had occupied. From a private collection.

The role of prototypes was discussed because these sources are important in the process of creation. Nevertheless, an analysis of the prototypes for particular carvings does not complete our understanding of their role; the Córdovan artists have an explicit theory of the role of prototypes that greatly influences the manner in which they interpret the work of particular artists. Their theory revolves around the way in which a carver abstracts a set of symbols from a more inclusive level of Hispano symbolism for incorporation into a particular image.

According to the carvers, this process can take place in any of three ways. First, the most highly esteemed manner of symbolic abstraction involves the embodiment of spiritual inspiration in the act of carving. This view holds that a particular carver utilized no material prototype whatsoever in the production of a certain image. Furthermore, the mental representation is deemed a product not of mundane experience but rather of divine inspiration. Nicudemos López described his father's carving in such a manner:

> Once some Anglos who knew of his [José Dolores López's] carving came up to Córdova and said, "José, who taught you how to carve? Which school did you go to to learn? Who taught you?" Well, these Anglos think that you have to learn everything in school. But that's not the way it is. My father wasn't taught in any school, it came from his own head [de pura mente]. God in heaven put the right way to do it into his mind. My father didn't have anything to show him how to carve and that's why he was so good.

Nicudemos' statement is especially interesting for its explicit contrast of the Anglo-American model of artistic creation with the Córdovans' notion of this process. While the Anglo-American view presupposes the necessity of prototypes, the Córdovans regard them as optional.[4]

The second means of encoding symbols in the production of saints also involves, according to Córdovans, an intellectually demanding process of abstraction. Here tangible graphic and plastic prototypes are used in the production of images. This practice is separated from the act of copying (which the carvers view pejoratively) by the fact that the materials used do not depict contemporary unpainted images but consist rather of prints, lithographs, paintings, religious texts, and other representations. Such sources were mentioned by José Dolores' nephew, Federico Córdova, when he spoke of his uncle's work:

> Once I asked my Uncle José Dolores, and this is true, "How do you make your carvings, Uncle?" And he replied, "At night I go to bed, but I keep thinking, and thoughts come into my head." He got ideas for carvings such as the Adam and Eve tempted in Paradise that he made. These ideas came to him through reading some books that he had. He had the Bible, but in those days they didn't use the Bible much. What they used more were catechisms and other books that the priests gave out, such as religious writings. And there were descriptions of things, such as this Paradise that he did. He used such writings as those on the Death cart that he carved. In addition to the writings, he used photo-

graphs that accompanied the lessons. He read all this, learned it all very well, and then he figured out how to make them. My uncle knew how to read and write Spanish, you know.

Although this type of extrapolation was not as highly esteemed as was divine inspiration, the view that active symbolic abstraction preceded the production of images rendered the use of such prototypes quite respectable nevertheless. This class of prototypes also includes traditional polychromed images, which were considered far less desirable than graphic models, although use of the polychromed images was still believed to entail a process of abstraction.

Finally, the use of contemporary Córdovan images as prototypes was viewed in a highly derogatory fashion by the carvers. Although informants considered the first two processes to be creative, copying from models in the same style was seen as a purely mechanical procedure involving no abstraction whatsoever. Although this method was deemed the least desirable, gradations of preferability were evident in the three recognized ways of copying from the work of other contemporary carvers. The use of photographs of contemporary images as prototypes was somewhat preferred to the direct observation of such works, and the examination of finished images was considered slightly preferable to instruction in the requisite techniques by a recognized carver.

The manner in which this view of the role of prototypes manifested itself in particular instances depended upon the time, place, and purpose of the conversation and the statuses of speaker, hearer, and the person mentioned. In other words, a person characterized the prototypes he used quite differently if he kept a "table," lived in a house in which a "table" was kept, or sold his carvings through another's "table." Such descriptions also varied according to the position of the hearer and the person(s) referred to with regard to a "table." I noted above that the "table" structured the competition between Córdovan carvers. Local opinions about the use of different prototypes in carving provided the primary means by which the hostility generated by competition between established carvers was vented. Carvers with "tables"[5] would not admit to having copied contemporary images or to having been taught by other carvers. "I thought it all up" and "God put the idea in my head" were common claims. José Dolores López was generally regarded as having produced exclusively original work. With this exception, however, carvers with tables never referred to their peers as having done such original carving. For the most part, other artists with their own tables were said to have copied from material prototypes, and the claim that one carver had taught the rest or that the others had copied the informant's work was not unusual.

One of the most interesting aspects of this competition is that it does not extend far beyond the households that keep tables. Carvers who have never had their own "table" often commented that one or more of the recognized carvers was entirely original in his work, and most admitted freely that they had received informal instruction from their relatives.

Unrecognized carvers who lived in a household that kept a table took an intermediate position. Although they generally refused to credit opposing recognized carvers with original work, they acknowledged their artistic debt to the recognized carver in their household and maintained that his or her work was genuine.

The data on prototypes, both in terms of the Córdovans' view of these models and as reflected in the carvings, indicate that the symbolism of the contemporary carving art has changed greatly. It is nevertheless somewhat difficult to assess the direction and the extent of the changes. On the one hand, the Córdovan carvers initiated a number of changes in the means of image production. Despite continual reassertions of the value of carving with *la pura navaja* (just a pocketknife), band and jig saws are now utilized by most of the carvers. Second, although divine inspiration is much more highly esteemed than the use of material prototypes, many artists utilize published drawings and photographs of images. Third, as noted in Chapter 5, the carvers' patrons place great emphasis on the originality and creativity of the work. Statements by the artists as to how they and their competitors use prototypes suggest that to some extent they have adopted their customers' abhorrence of copying. Finally, the carvers often jest about the importance that their patrons place on the recognition received by individual artists, especially with regard to the customers' emphasis on the presence of a particular artist's signature on the bottom of a piece. The recognized carvers now clamor for such acknowledgment, however, and often accuse each other of attempting to monopolize access to publicity.

In short, the carvers are well aware of outside intervention in the development of their industry. Nevertheless, by emphasizing their links to the old *santeros*, and by valuing work said to be based on this tradition, they assert their adherence to an ideal image of the carving industry as reflecting traditional Córdovan patterns rather than market dictates. The juxtaposition of traditional values and contemporary interests thus generates an *internal contradiction* within the industry. The symbolism of the Córdovan image-carving art revolves around a *search for meaning* rather than a set of static interpretations. The presence of an internal contradiction leads to the emergence of competing interpretations of images, and this indeterminacy is apparent even at a most basic level—that of the ethnotheologic status of the images.

A series of interviews initiated early in the study asked Córdovans to interpret the nature of the relationship between the images and the holy personages they represent. The two contradictory tendencies in the art—Anglo-American influence versus adherence to tradition—were reflected both in the responses and by their differences. For example, a close friend of both José Dolores and George López was asked to comment on the work of the traditional image makers, especially in relation to the way these artists felt about their work. The following is a translation of his response:

The *santos* in the chapel are different from the *santos* they make today. I remember talking to José Dolores, George's father, before he died. He told me that the *santos* he was making weren't from the heart, they weren't religious, but "God won't mind if I make enough money to live. God is happy for anybody who has the initiative to work his own way. This way was good," José Dolores said, "because you were working for yourself."

This informant, among others, also quoted the elder López as using the term *monos* (dolls or figures, especially as deformed) to refer to his images.

From this account it appears that when José Dolores López spoke with relatives and neighbors, he did not assert the presence of a symbolic link between the traditional image-carving art and the industry he started in the 1920s and 1930s. Although he sought to justify the merit of his pursuit to his fellows, as have many of his followers, he did not base his claim on a sacred status for the images, which he disavowed. He did not fail, however, to make recourse to tradition; the goal of working for oneself is a central Hispano value, and the theme of the independent rancher-farmer as a cultural ideal has not disappeared with growing dependence on wage labor.

George López articulates his claim to the validity of his occupation in a remarkably different manner. His explanation of the ethnotheologic status of images draws upon Catholic theology in linking the contemporary carving art with that of the traditional period. López's statement essentially shifts the burden of responsibility for the religious status of the carvings from the shoulders of the artist to those of the patron:

What happens when people who don't believe in God buy the carvings? Well, nothing. This block of wood is nothing more than wood. It's the same thing to make a carving for those people [tourists] or for a church. The difference is not in the wood or in the way in which one carves it. If you were baptized Catholic, then the father has your name in a book there in the church. And if your name is there, then you can take your carving to the father so that he will bless it. It does not do anything to pray to the carvings, because they are not holy, they have not been blessed. But if the father blesses them, well, then, they are images of the Apostles in Heaven. It's the same thing when the father blesses your car, or if you put a rosary on the windshield. This way the witches can't throw the car off the road. Do you know that they can do this? Also, if they baptized you as a child, you are baptized for life. It's the same with an image of a saint. If you sell or steal a blessed image, well, it's a very bad sin and you will pay for it. He who sells it is responsible.

I have never taken one of my carvings to have it blessed, but I think that all the Catholics who buy them take them to the priest. If not, they are just blocks of wood, no more. It's the same with you, if you are not baptized, then you are the same as a block of wood. I believe that Eluid and the Caballeros[6] blessed the Our Lady of Conquest that they bought. But the carvings here on this table have not been blessed, and for this reason I can sell them. But it's not the same with this Our Lady of the Immaculate Conception that my wife's *comadre*[7] Liria gave her. The father came after mass and blessed it, so now it is holy. But I could never sell one of these.

You must be baptized and have faith. It is the same thing to see a blessed image as a picture of your grandfather. You know that it is him, and you also know that he exists, and thus you have faith that it is his picture. It's the same with the images; you see the images, and you know that they represent the Apostles in Heaven. Some say that because they can't see God that He doesn't exist. But even though you don't see Him, if you have faith you will see Him with the eyes of your faith.

George López's view of the production and sale of contemporary images has clearly been well thought out, and its systematicity reflects his long involvement in the pursuit. His view largely derives from the common practice of blessing an image, a custom still carried out by López and other Córdovans in the case of newly purchased plaster of Paris statues (see Plate 104). Arrangements will be made with a priest before he begins one of Córdova's semi-weekly masses. After the mass, the priest, the owner of the image, and one or two individuals chosen as the sponsors (*padrinos*) of the statue will gather either in the chapel or in the owner's home. The priest recites the blessing for a sacred statue or picture from a ritual or similar compendium, making the sign of the cross over the object and blessing it with holy water.[8] Among Córdovans it is customary for the owner to make a small contribution to the church following the ceremony.

Plate 104

The central feature of López's interpretation of this set of events should be borne in mind: the blessing is seen as transforming the statue. According to López, unblessed images, including the ones he displays on his table, are not "religious" or "holy" in any sense. Once sanctified by a priest, however, they become wholly given over to a sacred function and must receive special treatment. López's justification of the modern carving art thus draws upon both Hispano tradition in particular and Catholic practices in general. Unlike his father's explanation, that of George López incorporates traditional knowledge concerning the production and use of images. His citation of the sin of simony (Acts 8:18–24), the sale of blessed objects, is also canonical, although the naming of sponsors derives from folk practice rather than church doctrine. José Dolores equated traditional images with the sacred and contemporary images with the secular; George López again departs from his father's interpretation by allowing for the presence of both sacred and secular images simultaneously.

Nevertheless, George López's view of the ethnotheologic status of contemporary images is not the only view held by Córdovan carvers. Another of José Dolores' sons, for example, appears to echo his father's attitude: "My father and I used to make the carvings, but we didn't believe in them. But others [i.e., outside patrons] believed in them." Similarly, Ricardo López, who fashioned images during the first decades of the new industry's existence, refuses to carve anything but birds, animals, trees, and the like today. It is a sin, he maintains, to sell images to nonbelievers.

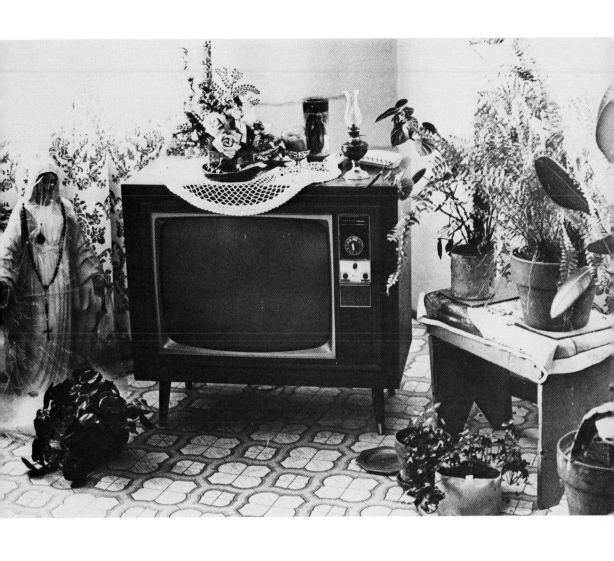

Plate 104. A Plaster of Paris Image of Our Lady of the Immaculate Conception, in the Lópezes' Front Room. This image was given to Silvianita by her *comadre*. It was subsequently blessed by a priest, and unlike the images on the Lópezes' "table," it is a *santo* (holy object).

Furthermore, the carvers' neighbors and relatives are divided as to their evaluation of the religious and moral implications of the contemporary image-carving art. Most informants appeared to accept the type of rationale that José Dolores proffered, and they considered the pursuit a respectable occupation. The established carvers were often termed "smart" or "very rich," and a number of persons spoke enviously of their presumed financial standing. A minority of residents viewed the industry with disfavor, however, and deemed the sale of images to nonbelievers to be improper. A few were sufficiently moved by the perceived sacrilegious nature of these activities to claim that several carvers had sold traditional images that belonged to the community. Residents who were not carvers were in agreement that there was no religious motive for the artists' work.

The internal contradiction apparent in the contemporary phase of the image-carving art is evident in the local use of images. Blessed images, traditional polychromed statues, and plaster of Paris statues as well as prints continue to serve as central vehicles of Córdovan worship. George López has stated that all blessed images are of equal religious merit, and accordingly we would expect Córdovans to acquire the carvers' statues and to use them, once sanctified, in their homes. Any of the carvers will tell you, however, that Córdovans are not among their customers. The reader may recall, nevertheless, that both José Dolores' and George López's works are used in community devotion: George's offertory box and image of St. Isidore reside in the chapel, while José Dolores' candelabras, Bible stand, Nativity, and the traditional images that he repaired stand in the same structure.

In short, it appears that many Hispanos depart from George López's view of the status of images by recognizing an inherent connection between the image maker and his products. This association appears also to have characterized reactions to the work of the traditional artists, judging by evidence collected outside Córdova. Steele (1974:36–43), for example, asserts that the traditional image maker of New Mexico had to be a holy man in order for his images to be effective. The desired personal characteristics related to both the virtue of his ordinary conduct and the intensity of his religious devotion. Wallrich (1951:157–60) corroborates all of these observations on the basis of interviews with residents of the San Luis Valley of southern Colorado with regard to image makers in their own and in the last several generations. He even reports one instance in which residents claimed that a group of images had been rendered inefficacious when their sculptor converted to Pentecostalism (1951:160).

A second implication of López's statement conflicts with extant data on the Hispano use of images. López has argued that all images, once they have been blessed, are equally suitable for devotional purposes. It is evident, however, that many Hispanos do not agree with him. First, there is ample support for the proposition that many villagers believe the effectiveness of an image to be contingent upon its aesthetic merit. Ellis (1954:346) reports the belief of Tomé area residents that ". . . one who

196   *The Symbolism of the Art*

made an ugly *santo* would suffer a period of purgatory in proportion to his bad artistry." Second, differences in materials were often reflected in the willingness of Hispanos to utilize images in worship. Although plaster of Paris statues are common, it appears that older villagers are still partial to the "old saints." Accounts such as those recorded by Jaramillo (1941:61) and Applegate and Austin (n.d.:165–66) indicate that during the first half of this century, many Hispanos considered the traditional images to be their special protectors. Plaster of Paris statues, on the other hand, represented an alien society.

Taken as a whole, the data on the symbolism of the contemporary Córdovan image-carving art do not, at first glance, permit one to draw any clear conclusions. Some features of the traditional art have been maintained, while others have been almost entirely supplanted. Furthermore, the interpretations of changes—even those recorded in one community alone—are frequently contradictory. The seeming chaos disappears, however, once one penetrates the surface. Indeed, this information on the symbolism of the contemporary art merely strengthens the picture that emerged from material on the carvers and the manner in which they make and sell their products.

Significant departures from the traditional phase of the art are apparent in all of these areas. Like José Dolores López, many of the most successful carvers have been individuals who were more used to dealing with the outside (and especially the Anglo-American) world than were the majority of their neighbors. Some of these individuals have adopted the use of labor-saving power tools in spite of the value traditionally placed on doing things by hand. Most important, the carvers' works, unlike those of the traditional image makers, are not purchased by their neighbors or by the residents of similar communities. Their customers are largely persons of a different social class and cultural background, most of whom do not embrace the carvers' faith.

Furthermore, these outside patrons have affected the evolution of the contemporary Córdovan industry throughout its history. Their evaluation of the art in periodic competitions, in the selection of pieces for inclusion in markets, shops, and exhibitions, and in the marketplace generally has influenced the carvers' styles and repertoire, as have the suggestions that patrons often make to the artists. The carvers' perception of the image-carving tradition as a whole has also been influenced by their use of publications on the subject.

These changes may be summarized as a movement from the *internal* focus of the traditional image makers to the *external* orientation that characterizes the contemporary phase. In the eighteenth and nineteenth centuries, the artists' patrons were fellow Hispanos, and the artist and his audience thus shared a vast array of religious and cultural assumptions.[9] In the twentieth century, however, the Córdovan carvers have had to comply with the tastes of individuals with whom they have very little in common. This hiatus between image maker and patron became much more pronounced after World War II. About this time the Santa Fe artists and writers, many of whom had studied Hispano art in the villages as well as in the museums, were largely replaced as carving patrons by myriad newcomers and tourists, most of whom had little knowledge of the image-making tradition.

Once the contemporary Córdovan carving industry has been located within the larger context, it becomes possible to understand the question of change versus continuity in the contemporary image-carving art. In the eighteenth and nineteenth centuries, images served as powerful mediators, bridging the gap between man and God, European and Mexican iconography and local traditions, legends of the saints' lives and powers and their ritual recognition, and other religious and sociocultural forces. The most fundamental similarity between the two phases of image production lies in the fact that the contemporary images continue to function as effective mediators. Rather than mediating between different aspects of the same culture and society, however, the twentieth-century images link individuals of dissimilar traditions. Carver and patron differ in their interpretations of and motivations for the exchange, and this difference constitutes the major dissimilarity between the contemporary and traditional phases. In somewhat more technical terms, the structure of the images' function has remained constant in spite of a radical change in the content.

8.

The Future of the Art

As noted in the last chapter, the image-carving art in New Mexico has undergone a profound change in this century—the transformation from an internal to an external focus. It was further argued that this change constitutes a reapplication of the traditional function of the images—that of mediation—rather than a complete displacement of their role in society. Indeed, one may recall the iconographic and stylistic changes that occurred in the traditional art between the seventeenth and nineteenth centuries. These modifications kept the evolution of the art closely in line with the development of Hispano society. This fact hardly seems surprising in view of the function of the images as mediators of ongoing social relations. The traditional image-carving art thus exhibited great fluidity and responsiveness to the needs of the Hispanos of the traditional period.

It would indeed be misleading to suggest that the function of contemporary carvings in mediating between Hispano and Anglo-American cultures is an isolated phenomenon. The extent of this form of intercultural articulartion is apparent in two ways.

First, the so-called ethnic or tourist arts, those sold by natives to outsiders, have sprung up in nearly every part of the world and have become the subject of scholarly interest in recent years. Graburn (1969; 1976) and others have demonstrated that a number of features are held in common by the works of artists from relatively small subordinate groups that are sold to members of superordinate societies. Several aspects of the Córdovan industry that have been discussed above appear to be common elements of art forms resulting from contact between such societies. Modifications of technique, such as the disappearance of paint on contemporary Córdovan images, are quite widespread, as are extensions of the subjects or genres of the traditional art form. Similarly, many artists attempt, as do the Córdovans, to make items that satisfy the consumers' stereotypes of the producers' society (Graburn 1976:1-32; also see Dawson, Fredrickson, and Graburn 1974). Entrepreneurial artists (such as José Dolores López) and cultural mediators or go-betweens (like Lorin Brown) frequently play important roles in artistic innovation (Graburn 1969). The patrons' concern with the individualization of artistic production often confers symbolic significance upon the worker's signature and leads to the emergence of competitiveness and "the emulation of the successful for his success rather than for the beauty or utility of his product" (1976:22).

Second, it would be myopic to claim that the sale of contemporary wood carvings alone mediates between Hispano and Anglo-American cultures or represents the only point of contact between the two groups. Anglo-American contact has been important in Hispano society since the United States conquered the area in 1846, and the intensity of Hispano involvement in American society has been increasing steadily. An examination of the historical record reveals that a number of material objects have played a central role in this interaction.

Spanish and Mexican land policy granted settlers a variety of rights to different types of land that were intended to provide for their subsistence. As noted in Chapter 4, the exploitation of these resources in gaining one's livelihood formed an important element of personal, familial, and community identity. Indeed, the units of traditional rural Hispano social organization and the ways in which they were bound together are very clearly indicated by the individual and communal activities involved in growing and harvesting crops, herding livestock, maintaining the ditches, and the like. Like religious images, rights to land and water thus served as mediators among persons, families, communities, activities, and the like long before the coming of the *Americanos*. Communal units consisting of several households and the important ditch associations were formed on the basis of a shared interest in and exploitation of land and water resources, for example, and such activities as the annual spring cleaning of the ditches brought together the members of these groups in the accomplishment of common ends.

Under the Treaty of Guadalupe Hidalgo of 1848, the United States agreed to respect rights granted under Spanish and Mexican law. As subsistence agriculture and farming were increasingly displaced by commercial interests, however, rights to New Mexico's land and water came to be of great importance to Anglo-Americans as well. Accordingly, the newcomers gained control over vast sections of territory formerly held by Spanish and Mexican grantees and their inheritors. Capitalism had become the driving force of the economy, and land speculation, cash cropping, and large-scale commercial ranching were its favored means of exploiting these resources.[1]

Just as land and water were highly valued by the two groups, control over rights to these "commodities" became a central focus of relations between the members of both. The acquisition of rights to the land and water that supported communities such as Córdova plainly brought economic control over their residents. As I noted above, land and water were important mediators of Hispano social relations prior to the American conquest. As a result of their later importance to both Hispanos and Anglo-Americans, they became central mediators of relations between the two groups. In other words, the utilization of land and water became a primary vehicle for the expression of Hispano/Anglo-American cooperation and antagonism as well as an issue capable of modifying the disposition of members of each group with regard to those of the other. The similarity between the intercultural role played by land and water and that of contemporary wood carvings is striking; the Anglo-Americans' preferred means of appreciating these entities was to possess them. In seeking to possess them, Anglo-Americans succeeded in forming a bond between the two groups through the use of entities that had different meanings in each. Furthermore, the political and economic hegemony of the newcomers enabled them to dictate the terms of the relationship to a substantial degree.

The analogous functions of wood carvings and land and water in mediating in social relationships reveal a further dimension of the role of the contemporary carving industry in the past two decades. A number of Hispanos have not been content to observe passively the appropriation of their basic resources. Violence directed against such exploitation occurred in San Miguel and neighboring counties in the 1880s and 1890s (Schlesinger 1971) and in Río Arriba County in the 1920s and 1950s (Gardner 1970; Knowlton 1976). A group first known as the Alianza Federal de Mercedes (Federated Alliance of Land Grants) was founded in 1963 by Reis López Tijerina and others who sought an equitable solution to the problems created by the alienation of grant lands.[2] In addition to calling attention to the injustices committed against Hispanos, the movement as a whole succeeded in consolidating Hispano concerns with the maintenance of Hispanic identity. Part of this struggle involved the examination of Hispano history and culture to select symbols that could facilitate a unification and mobilization of Hispanos in combatting Anglo-American hegemony. Great value had been placed on rights to land and water throughout Hispano history, and these resources were adopted as the central symbols of the movement.

The crystallization of efforts to maintain Hispano identity has resulted in a nascent transformation of the contemporary wood-carving art in New Mexico. Conflicting values in the Córdovan artists' conception of their work have created a certain tension in the industry; as I argued above, the fact that the images have retained their traditional function as mediators does not prevent the generation of a number of internal contradictions as the carvers turn from an internal to an external market.

It is indeed true that the internal tensions in the contemporary wood-carving industry have not been entirely resolved—carvings are still sold to nonbelievers, and the ethnotheological status of the images still retains its ambiguity. The Hispano ethnicity movement has succeeded, nevertheless, in initiating a resolution of the dilemma: I noted above that during the first half of the twentieth century, traditional polychromed images of the saints produced in New Mexico appear to have served, in their opposition to plaster of Paris statues, as symbols of Hispano ethnicity. Similarly, the more recent movement toward ethnic identity has reincorporated the traditional images along with land and water as symbols of Hispano history and religion. The association of the contemporary images with the tourist trade has prevented their wholehearted adoption in a manner analogous to that of the traditional images. Recently, however, the twentieth-century images have begun to break away from this identification and to join the traditional images as emerging symbols of Hispano ethnicity. Their adoption appears to have been initiated not by the residents of Córdova and similar communities but by their more urban and acculturated kinsmen. The contemporary images have gained a great deal of prominence and have received much publicity in the last several years, and their importance has not ceased to grow.

Three prima facie reasons for the effectiveness of images as symbols of Hispano ethnicity are apparent. First, the fluidity of the images' long-standing role as mediators permits their incorporation into a variety of new situations. Second, Hispanos have been familiar with religious images for centuries, and many Anglo-Americans have become accustomed to the images since the 1920s. This promotes their utility as a sort of lingua franca for intercultural communication. Finally, as moveable material objects, the images are highly visible and can be utilized in a number of contexts. This aspect increases their effectiveness as vehicles for communicating messages between the artist and the viewer, between participants and viewers (as in a procession), and between Hispanos and Anglo-Americans in general.

The emergence of contemporary image carving in this new context has clearly modified the art in various ways. If we turn initially to the changes that have occurred with regard to the carvers, a number are apparent. First, the growing popularity and political importance of the contemporary images have led to a tremendous increase in the number of image carvers. This growth has been less pronounced in Córdova, where the proportional increase in the last several years has not been as overwhelming as it has been in Santa Fe, Española, Albuquerque, Taos, and elsewhere. Furthermore, new carvers are continually coming into public view, and persons who dabbled in the art in previous years are devoting more and more time to their work and its promotion.

Second, as the transmission of the image-carving tradition becomes more closely connected with the maintenance of Hispano ethnic identity, self-instruction and informal training (which are of primary importance in Córdova) are giving way to more formal instruction. For example, Savinita Ortiz, George López's niece, was invited to teach a class at the Española Center of the College of Santa Fe in 1973.[3] López himself has given several demonstrations, and small groups occasionally arrange to have a short lesson in the artist's home. Similarly, John Lucero, who now lives in Albuquerque, supplemented the display of images included in "The Santero Experience," an exhibition at the Museum of Albuquerque, by demonstrating the production of polychromed images. Max Roybal, a retired dentist also from Albuquerque, has taught classes at the University of New Mexico, at the Ghost Ranch near Abiquiú, New Mexico, and elsewhere.

Finally, many of the new image makers, particularly those who emerged in the 1970s, are drawn from segments of the Hispano population different from those to which earlier artists like José Dolores López and Celso Gallegos belonged. Many reside in New Mexico's more urban centers—Albuquerque, Santa Fe, Española, and Taos—and their backgrounds reflect the increased Hispano-Anglo contact in these places. Furthermore, their level of educational attainment is generally much higher than that of their predecessors, and some hold B.S., M.S., and D.D.S. degrees. Several are active or retired professionals; a teacher, an engineer, and a librarian do some of the best work. Their greater fluency in Anglo-American culture goes hand in hand with greater knowledge of modern Western art, gained both in the studio and in the study of art history. Several are also familiar with the scholarly literature on the images.

These changes in the composition of New Mexico's contemporary image makers have been accompanied by modifications in the process of image production itself. Research into museum and church collections of traditional images resulted, for example, in the appearance of many copies of pieces featured in museum catalogs and other scholarly publications.[4] Several of the artists claim to derive their subject matter from research into European and Mexican iconography, and some of their products represent subjects outside the traditional New Mexican repertoire.

A recent change in materials and technique promises to usher in a new era in the image-making art. One may recall that Celso Gallegos used small amounts of paint on some of his images, and that José Dolores López painted his early furniture and occasionally other pieces upon request (Boyd 1969:22; unpublished and undated notes on the López family). López's later work, like that of Patrocinio Barela, was almost entirely unpainted, however. Most patrons found the commercial house paints that decorated López's pieces "too gaudy," and this may have accounted, at least in part, for their scarcity in collections outside Córdova.

A number of recent image makers have felt the need to work in a style closer to that of the traditional artists than are the Córdovan and similar techniques. Some image makers have therefore experimented with paints, and several have developed personal styles using commercial gesso and acrylics. Images by Horacio Valdez of Lyden, New Mexico near Dixon (see Plate 105) and by Luis Tapia of Santa Fe (Plate 106 and Color Plate 4) provide examples of recent polychromed work. Polychromed images are important in the contemporary art in two ways that concern the function of the images as symbols of Hispano ethnicity.

Plate 105
Plate 106

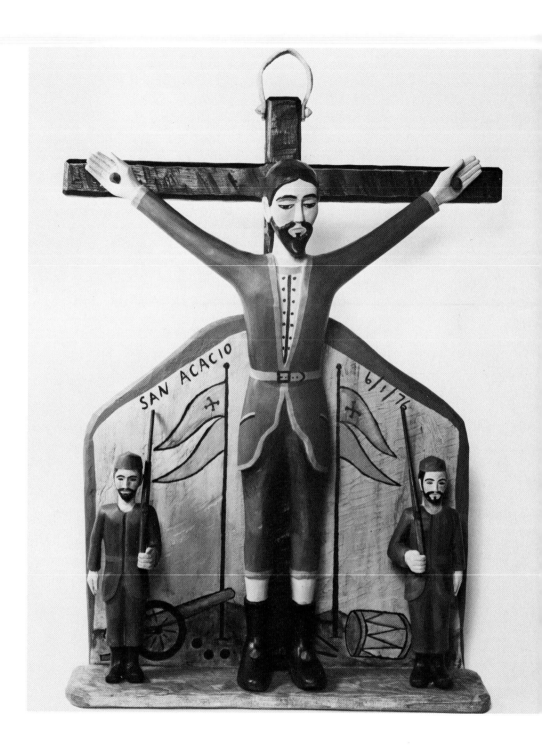

Plate 105. A Polychromed Image of St. Acacius by Horacio Valdez (base 37 x 8.5 cm. or 14.8 x 3.4 in., figure 44 cm. or 17.6 in. in height). This image, like most of the contemporary polychromed work, is painted with commercial acrylics. In the collections of the Museum of International Folk Art, a unit of the Museum of New Mexico, Santa Fe.

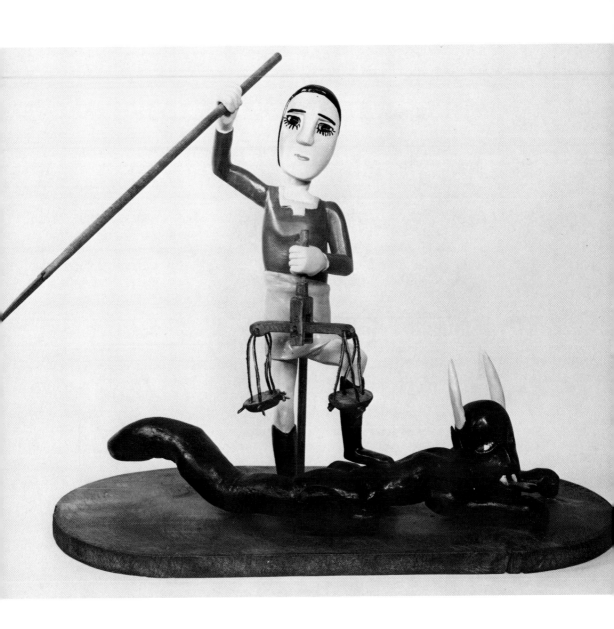

Plate 106. A Polychromed Image of St. Michael and the Dragon by Luis Tapia (height of figure 38 cm. or 15.2 in., length of dragon 40 cm. or 16 in.). Tapia uses much brighter colors than does Horacio Valdez. In the collections of the Spanish Colonial Arts Society, Inc., in the Museum of International Folk Art, Santa Fe.

First, the polychromed images are of substantial size. More care is taken in their construction, and they are sold at substantially higher prices than are most of the recent unpainted pieces. These characteristics assist in removing the images from the class of curios and enhancing their classification with more "serious" forms of artistic expression. Second, the polychromed images exhibit a closer proximity to the style of the traditional images and a more substantial departure from the stylistic canons of modern Western art (these images are brightly colored, highly polished, and more representational than the unpainted carvings). The Anglo-American customers who are drawn to polychromed works tend to be persons of greater knowledge of and respect for the canons of Hispano art. The simultaneous disassociation from mass-produced curios and association with traditional Hispano images makes the contemporary images more recognizable as symbols of Hispano ethnicity.

Another important result of the association of contemporary images with Hispano ethnicity is tied to their marketing and distribution. The idea that Hispano images should be reserved primarily for Hispano usage has gained currency in recent years. A number of communities have requested the return of traditional images that came into the hands of outsiders through thefts and sales, and some individuals have opposed the location of substantial collections of traditional images outside the state. This attitude has begun to extend to contemporary images as well. George López, for example, is concerned with the exodus of his works and those of his family from the area, and his nephew Eluid Martínez commissioned a number of images from López in order to keep a visual record within the family.

A number of the artists are more concerned that their images be used in Catholic worship than that their work command high prices. Some image makers give their works to friends and relatives, and it is becoming more common to donate an image to a church or brotherhood chapter or to sell it for a very modest fee to a devotee. Horacio Valdez, who is pictured in *Plate 107* Plate 107, is such an artist. Benjamín López of Española similarly reports: *Plate 108* "I have never sold a *santo*." (See Plate 108.) The López family, which has sold its works for more than four decades, has also been affected by this attitude. They were recently asked to replace a traditional image of St. Cajetan that had been stolen from the Santuario in Chimayó (refer back to Plate 102). Alex Ortiz produced a painted rendition of the work, asking reimbursement for the price of materials alone, and it now stands in the niche of the nineteenth-century *retablo* that housed its predecessor (see Plate 103). Alex, who had some art training in high school, has turned to *Plate 109* the production of polychromed *retablos* as well (see Plate 109).

The observer necessarily becomes aware of the need to relate these recent developments to the evolution of the image-making art in New Mexico as a whole. At the beginning of the chapter I suggested that the contemporary tradition was characterized by the presence of an internal contradiction. The ethnic identity movement of the last two decades paved the way for a partial resolution of this conflict in the utilization of

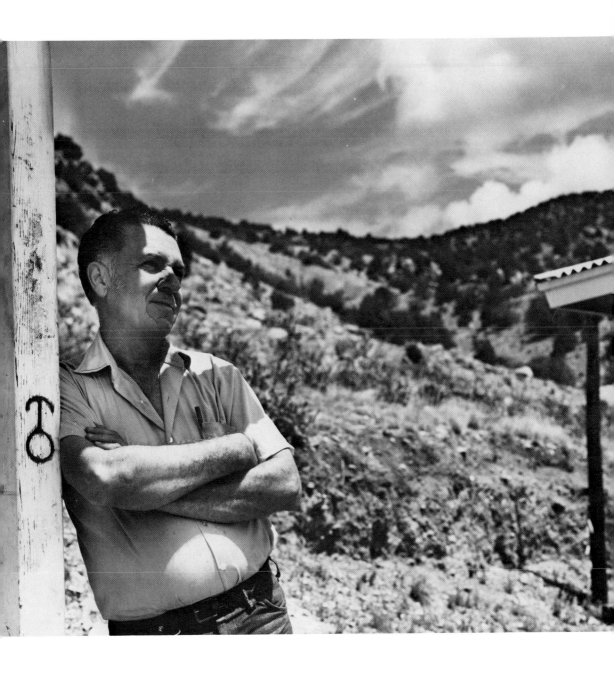

Plate 107. Horacio Valdez at His Home in Lyden, near Dixon, New Mexico, 1977.

The Future of the Art 207

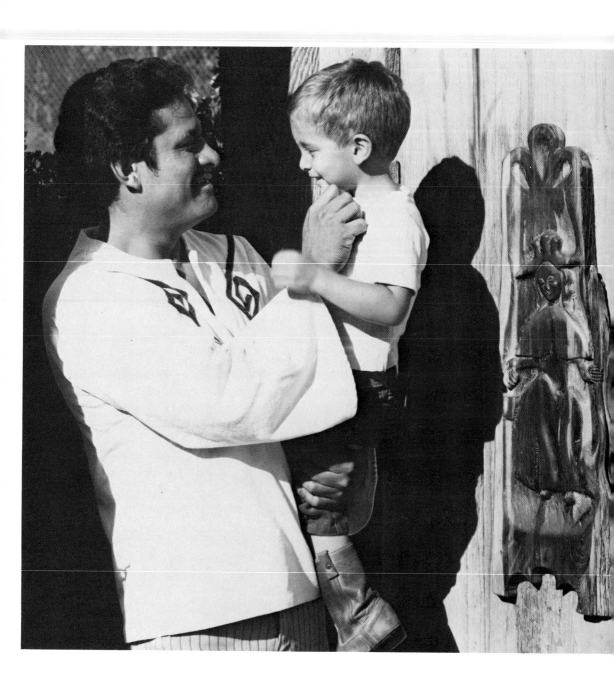

Plate 108. Benjamín López with His Bas-Relief Image of the Holy Child of Atocha and His Own Child, 1977.

The Symbolism of the Art

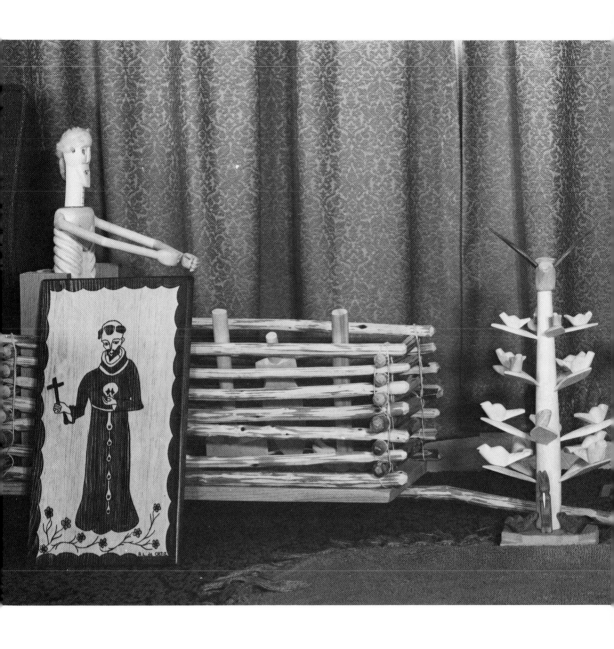

Plate 109. A Polychromed *Retablo* of St. Francis of Assisi by Alex Ortiz, 1977 (approximately 17.5 x 25 cm. or 7 x 10 in.). The carvings are by his brothers; Elvis made the Death cart and Lawrence carved the tree. From a private collection.

images, both traditional and contemporary, as important symbols of Hispano heritage. Although many of the artists who regard the images in this light are more highly involved in the Anglo-American world than were the early twentieth-century carvers, they conceive of their work as a provocative means of communicating their Hispano traditions to modern viewers.

The last two decades thus demonstrate the emergence in another form of the peculiar ability of the images to act as social mediators. The 1960s and 1970s found the Hispanos in the process of becoming integrated at a fairly rapid pace into another cultural and economic system. Many individuals discovered at this time that they were then more able to understand the internal workings of the Anglo-American system than ever before. They soon realized, however, that this perception did not enable them to overcome quickly the political and economic advantage of the Anglo-American majority. They also found that their attempt to overcome racism by adopting the tools and strategies of the superordinate society presented them with the risk of losing contact with their own language, culture, and history.

Confronted simultaneously with relative political and economic domination and a threatened loss of ethnic identity, a number of Hispanos attempted to consolidate their position by drawing upon the symbols of land, water, and New Mexican religious images. The visibility of these three entities permitted them to articulate the existence of their group and the seriousness of its grievances to the rest of the world. It also aided them in their efforts to establish a cultural identity. On both counts, the ability of the images to mediate in a variety of situations proved to be an invaluable asset.

The artists' desire to free their arts from Anglo-American control is increasingly being realized on more than an individual basis. Many Hispano artists, writers, musicians, and poets believe that the established patrons are largely unsympathetic to the changes which Hispano art has undergone in its dialogue with the ethnic identity movement. These artists are accordingly seeking to circumvent the influence of these outsiders over their work and have established organizations for the promotion of their artistic work. A prime example is the recently formed La Cofradía de Artes y Artesanos Hispanicos, consisting of Hispanos from throughout New Mexico. La Cofradía presented exhibitions and verbal art performances in Santa Fe in 1978 and 1979 and organized a fair in 1979.

Both La Cofradía itself and the events it has staged are specifically intended to support Hispano artistic freedom. Here artists can present work that is excluded from such forums as the Spanish Market of the Spanish Colonial Arts Society because of its departure from "traditional" or "Spanish colonial" canons in style, technique, or subject matter. Such efforts to unite Hispanos in combating artistic hegemony and in enhancing artistic expressions of contemporary cultural concerns appear to hold much potential for resolving the internal contradictions of twentieth-century Hispano image carving.

In a sense, the role of the images in the last two decades incorporates that of their entire previous existence. One element of their current utility clearly derives from the function of the images during the first half of this century as a mode of Hispano–Anglo-American communication. This intercultural function has combined with an intracultural role—Hispano past has been juxtaposed with Chicano present, and the images once again form a basis for relating the two. The external orientation of image carving during the first half of the twentieth century has combined with the internal, cultural focus characteristic of the traditional period. More than in any previous period, this complex mélange attests to the dynamism of the images as well as their ability to mediate.

These recent developments in the evolution of the art shed light on the role of the images in Hispano society, and they further permit one to draw some conclusions regarding the future of carving. It has become apparent that the persistence of image making in New Mexico is not contingent upon its association with any particular set of social conditions. As mediators, the images exhibit great dynamism and fluidity, and their position in society at any given time varies with the nature of their milieu and the needs and ends of the persons who make and appreciate them. It is invalid to attempt the explanation of the images in religious, aesthetic, or technical terms alone, as some writers have attempted to do. Both the form and the function of images simultaneously relate to all of these aspects, and any one may play a dominant role in the development of the art at a given time.

This account has followed the evolution of image making in New Mexico for nearly three centuries, and many periods of efflorescence and decline have been noted. Its findings should encourage observers who, like Chávez (in Espinosa 1960 [1967]), believe that the image-carving art in New Mexico has been dead for some time, to reconsider their position. Although the Hispano image-making tradition has periodically receded from public view for substantial stretches of time, its subsequent re-emergence demonstrates the fact that it had merely been dormant, not moribund. Indeed, the contribution of the images in the struggle to overcome the serious social and economic problems faced by Hispanos in the last half-century indicates that reports of the image carvers' demise have been greatly exaggerated.

The ability of the images to serve as social and cultural mediators, as well as the fluidity of the tradition and its capacity for revivification following sustained periods of dormancy, leads one to conclude that the images will continue to play an important role in Hispano society for many years to come. Although the image makers may from time to time be obscured by a lack of public attention and may even disappear altogether, the tradition that gives rise to their work will be ever ready to respond to the needs of the people who have sustained it through the centuries.

Appendixes

APPENDIX 1

Text of Cover Letter and Questionnaire Distributed by Carvers to Patrons

A. Cover Letter

Charles L. Briggs
P.O. Box 82
Córdova, NM 87523

July 4, 1976

Dear Visitor:

Please allow me to introduce myself. For several years now I have been conducting a study of the wood carvers of Córdova. So far I have spent a total of about a year living in the community and talking with the carvers and their neighbors about the wood-carving art.

One major gap remains, however, in my knowledge of the tradition: I have only spoken with a few of the carvers' customers, and at the present time I have little idea what these persons think about the carvings and who visits the Córdovan artists. As I am unable to sit in each of the carvers' shops all of the time in order to get to know the people who come to buy the carvings, I thought that I might leave this letter and a simple questionnaire in each of the workshops. So if you have a moment and would like to help me out with my study, please fill out the attached form and return it to me in the envelope which I have provided.

If you should choose to reply, please feel assured that your privacy will be fully protected. All questionnaires will be treated anonymously, and naturally, all questions are optional. The information will become part of a book on the Córdova carvers. These plans have been discussed with a number of carvers, and they agree that accurate published works on their art would benefit them directly by increased sales and indirectly in terms of a greater public awareness of the tradition which surrounds their work.

Finally, if you would place your name and address on the return envelope, I would like to send you a copy of a short history of the Córdova carving industry which I have compiled. This is, however, up to you. All correspondence is for research purposes and is not part of any promotional program.

   I thank you for your time, and I hope that you have a safe trip home.

Sincerely,
(signed)
Charles L. Briggs

B. Questionnaire Concerning the Cordova Wood-Carving Industry

1. Please relate your general impression of the wood carvings which you found in this shop. _____

2. Did any particular figures strike you as especially pleasing? (list) ___

3. What size of carving would you most like to have in your home? __

4. Did your reaction to the images of the saints differ from your impression of the other figures? _____

5. Could you recognize any of the saints which were portrayed? _____ If so, which ones? _____
6. With respect to the images, what was your reaction to the a) facial features_____, b) overall shape_____, c) the incised lines on the surface of the carvings_____, and d) the hands and feet? _____
7. Do the prices seem fair to you?_____If not, how should they be changed?_____
8. Did you buy any carvings?_____If so, please list _____

9. Intended use of carvings: gift?_____ own home?_____other?_____
10. Was your visit to Córdova part of a trip a) longer than a day?_____b)longer than a weekend? _____
11.Was your visit in connection with any professional interest in the carvings?_____ If you purchased any pieces, will these become a part of any institutional collections?_____If you care to list an institutional affiliation, please do so here_____
12. Where do you live? City_____State _____
13. Religious preference _____
14. Had you visited this carver previously?_____ Have you visited any other carvers? (Please list)_____
15. How did you first learn about the Córdova carvers? _____

If you need more space for any of the above questions or if you have any additional comments, please write them on the back of this page. Thank you for your assistance.

APPENDIX 2

Selected Data on Patrons

Question 8: Purchases of carvings
Total: Yes—27   No—6   No Response—3
Specified: *corona* (crown)   2
            Christmas tree   8
            bird   24
            burro   3
            rabbit   5
            squirrel   1
            mouse   1
            animals   23
            cross   2
            necklace   1
            fish   1
            St. Rafael   1
            St. Francis   4
            St. Pascual   2
            St. Michael with the Devil   1

Question 9: Intended use of purchases
            gift   14
            own home   26
            other   4 (for sale 1, teaching aid 2,
                                 school project 1)

Question 10: Duration of visit to area
            one day only   9
            longer than one day, but not longer than weekend   6
            longer than one weekend   20
            no response   1

Question 11: Visit connected with professional interests
            yes   3
            no   32
            purchases to become part of institutional collection   1

Question 12: Place of residence
<pre>
        Alabama   1
        Arizona   1
        California   4
        Colorado   8 (Denver area 5, Colorado Springs 2)
        Florida   1
        Kansas   1
        Illinois   3
        Indiana   1
        Massachussetts   1
        New Mexico   11 (Albuquerque 5, Los Alamos 3,
                              Santa Fe 3)
        Texas   1
        Utah   1
        Washington, D.C.   1
        Wyoming   1
</pre>

Question 13: Religious preference
<pre>
        Protestant   18
        Society of Friends 2
        Roman Catholic   6
        none   9
        no response   1
</pre>

Question 14: Record of respondent's past visits
<pre>
        had visited carver previously   20
        had not visited carver previously   16
        had visited other carvers previously   21
        had not visited other carvers previously   15
        number of first visits to Córdovan carvers   6
</pre>

Question 15: Manner in which respondent learned of carvers
<pre>
        saw work in museums   3
        publications   10
        from friends   12
        saw road signs   2
        from local people   3 (i.e., Chimayó weavers)
        found shop (road signs not mentioned)   6
        research trip   1
        school class   1
        no response   1
</pre>

APPENDIX 3

Partial Genealogy
of the López and Aragón Families

SOURCES: Archives of the Archdiocese of Santa Fe in the State Records Center and Archives, Santa Fe; the Holy Cross Parish, Santa Cruz, New Mexico, and the Holy Family Parish, Chimayó, New Mexico; baptismal, marriage, and burial records.

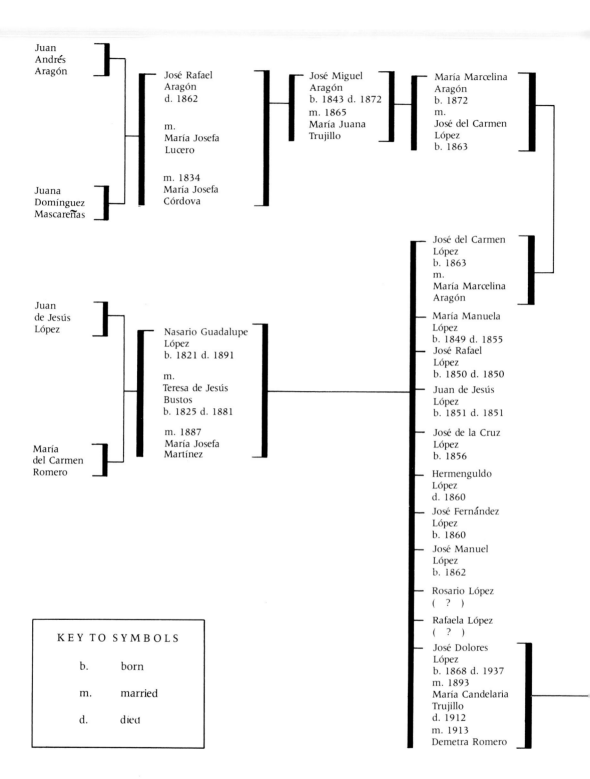

Juan
Andrés
Aragón

José Rafael
Aragón
d. 1862

m.
María Josefa
Lucero

m. 1834
María Josefa
Córdova

Juana
Domínguez
Mascareñas

José Miguel
Aragón
b. 1843 d. 1872
m. 1865
María Juana
Trujillo

María Marcelina
Aragón
b. 1872
m.
José del Carmen
López
b. 1863

Juan
de Jesús
López

Nasario Guadalupe
López
b. 1821 d. 1891

m.
Teresa de Jesús
Bustos
b. 1825 d. 1881

m. 1887
María Josefa
Martínez

María
del Carmen
Romero

José del Carmen
López
b. 1863
m.
María Marcelina
Aragón

María Manuela
López
b. 1849 d. 1855
José Rafael
López
b. 1850 d. 1850
Juan de Jesús
López
b. 1851 d. 1851

José de la Cruz
López
b. 1856

Hermenguldo
López
d. 1860

José Fernández
López
b. 1860

José Manuel
López
b. 1862

Rosario López
(?)

Rafaela López
(?)

José Dolores
López
b. 1868 d. 1937
m. 1893
María Candelaria
Trujillo
d. 1912
m. 1913
Demetra Romero

KEY TO SYMBOLS

b.   born

m.   married

d.   died

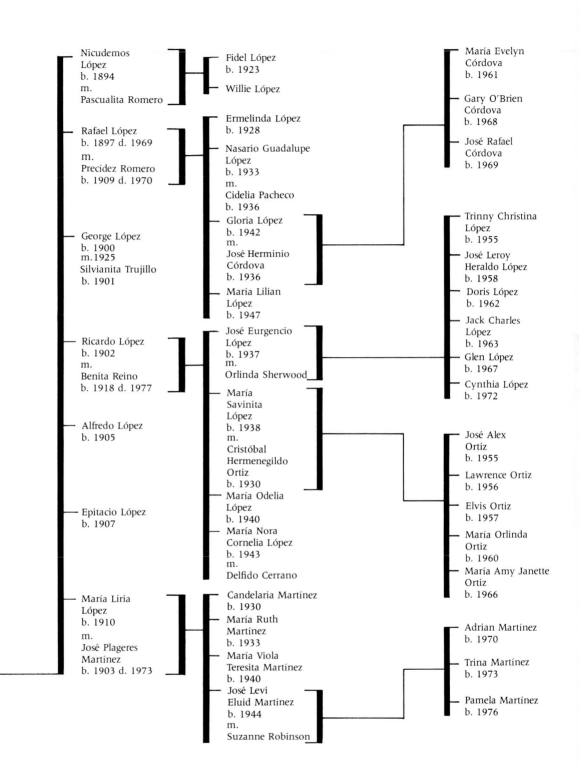

Nicudemos López
b. 1894
m.
Pascualita Romero

Fidel López
b. 1923

Willie López

Rafael López
b. 1897 d. 1969
m.
Precídez Romero
b. 1909 d. 1970

Ermelinda López
b. 1928

Nasario Guadalupe
López
b. 1933
m.
Cidelia Pacheco
b. 1936

George López
b. 1900
m.1925
Silvianita Trujillo
b. 1901

Gloria López
b. 1942
m.
José Herminio
Córdova
b. 1936

María Lilian
López
b. 1947

María Evelyn
Córdova
b. 1961

Gary O'Brien
Córdova
b. 1968

José Rafael
Córdova
b. 1969

Ricardo López
b. 1902
m.
Benita Reino
b. 1918 d. 1977

José Eurgencio
López
b. 1937
m.
Orlinda Sherwood

María
Savinita
López
b. 1938
m.
Cristóbal
Hermenegildo
Ortiz
b. 1930

Trinny Christina
López
b. 1955

José Leroy
Heraldo López
b. 1958

Doris López
b. 1962

Jack Charles
López
b. 1963

Glen López
b. 1967

Cynthia López
b. 1972

Alfredo López
b. 1905

Epitacio López
b. 1907

María Odelia
López
b. 1940

María Nora
Cornelia López
b. 1943
m.
Delfido Cerrano

José Alex
Ortiz
b. 1955

Lawrence Ortiz
b. 1956

Elvis Ortiz
b. 1957

María Orlinda
Ortiz
b. 1960

María Amy Janette
Ortiz
b. 1966

María Liria
López
b. 1910
m.
José Plageres
Martínez
b. 1903 d. 1973

Candelaria Martínez
b. 1930

María Ruth
Martínez
b. 1933

María Viola
Teresita Martínez
b. 1940

José Levi
Eluid Martínez
b. 1944
m.
Suzanne Robinson

Adrian Martínez
b. 1970

Trina Martínez
b. 1973

Pamela Martínez
b. 1976

Notes

Chapter 1: Introduction: The Art of the Image Maker in New Mexico

1. The phrase was coined by Fray Angélico Chávez (in Espinosa 1960 [1967]:ix).

2. One author differs from the views presented by most of his colleagues on this point. Espinosa (1960 [1967]:12, 20) believes that paintings on hide of both Mexican and New Mexican origin were present before 1680.

3. One conspicuous exception to this generalization is the nineteenth-century image maker Molleno, who made several paintings on hides (Boyd 1974:127).

4. This apparent training of the artists and the greater adherence of these images to formal canons of artistic composition, perspective, and anatomy prompted Boyd (1974:118) to claim that they were Franciscans, while Espinosa (1960 [1967]:21) reaches the conclusion that the paintings were executed in Mexico.

5. Although some early writers believed the traditional images to have been produced by Indians, later authors such as Boyd (1950:137) were strongly convinced that this was not the case: the image makers were Hispanic. Nevertheless, the issue is hardly as clear as the literature might suggest. Stoller (1976) has suggested that some of the image makers of the first two periods might have been Indians or Hispanicized Indians.

6. Shalkop (1969) provides a good description of two private chapels in Arroyo Hondo (near Taos) and their contents.

7. Espinosa (1960 [1967]:83) suggests a general explanation of the origin of Hispano place names and corresponding patron saints: "In most cases the geographic name is the key to the date upon which it was applied, for often a place or landmark was given the appellation of the saint or the name of the feast on whose day it was reached or observed." Also see Chávez (1949:323-35) on the saints in New Mexico geography.

222   *Notes to pages 6–15*

8. Aurora Lucero-White (1936:5) writes: "The *velorio de santos* being a community enterprise, it includes all the *santos* in the community. No one may refuse to lend his or her *santo* for the occasion, including the sacristan who has custody of the church's images."

9. In addressing the subject of the role of the saints in Catholic prayer, Hill and Stone (1964:281) write:

> The devout custom of praying to the saints is in keeping with a very old tradition of the Church. The saints are united with Christ in glory and with Him make intercession for us before the throne of the Father in Heaven. There they are able to plead for us to the Father as Christ Himself does. We pray to them to continue their pleading for us, their brothers and sisters on earth.

10. If further research lends support to Stoller's hypothesis (1976) regarding the Indian identity of the earliest image makers, then an additional dimension of the mediating role of images in Pueblo-Hispano relations will become apparent.

Chapter 2: Beginnings: Saint Carving in Córdova from 1820 to 1917

1. A petition of 1748 requests permission for the withdrawal of the settlers of three communities, Abiquiú, Ojo Caliente, and Pueblo Quemado, to more secure locations (SANM I: #28, SRCA). Taken as a whole, the documentary references to Pueblo Quemado (Córdova's name until 1900) suggest that it once received a community land grant. Accordingly, José de Gracia Trujillo and three other Córdovans petitioned the U.S. Court of Private Land Claims in 1893 for confirmation of the Pueblo Quemado grant. The original petition and the title of possession have not come to light, however, and the case was dismissed in 1898 (CPLC, Case #212, SRCA). Córdovans do retain rights to use of the Nuestra Señora del Rosario, San Fernando y Santiago grant on which the community lies. The grant was requested by Juan de Dios Romero and ten other residents of Chimayó in a petition to Governor Tomás Veles Cachupín of 1754 Cachupín granted the lands requested by Romero and the Las Truchas settlers on March 18, 1754, subject to their establishment of a fortified community (SANM I: #771, SRCA). On Aug. 13, 1892, Pedro José Gallegos filed suit inthe Court of Private Land Claims on behalf of the claimants of the grant, seeking confirmation of their interest. The U.S. Surveyor General's Office declared the grant to contain 14,786.58 acres, and a patent was issued on May 5, 1905 (CPLC, Case #28, SRCA).

2. Boyd does not concur with Chávez's date. After quoting from the inventory, Boyd writes: "The original document is undated and was classified by Fray Chávez with others of the year 1821. In view of the licensing of the chapel at Durango in 1832, it is probable that this report was made in that year or when the Quemado chapel was newly completed" (1974:407). It is true that new licenses were issued to recently remodeled churches and chapels; the wording of the document of January 1, 1832 does not, however, lend itself to this interpretation.

3. This letter acknowledges the receipt of licenses of three chapels: El Señor de Esquipulas (Chimayó), Nuestra Señora del Rosario (las Truchas), and San Antonio de Padua (Córdova), the latter being listed as nearing completion. It was addressed to Father Alcina of Santa Cruz (AASF, Patentes, Reel 55, frames 222-23).

4. A photograph of the exterior of the chapel taken on Feb. 15, 1939 by B. Brixner (in the Photographic Archive, Museum of New Mexico, Santa Fe) reveals that the annual mud plastering was discontinued and that after that time the chapel was given a more permanent coat of plaster.

5. The wood stove is shown in a photograph of the nave taken from the sanctuary; it was published as Plate 183 of Kubler (1940).

6. These contrasts are evident in the comparison of Plate 9, which dates to 1976, with a photograph made about 1935 by T. Harmon Parkhurst in the Photographic Archive, Museum of New Mexico, Santa Fe.

7. The date of José Rafael Aragón's death, January 3, 1862, is contained in the Archdiocese of Santa Fe records for Santa Cruz de la Cañada, Book of Burials for 1860–1924, p. 27. Thanks are extended to Christine Mather for making me aware of this document. Interestingly, Aragón was first buried in the San Antonio de Padua del Pueblo Quemado Chapel, but his remains were later reinterred in the Chapel of our Lady of Carmel in the Holy Cross Parish Church in Santa Cruz, New Mexico (ibid.).

8. The link between the López and Aragón families in Córdova that is most frequently cited by the contemporary Lópezes is the marriage of José del Carmen López, Nasario's next-to-last child (AASF, Baptisms, 16 Sept. 1863, SRCA), to Marcelina Aragón around 1891. Marcelina was Miguel Aragón's daughter, and was thus a granddaughter of José Rafael Aragón (AASF, Baptisms, Feb. 24, 1872, SRCA).

Chapter 3: The "Discovery" and "Encouragement" of José Dolores López

1. Ahlborn (1968), Boyd (1974:459-66), and Weigle (1976) provide substantial descriptions of the structure, contents, and functions of *moradas*.

2. Also see Writers' Program (1940:165-66).

3. The interest of the Santa Fe artists in Spanish colonial art in general and in the images specifically has also been noted briefly in recent works by Robertson and Nestor (1976:140-42; Nestor 1978).

4. One report from the community of Abiquiú, west of the Río Grande, indicates that in 1923 between 100 and 125 outsiders swarmed into the village on Good Friday. Interestingly, William Nash, Will Shuster, Frank Applegate, and Josef Bakos accompanied Governor and Mrs. Hinkle on the trip (*Santa Fe New Mexican*, March 31, 1923, p. 5).

5. Although Brown has published a brief account of his experiences in Córdova (1972), most of the material reported here is drawn from a set of tape-recorded, unpublished interviews with Brown conducted by Marta Weigle and the author. These are summarized in the introduction to a volume containing Brown's contributions to the New Mexico Writers' Project (Brown, Briggs, and Weigle 1978).

6. For example, see Anonymous (1928), Anonymous (1930), Austin (1933), Twobridge (1926), McCrossen (1931), and *El Pasatiempo* (1931). The last reference provides a case in point: "The Society for the Revival of Spanish Colonial Arts and Handicrafts sprang up naturally six years ago, as soon as it was realized at Santa Fe that an important contribution to the folk arts and crafts of the United States was being allowed to lapse *for lack of organized appreciation*" (*El Pasatiempo* 1931:4; italics added).

7. Coan (1935:52) similarly lauds the efforts of students in vocational schools: "here they can give vent to the spirit of individuality which has been crushed in hastily manufactured articles . . . ."

8. The efforts of the society, which was also known as the Society for the Revival of the Spanish Arts, were interrupted however, by a period of inactivity beginning about the time of the deaths of Applegate (in 1931) and Austin (in 1934). The society was revived in 1952 by E. Boyd (Alan Vedder 1977: personal communication). T.M. Pearce's introduction to the University of New Mexico's copy of the Applegate-Austin manuscript (n.d.)should be consulted for additional information on the two individuals' involvement in Hispano folk art. Austin and Applegate led in the formation of the Spanish Colonial Arts Society and in the planning of its activities, but they were hardly the only two participants. Mauzy (1935:67) credits Dr. F.E. Mera, John G. Meem, George M. Bloom, and unnamed others with initiating the "revival." The *Hand List of the Collection of the Spanish Colonial Arts Society, Inc.* also shows the following persons as contributing to the effort: Mrs. Ruth Laughlin Alexander, Mr. and Mrs. A.S. Alvord, Mr. and Mrs. Gerald Cassidy, Dr. Kenneth Chapman, Mrs. Thomas Curtin, Senator Bronson M. Cutting, Mr. Andrew Dasburg, Mr. and Mrs. John DeHuff, Mrs. Charles H. Dietrich, Mrs. Lois Field, Mrs. William Field, Mrs. Alice Corbin Henderson, Mr. Wayne Mauzy, Mr. and Mrs. Cyrus McCormick, Mr. George McCrossen, Mr. Preston McCrossen, Mrs. Alice Clark Myers, Mrs. Leonora Curtin Paloheimo, Mr. Sheldon Parson, Dr. Francis Proctor, Mrs. Marie Robinson, Mr. H. Cady Wells, and Miss Mary C. Wheelwright.

9. Some flexibility is evident in the terminology involved in the two events. The outdoor event was termed the "Spanish Market" in reports on the 1919, 1928, and 1930 fiestas (Anonymous 1919:103; 1928:183; 1930:142) but the indoor competition was referred to as the "annual prize competition of Spanish Colonial Arts" in 1927 (1927:337), the "Spanish Colonial Arts and Crafts Exhibition" in 1928 (1928:183), the "Colonial Arts Exhibit" in 1930 (1930:142), and the "Annual Spanish Fair" in 1933 (1933:126). It is also possible that separate outdoor and indoor events were not held in some years.

10. Nestor (1978:8) gives 1925 as the date of the initial Spanish Market of the Spanish Colonial Arts Society, which "offered the possibility of sales and prize money." An anonymous article in *El Palacio* cites the 1927 Exhibition as "the second annual prize competition of Spanish Colonial Arts," and other sources indicate that 1926 was the date of the first competition as well (e.g., Anonymous 1926:97).

11. Similarly, Nestor (1978:8) reports that the Spanish Arts Shop was opened in May 1930. Both *El Pasatiempo* (1931:4) and Mauzy (1935:67) indicate, however, that the shop was established in 1929.

12. Interestingly, the resident expert in wood carving at the Native Market was David Villiaseñor from Mexico (Nestor 1978:21).

13. Mauzy (1935:70) has commented on this feature of Native Market policy: "This competetive spirit is very real, for the designs and workmanship meeting with most favor with the public naturally result in greater sales for the producing workman. This is true also of woodworking and weavings, making a constant economic pressure on the craftsman to improve his output."

14. These data concerning the López highchair are found in unpublished notes by E. Boyd and Alan Vedder that are contained in the catalog entry for this piece. Another member of the López family, Eluid L. Martínez, claims that the chair was made for Fidocio López, a Córdova orphan who was adopted by José Dolores López about 1924. Fidel's birthdate of April 25, 1923 (as registered with the Vital Records Section of the Health and Environment Department in Santa Fe) suggests that Nicudemos López's claim that it was presented to Fidel as a Christmas present when he was about one year of age may be accurate.

15. This information about Gallegos is drawn from an anonymous article in *El Palacio* (1927:337), Boyd (1969:22), *El Pasatiempo* (1931:6), McCrossen (1931:456-58), and Stevens (1974:6). Apropos of Gallegos' own religious bearing, McCrossen and Stevens laud his prayerful demeanor and his role as sacristan of the chapel and as *resador* or prayerleader, while Hare (1943:21) baldly states, "López was a Penitente."

16. López's son Ricardo claims, however, that José Dolores was not the first Córdovan to carve images for sale to Anglo-Americans. He states that *he* innovated the carving of monotone images, that he produced the first examples, and that his father and brothers learned from him. After carving this first group of images, however, Ricardo decided that such work was sacrilegious; he never carved images again.

This claim is rather difficult to assess. The remainder of the family, along with patrons and scholars, assert that José Dolores was the first, and I have not discovered any evidence that would support Ricardo's view. It is, however, a distinct possibility. Artistic recognition mattered little to the carvers at first, but they soon learned that it was of great importance to their customers. The entire family accordingly sold the carvings under the name of José Dolores López, who was present to greet his patrons. Since his father had been selling furniture and animal and bird figures for some time, Ricardo might simply have asked his father to sell his images along with the rest of the carvings. The identity of the initial image carver does not, however, affect the thrust of my argument. Hispanos still initiated the sale of unpainted images to Anglo-Americans in response to the suggestion of an Anglo-American patron as a means of obtaining cash income.

17. It is not clear that the two pieces illustrated in Plates 33 and 34

were carved as a set. They have been photographed together because they are contained in the same collection and because they appear relatively close stylistically. Nevertheless, the collection contains a second Adam and Eve, and this somewhat idiosyncratic piece differs stylistically from the other two. It was, however, cataloged with the angel shown in the photograph when the atypical set was given to the New Mexico Historical Society, and the two may have been carved as a set. Unfortunately, the lack of information in the pertinent record books prevents the resolution of this difficulty.

18. It is possible that the image represents the Seven Brothers and St. Felicity, Symphorosa and her Seven Sons, or the Holy Machabees (seven brothers).

19. Some controversy surrounds the precise date of his death. Boyd (1969:23; 1974:265) and Wilder with Breitenbach (1943:text opposite Plate 43) maintain that he died in 1938. Unfortunately, the pertinent book of burial records at the parish church does not include an entry for López's burial. The date in the text was, however, supplied by the López family and is visible on his present (cement) grave marker. It is confirmed by an obituary for López in the *Santa Fe New Mexican* dated May 17, 1937 and by a mention of López by the Writers' Program (1940:299).

Chapter 4: The Expansion of the Industry

1. Briggs (1974b:98-126) should be consulted for a more complete autobiographical sketch along these same lines. The Spanish original of the quoted material in the text is available in Briggs (1974b:221).

2. In 1935 the number of persons finding work outside the state had dropped to fewer than 2,000, and their earnings were estimated at $350,000 (Harper, Córdova, and Oberg 1943:77). Although earnings rose in the following years (Soil Conservation Service 1937a:5), a large gap was left between the income of most villagers and the amount needed for subsistence. This gap was filled by relief dollars from the Works Projects Administration, the Soil Conservation Service, Civilian Conservation Corps, the Farm Security Administration, the Water Facilities Administration, Rural Rehabilitation Administration, and many other governmental relief projects. Estimated relief income for Hispanos in the Middle Río Grande Valley in 1936 was $1,143,051 (Soil Conservation Service 1937a:5). A number of sources have reported on this situation; the most notable include the Conservation Economics Series of the Soil Conservation Service, especially (1937a:2) and Weigle (1975). Siegel (1959:38), Harper, Córdova, and Oberg (1943), and Hurt (1941) should also be consulted.

3. MacDonald (1969) should be consulted with regard to the F.A.P. He summarizes its functions as consisting of ". . . three types: production of works of art, which never employed less than 50 percent of the personnel; art education, including the establishment of community art centers,

which employed 10 percent of the personnel in 1936 and, as the popularity of the device increased, 25 percent in 1939; and art research, the great effort of which was the Index of American Design, which employed approximately 10 percent of the personnel" (1969:422). McKenzie (1973) should also be consulted.

4. The community vocational schools were located in Taos, Galisteo, Los Lunas, Roswell, Costilla, Peñasco, Anton Chico, Española, Santa Cruz, Chupadero, San José, Grants, Atarque, Mora, Cundiyó, Limitar, Socorro, Abiquiú, Puerto de Luna, Bernalillo, Portales, Las Vegas, Cienega, and Agua Fría, while public schools such as the Normal at El Rito adopted the program as well (Coan 1935:14; Mauzy 1935:66; Nestor 1978:17; Sewell 1935:49).

5. This information comes from Córdovan oral history, a set of unpublished and undated notes by E. Boyd, and the catalog of an F.A.P. Exhibition in Washington (Public Works of Art Project 1934:14, 78).

6. This information was provided by Charles Hart (1973:personal communication) on the basis of a public voucher for work performed under provisions of the Federal Aid and Federal Highways Acts, as amended. The voucher was filed with the New Mexico State Highway Commission in 1955.

7. Baptismal and marriage certificates verify these dates. The microfilmed copies of the Archives of the Archdiocese of Santa Fe in the State Records Center and Archives list baptismal certificates as follows: Rafael, Oct. 24, 1897; George [sic], April 28, 1900; Ricardo, Dec. 28, 1902; Alfredo, June 18, 1905; Epitacio, Nov. 12, 1907; and María Liria, Aug. 28, 1910. A baptismal certificate for Nicudemos is not included in these documents. José Dolores López's marriages are cited in the Santa Cruz Parish records for Nov. 21, 1893 and June 9, 1913.

8. This conclusion is based upon the results of a survey of the Córdovan wood carvers' patrons, on which I report in Ch. 5.

9. This date is based on the recollection of other family members. See Note 16 of Ch. 3 for Ricardo's interpretation.

PART II: THE CONTEMPORARY PERIOD

Chapter 5: The Marketing of Contemporary Wood Carvings

1. In the summer of 1977 the Lópezes had moved the carvings table into the (east) living room, and they no longer covered the carvings. Such changes of location of the articles between the two front rooms do occur occasionally, but this is the first time that I saw them leave their table uncovered for any length of time.

2. Silvianita Trujillo de López does not suffer from any difficulty in language acquisition—she has simply not participated in the activities that prompted members of her generation to learn English. Many elderly men such as George López gained experience in the English language

through employment with Anglo-American coworkers and supervisors in the track-laying camps and elsewhere. The women of this generation generally remained at home while their fathers or husbands left in search of work, and nearly all of the people with whom the women interacted spoke Spanish.

3. This portrait, which is the work of Ernie Knee, is reproduced in Briggs (1974a:41).

4. An exception was noted as this study was going to press. A young carver who had just set up a table for the first time utilized the "we're closed" side of his sign. This was not, however, intended to convey the idea that business hours were over; the man was out of carvings and did not want to disappoint his customers.

5. Due to the problems involved in sampling, no attempt will be made to perform elaborate statistical analysis of the data, nor would the application of such procedures be appropriate in view of the nature of these data.

6. In 1976, for example, only Benita López and Orlinda López attended. George López and the Ortizes have not gone for several years.

7. The Santa Fe Fiesta has been held on Labor Day Weekend for decades. In 1977, however, the fiesta council pushed the date back two weeks in order to encourage greater hometown participation and to reduce the threat of violence. If this change becomes permanent, it could further affect the extent of the Córdovan carvers' participation in the arts and crafts market, as the smaller fiestas include many fewer tourists.

8. This is true only of the carvings currently being produced. Although José Dolores López's works are seldom offered for sale, they are highly valued and would command high prices.

Chapter 6: The Technology of Contemporary Carving in Córdova

1. The comparison between the attributes used on traditional images and those of contemporary images is extended in Ch. 7.

2. Special orders are generally stored in another room to prevent difficulties that could arise if another patron wished to purchase the piece. Special orders are thus deemed to be "not for the table."

3. This situation has been noted as well in the case of Mexican popular image makers (Giffords 1977:21-23).

PART III: THE SYMBOLISM OF THE IMAGE-CARVING ART

Chapter 7: The Search for Meaning

1. George López's version of this hymn is contained in the John Donald Robb Folk Music Recordings Collection in the Fine Arts Library of the University of New Mexico. The transcription and translation are my own.

2. The reader may wish to refer back to Plates 10, 43, 44, and 45.

3. Juan Sánchez's copy of this image appears in Plate 54.

4. In a sense, the carvers do recognize the role of prototypes in the production of images by emphasizing the concept of "getting the cuts." The "cuts" consist, however, of a set of proportions rather than a group of material representations. Furthermore, the carvers believe that a person may "think up" the cuts and need not receive them from another artist. For this reason the concept of the cuts appears relatively remote from most definitions of the prototype.

5. Unless otherwise specified, the expression "carvers with tables" refers to the individual(s) responsible for the management of particular tables and not to the sum total of persons who sell their works under the auspices of established carvers.

6. Los Caballeros de Vargas, a lay confraternity in Santa Fe, purchased a carving of Our Lady of the Conquest carved by George López and raffled it off following the Spanish Market in 1972. The Caballeros and their activities are mentioned in Grimes (1976:58, 60, 69, 101-13, 164, 170).

7. The *comadre* relationship is formed between two women and their husbands when one couple serves as godparents for the other's child. A man or woman may address or refer to a woman as his or her *comadre* if she is the godparent of their child or if the speaker is a godparent of the woman's child. (See Vincent 1966 for an excellent description of ritual sponsorship in Martíneztown, a section of Albuquerque.)

8. See Briggs (1974a:48-49) for the text of the blessing.

9. In somewhat more technical terms, the traditional artists shared a number of cultural codes with their patrons, including the code that enabled persons to interpret the iconography of the images.

Chapter 8: The Future of the Art

1. A great deal of scholarship has recently focused on questions relating to the appropriation of Spanish and Mexican land grants, and substantial results are emerging. The reader should consult Harper, Córdova, and Oberg (1943), Leonard (1943), Leonard and Loomis (1941), Soil Conservation Service (1937b), and Weigle (1975) for the early work on the land grants issue. With regard to more recent studies, González (1967 [1969]:215-35), Swadesh (1973:73-77), and Weigle (1975:267-68, 277) provide useful bibliography, while the following studies provide valuable data: Atencio (1964), Bowden (1969), Eastman, Carruthers, and Liefer (1971), Jenkins (1961), Knowlton (1961; 1967a; 1967b; 1976), Liefer (1970), Reynolds (1976a; 1976b), Rock (1976), Smith (1973), Swadesh (1974), Van Ness (1976a; 1976b), Westphall (1965; 1973; 1974), and White et al. (1971).

2. Blawis (1971), González (1967 [1969]), Knowlton (1970, 1976), Nabakov (1969), and Swadesh (1968; 1974:129-32) present interesting information on the Alianza and other efforts to resolve questions concerning land grants in New Mexico.

3. Ortiz's course was listed in a schedule of classes for the Española Center which appeared in the *Santa Fe New Mexican* for Sept. 24, 1973. The article reads in part: "The wood-carving course also is scheduled to begin tomorrow evening, and can accept additional enrollees. Mrs. Savinita Ortiz, daughter [sic] of nationally-known wood carver George López of Córdova, will instruct the class." Unfortunately, the enrollment did not meet the quota, and the class was canceled.

4. I will cite just two examples. A *retablo* exhibited at the 1976 Spanish Market was an exact copy of the photograph of a *bulto* of the crucified Christ that appears on the cover of Mills [1967]. The transformation from a three-dimensional object to a two-dimensional surface was thus accomplished by the photographer rather than by the artist. Similarly, one of the first images to appear on tanned hides in the very recent revival of this form of image making was a nearly exact copy of the painting of St. Francis of Assisi included in Boyd (1974:126). The copy was shown at the 1977 Spanish Market.

References Cited

(AASF) Archives of the Archdiocese of Santa Fe, microfilm copies in the State Records Center and Archives, Santa Fe. Baptismal records for Holy Cross Parish, Santa Cruz, New Mexico, dated Sept. 10, 1843; May 4, 1856; Sept. 16, 1863; April 5, 1868; Feb. 24, 1872; Oct. 24, 1897; April 28, 1900; Dec. 28, 1902; June 18, 1905; Nov. 12, 1907; Aug. 28, 1910. Marriage records for Holy Cross Parish, Santa Cruz, dated Sept. 30, 1844. Original copies in the Holy Cross Parish, Santa Cruz, Marriage records dated Nov. 21, 1893; June 9, 1913. Burial records dated Jan. 3, 1862; Oct. 28, 1872; June 28, 1891; Patentes, Reel 54, frame 463 and Reel 55, frames 222-23, 230.

Adams, Ansel
    1976 *Photographs of the Southwest.* Boston: New York Graphic Society.

Adams, Eleanor B., and Chávez, Fray Angélico (eds.)
    1956. *The Missions of New Mexico*, 1776. Albuquerque: Univ. of New Mexico Press.

Ahlborn, Richard E.
    1958. "Spanish Colonial Wood Carving in New Mexico, 1590–1848." Master's thesis, Univ. of Delaware.
    1968. "The Penitente Moradas of Abiquiú." *Contributions from the Museum of History and Technology*, Paper 63. Washington, D.C.: Smithsonian Institution Press.

Anonymous
    1919. "The Santa Fe Fiesta," *El Palacio* 7(5-6):99-132.
    1924. "The Santa Fe Fiesta," *El Palacio* 17(2):23-24.
    1926. "The Santa Fe Fiesta—1926," *El Palacio* 21(3-4-5):73-105.
    1927. "Museum Events: Spanish Colonial Arts," *El Palacio* 23 (12): 337-38.
    1928. "Santa Fe Fiesta: Events at Gallup and Albuquerque," *El Palacio* 25(8, 9, 10, 11):183.
    1930. "Fiesta Event: The Spanish Colonial Arts Society," *El Palacio* 29(3):105-6, 142.
    1932. "Spanish Arts: Wood Carving Group," *El Palacio* 33 (11-12):120.
    1933. "Arts of the Southwest," *El Palacio* 34(15-16):126.
    1935. "WPA Art Work Shown in Museum," *El Palacio* 40(16-17-18):92-94.

Applegate, Frank

1931. "New Mexico Legends," *Southwest Review* 17(1):199-208.

———and Austin, Mary

n.d. "Spanish Colonial Arts and Crafts." Unpublished ms. in the T.M. Pearce papers, Univ. of New Mexico General Library, Albuquerque.

Atencio, Tomás C.

1964. "The Human Dimensions in Land Use and Displacement in Northern New Mexico Villages." *In* Clark S. Knowlton, ed., *Indian and Spanish American Adjustments to Arid and Semiarid Environments*. Lubbock: Texas Technological College. Pp. 44-52.

Austin, Mary

1924. *The Land of Journeys' Ending*. New York: Century.

1931. *Experiences Facing Death*. Indianapolis: Bobbs-Merrill.

1932. *Earth Horizon*. Boston: Houghton Mifflin.

1933. "Spanish Colonial Furnishings in New Mexico," *Antiques*, Feb., 46-49.

Barker, Ruth Laughlin

1926. "Sentiment a Santa Fe Asset: Interview with Dr. Lummis," *El Palacio* 21(12):319-25.

Berg, Margaret

1965. "Patrocinio Barela, Wood Carver of Taos, 1900–1964," *Museum of New Mexico Newsletter*, Jan.

Blawis, Patricia Bell

1971. *Tijerina and the Land Grants: Mexican Americans in Struggle for Their Heritage*. New York: International Publishers.

Blumenschein, Ernest L.

1926. "Origin of the Taos Art Colony," *El Palacio* 20(10):190-93.

Bodine, John J.

1968. "A Tri-Ethnic Trap: The Spanish Americans in Taos." *In* June Helm, ed., *Spanish-Speaking People in the United States: Proceedings of the 1968 Annual Spring Meeting of the American Ethnological Society*. Seattle: Univ. of Washington Press. Pp. 145-53.

Bowden, J.J.

1969. "Private Land Claims in the Southwest." L.L.M. thesis, Southern Methodist Univ.

Boyd, E.

1946. *Saints and Saint Makers*. Santa Fe: Lab. of Anthropology.

1950. "The Literature of Santos," *Southwest Review* 35(2):128-40.

1954a. "Addendum to Paper on José E. Espinosa's Ramón Velasquez," *El Palacio* 61(6):190-91.

1954b. Unpublished notes, report of conversation with Apolonio Rodríguez, April 6.

1969. *The New Mexico Santero*. Santa Fe: Museum of New Mexico Press.

1974. *Spanish Colonial Popular Arts*. Santa Fe: Museum of New Mexico Press.

Breese, Frances, and Boyd, E.

1966. *New Mexico Santos: How to Name Them*. Santa Fe: Museum of New Mexico Press and the International Folk Art Foundation.

Briggs, Charles L.

1974a. "What is a Modern 'Santo'?" *El Palacio* 79(4):40-49.

1974b. "An Ethnographic Study of Wood Carving in Córdova, New Mexico." Bachelor's thesis, Colorado College.

1974c. "A Modern Santero," *New Mexico Magazine* 52(11-12):38-40.

1976. "To Sell a Saint: The Manipulation of Religious Symbols in the Evolution of a Sacred Art," *Papers in Anthropology* 17(2):201-21.

Brody, J.J.

1971. *Indian Painters and White Patrons*. Albuquerque: Univ. of New Mexico Press.

1976. "The Creative Consumer: Survival, Revival, and Invention in Southwest Indian Arts." *In* Nelson H. H. Graburn, ed., *Ethnic and Tourist Arts: Cultural Expressions from the Fourth World*. Berkeley: Univ. of California Press. Pp. 70-84.

Brown, Lorin W.

1941. "Fiestas in New Mexico," *El Palacio* 48(11):239-45.

————Briggs, Charles L., and Weigle, Marta

1978. *Hispano Folklife of New Mexico: The Lorin W. Brown Federal Writers' Project Manuscripts*. Albuquerque: Univ. of New Mexico Press.

Cabeza de Baca, Fabiola

1954. *We Fed Them Cactus*. Albuquerque: Univ. of New Mexico Press.

Carroll, Charles D.

1943. "Miguel Aragón, a Great Santero," *El Palacio* 50(3):49-64.

Cassidy, Ina Sizer

1936. "Art and Artists of New Mexico: Wood Carver," *New Mexico Magazine* 14(11):25,33.

Chávez, Fray Angélico

1948. *Our Lady of the Conquest*. Santa Fe: Historical Society of New Mexico.

1949. "Saints' Names in New Mexico Geography," *El Palacio* 56:323-35.

1957. *Archives of the Archdiocese of Santa Fe, 1678–1900*. Washington, D.C.: Academy of American Franciscan History.

Coan, Mary W.

1935. "Handicraft Arts Revived," *New Mexico Magazine* 13(2):14-15, 52.

Coke, Van Deren

1963. *Taos and Santa Fe: The Artist's Environment, 1882–1942*. Albuquerque: Univ. of New Mexico Press.

1965. "A Saint-Carver in New Mexico," *Art in America* 53:124-27.

1967. "A Note on B. J. O. Nordfeldt's 'Penitente Crucifixion,' " *University of New Mexico Art Museum Bulletin* 2:6-11.

1972. *Nordfelt the Painter*. Albuquerque: Univ. of New Mexico Press.

Córdova, Gilberto Benito

1973. *Abiquiú and Don Cacahuate: A Folk History of a New Mexican Village*. Cerrillos, N.M.: San Marcos Press.

Córdova, Lorenzo de (pseudonym for Lorin W. Brown)

1972. *Echoes of the Flute*. Santa Fe: Ancient City Press.

Crews, Mildred T.

1968. "Patrocinio Barela: Woodcarver of Taos," *Presbyterian Life*, Feb. 15, 1968, pp. 7-11.

Crews, Mildred, Anderson, Wendell, and Crews, Judson
  1962. *Patrocinio Barela: Taos Woodcarver*. Taos, N.M.: Taos Recordings and Publications.
Dawson, Lawrence E., Fredrickson, Vera-Mae, Graburn, Nelson H.H.
  1974. *Traditions in Transition: Culture Contact and Material Change*. Berkeley: Lowie Museum of Anthropology.
DeHuff, Elizabeth Willis
  1948. *Say the Bells of Old Missions: Legends of Old New Mexico Churches*. St. Louis: B. Herder Book Co.
Dike, Sheldon Holland
  1958. *The Territorial Post Offices of New Mexico*. Albuquerque: Dr. S.H. Dike.
Eastman, Clyde, Carruthers, Garrey, and Liefer, James A.
  1971. *Evaluation of Attitudes toward Land in North-Central New Mexico*. Agricultural Experiment Station Bulletin 577. Las Cruces: New Mexico State Univ.
Ellis, Florence Hawley
  1954. "Santeros of Tomé," *New Mexico Quarterly* 24(3):346-53.
El Pasatiempo
  1931. "José Dolores López, Grabador de Maderas" and "Celso Gallegos, Fabricador de los Santos de Bulto," Sept. 5, pp. 6, 9.
Espinosa, José Edmundo
  1954. "The Discovery of the Bulto-Maker Ramón Velásquez of Canjilón," *El Palacio* 61(6):185-90.
  1960. *Saints in the Valleys: Christian Sacred Images in the History, Life and Folk Art of Spanish New Mexico*. (Rev. ed., 1967.) Albuquerque: Univ. of New Mexico Press.
Forest Service, U.S. Department of Agriculture
  1970. *Regulations Governing Livestock Grazing on National Forest System Lands and Other Lands under Forest Service Control*. Washington, D.C.: Government Printing Office.
García Villada, Zacarías, S.J.
  1922. *San Isidro labrador en la historia y en la literatura*. Madrid: Administración de "razón y fe."
Gardner, Richard
  1970. *¡Grito! Reis Tijerina and the New Mexico Land Grant War of 1967*. Indianapolis: Bobbs-Merrill.
Gettens, Rutherford J., and Turner, Evan H.
  1951. "The Materials and Methods of Some Religious Paintings of Early Nineteenth-Century New Mexico," *El Palacio* 58(1):3-16.
Giffords, Gloria Kay
  1974. *Mexican Folk Retablos: Masterpieces on Tin*. Tucson: Univ. of Arizona.
  1977. "Mexico's Last Saint Makers," *El Palacio* 83(3):11-27.
González, Nancie L. Solien de
  1967. *The Spanish-Americans of New Mexico: A Heritage of Pride*. (2nd ed., 1969.) Albuquerque: Univ. of New Mexico Press.
Graburn, Nelson H.H.
  1969. "Art and Acculturative Processes," *International Social Science Journal* 21(3):457-68.
  1976. (ed.) *Ethnic and Tourist Arts: Cultural Expressions from the Fourth World*. Berkeley: Univ. of California Press.

Grimes, Ronald L.
    1976. *Symbol and Conquest: Public Ritual and Drama in Santa Fe, New Mexico*. Ithaca, N.Y.: Cornell Univ. Press.
Hare, Elizabeth Sage
    1943. "The Wood Carver of Córdova," *Travel* 81:20-21, 32.
Harper, Allan G., Córdova, Andrew R., and Oberg, Kalervo
    1943. *Man and Resources in the Middle Río Grande Valley*. Albuquerque: Univ. of New Mexico Press.
Hill, Rev. John J., and Stone, Rev. Theodore C.,
    1964. *A Modern Catechism*. Np.: ACTA Foundation.
Horwitz, Elinor Lander
    1975. *Contemporary American Folk Artists*. Philadelphia: Lippincott.
Houghland, Willard
    1946. *Santos: A Primitive American Art*. New York: Jan Kleijkamp and Ellis Monroe.
Hurt, Wesley Robert, Jr.
    1941. "Manzano: A Study of Community Disorganization." Master's thesis, Univ. of New Mexico.
Jaramillo, Cleofas M.
    1941. *Shadows of the Past*. (2nd ed., 1972.) Santa Fe: Ancient City Press.
Jenkins, Myra Ellen
    1961. "The Baltasar Baca 'Grant': History of an Encroachment," *El Palacio* 68:47-64, 87-105.
    1974. "Documentation Concerning Settlement of Pueblo Quemado (Córdova)." Ms. in possession of the author, State Records Center and Archives, Santa Fe.
Kent, Kate Peck
    1976. "Pueblo and Navajo Weaving Traditions and the Western World." In Nelson H.H. Graburn, ed., *Ethnic and Tourist Arts: Cultural Expressions from the Fourth World*. Berkeley: Univ. of California Press. Pp. 85-101.
Knowlton, Clark S.
    1961. "The Spanish Americans in New Mexico," *Sociology and Social Research* 45(4):448-54.
    1967a. "Conflicting Attitudes toward Land Use and Land Ownership in New Mexico," *Proceedings of the Southwestern Sociological Association* 18:60-68.
    1967b. "Land-Grant Problems among the State's Spanish-Americans," *New Mexico Business* 20(6):1-13.
    1970. "Violence in New Mexico: A Sociological Perspective," *California Law Review* 58:1054-84.
    1976. "The Study of Land Grants as an Academic Discipline," *Social Science Journal* 13(3):3-7.
Kubler, George
    1940. *The Religious Architecture of New Mexico: In the Colonial Period and Since the American Occupation*. Colorado Springs: Taylor Museum.
    1964. "Essay." In *Santos: An Exhibition of the Religious Folk Art of New Mexico*. Fort Worth: Amon Carter Museum of Western Art.
Lange, Yvonne
    1974. "Lithography, an Agent of Technological Change in Religious Folk Art: A Thesis," *Western Folklore* 33(1):51-64.

1975. "Santos: The Household Wooden Saints of Puerto Rico." Ph.D. diss., Univ. of Pennsylvania.

Leonard, Olen E.
1943. *The Role of the Land Grant in the Social Organization and Social Processes of a Spanish-American Village in New Mexico*. Ann Arbor: Edwards Brothers.

————, and Loomis, C.P.
1941. *Culture of a Contemporary Rural Community: El Cerrito, New Mexico*. Rural Life Studies, 1. Washington, D.C.: U.S. Dept. of Agriculture, Bureau of Agricultural Economics.

LeViness, W. Thetford
1958. "He Carves the Santos—In the Land of the Penitentes," *Desert Magazine*, Jan., 10-12.
1963. "George López: A Carver of Santos," *American Artist*, April, 25-29, 78-79.

Liefer, James Arnold
1970. "Attitudes toward Land Ownership and Usage in Northcentral New Mexico." Master's thesis, New Mexico State Univ.

Lucero-White, Aurora
1936. "El Velorio (The Wake)." Unpublished ms. in the files of the W.P.A. New Mexico Writers' Project, History Library, Museum of New Mexico, Santa Fe.

McCrossen, Helen Cramp
1931. "Native Crafts in New Mexico," *The School Arts Magazine* 30(7):456-58.

McDonald, William F.
1969. *Federal Relief Administration and the Arts*. Columbus: Ohio State Univ. Press.

McKenzie, Richard D.
1973. *The New Deal for Artists*. Princeton, N.J.: Princeton Univ. Press.

Martínez, Eluid L.
1978. *What is a New Mexico Santo?* Santa Fe: Sunstone Press.

Mauzy, Wayne
1935. "Santa Fe's Native Market," *El Palacio* 40(13-14-15):65-72.

Mills, George
[1967]. *The People of the Saints*. Colorado Springs: Taylor Museum.

Nabakov, Peter
1969. *Tijerina and the Courthouse Raid*. Albuquerque: Univ. of New Mexico Press.

Nestor, Sarah
1978. *The Native Market of the Spanish New Mexican Craftsmen, Santa Fe, 1933–1940*. Santa Fe: Colonial New Mexico Historical Foundation.

Public Works of Art Project
1934. *National Exhibition of Art by the Public Works of Art Project*. Washington, D.C.: Corcoran Gallery of Art.

Reau, Louis
1958. *Iconographie de l' art chrétien*. Vol. III. Paris: Presses Universitaires de France.

Reynolds, C. Lynn
1976a. "Economic Decision-Making: The Influence of Traditional Hispanic Land Use Attitudes on Acceptance of Innovation," *Social Science Journal* 13(3):21-34.

1976b. "Alternative Water Uses: The Impact of Proposed Non-Agricultural Uses for Water on Irrigation-Based Hispanic Villages," *Papers in Anthropology* 17(2):179-200.

Robertson, Edna, and Nestor, Sarah
1976. *Artists of the Canyons and Caminos: Santa Fe, the Early Years*. N.p.: Peregrine Smith.

Rock, Michael J.
1976. "The Change in Tenure New Mexico Supreme Court Decisions Have Effected upon the Common Lands of Community Land Grants in New Mexico," *Social Science Journal* 13(3):53-63.

(SANM) Spanish Archives of New Mexico
Cases numbered 28, 211, 718, 768, 771, and 1041 in the New Mexico State Records Center and Archives, Santa Fe.

Santa Fe New Mexican
1923. "Governor Sees Penitentes in Ceremonies at Abiquiú," *Santa Fe New Mexican*, March 31, 1923.
1973. "[College of Santa Fe] Española Center Course Openings Listed," *Santa Fe New Mexican*, Sept. 24, 1973.

Schlesinger, Andrew B.
1971. "Las Gorras Blancas, 1889–1891," *Journal of Mexican American History* 1:87-143.

Sewell, Brice H.
1935. "A New Type of School," *New Mexico School Review* 15(2):49-50.

Shalkop, Robert L.
1969. *Arroyo Hondo: The Folk Art of a New Mexican Village*. Colorado Springs: Taylor Museum.

Siegel, Bernard J.
1959. "Some Structure Implications for Change in Pueblo and Spanish New Mexico." *In* Verne F. Ray (ed.), *Intermediate Societies, Social Mobility, and Communication: Proceedings of the 1959 Annual Spring Meeting of American Ethnological Society.* Seattle: American Ethnological Society. Pp. 37-44.

Smith, Andrew T.
1973. "The People of the San Antonio de las Huertas Grant, New Mexico, 1767–1900." Bachelor's thesis, Colorado College.

Soil Conservation Service, United States Department of Agriculture
1937a. *Village Livelihood in the Upper Río Grande Area and a Note on the Level of Village Livelihood in the Upper Río Grande Area.* Regional Bulletin No. 44., Conservation Economics Series No. 17. Albuquerque: Soil Conservation Service.
1937b. *Notes on Community-owned Land Grants in New Mexico.* Regional Bulletin 47, Conservation Economics Series No.2. Albuquerque: Soil Conservation Service.

Spanish Colonial Arts Society
n.d. *Hand List of the Collection of the Spanish Colonial Arts Society, Inc.* N.p.

Spicer, Edward H.
1962. *Cycles of Conquest: The Impact of Spain, Mexico, and the United States on the Indians of the Southwest, 1533–1960.* Tucson: Univ. of Arizona Press.

Steele, Thomas J., S.J.
　1974. *Santos and Saints: Essays and Handbook*. Albuquerque: Calvin
　　Horn.
Stevens, Clifford
　1974. "Celso Gallegos: The Santero of San Ysidro," *Viva* (Sunday sec-
　　tion), *Santa Fe New Mexican*, Jan. 13, p. 6.
Stoller, Marianne L.
　1976. "The Early Santeros of New Mexico: A Problem in Ethnic Iden-
　　tity and Artistic Tradition." Paper presented at Annual Meeting
　　of American Society for Ethnohistory, Albuquerque, Oct. 9,
　　1976.
Swadesh, Frances Leon
　1968. "The Alianza Movement: Catalyst for Social Change in New
　　Mexico." *In* June Helm, ed., *Spanish Speaking People in the
　　United States: Proceedings of the 1968 Annual Meeting of the
　　American Ethnological Society*. Seattle: Univ. of Washington
　　Press. Pp. 162-77.
　1973. *20,000 Years of History: A New Mexico Bibliography*. Santa Fe:
　　Sunstone Press.
　1974. *Los Primeros Pobladores: Hispanic Americans of the Ute Fron-
　　tier*. Notre Dame, Ind.: Univ. of Notre Dame Press.
Tucson Museum of Art
　n.d. *Raices Antiguas/Visiones Nuevas: Ancient Roots/New Visions*.
　　Tucson: Tucson Museum of Art.
Twobridge, Lydia J.
　1926. "The Santa Fe Fiesta of 1926," *El Palacio* 21(7-8):179.
Van Ness, John R.
　1976a. "Spanish American *vs.* Anglo American Land Tenure and the
　　Study of Economic Change in New Mexico," *Social Science
　　Journal* 13(3):45-52.
　1976b. "Modernization, Land Tenure, and Ecology: The Costs of
　　Change in Northern New Mexico," *Papers in Anthropology*
　　17(2):168-78.
Vincent, María
　1966. "Ritual Kinship in an Urban Setting: Martíneztown, New
　　Mexico." Master's thesis, Univ. of New Mexico.
Wallrich, William J.
　1951. "The Santero Tradition in the San Luis Valley," *Western Folklore*
　　10:153-61.
Weigle, Marta
　1976. *Brothers of Light, Brothers of Blood: The Penitentes of the South-
　　west*. Albuquerque: Univ. of New Mexico Press.
　1975. (ed.) *Hispanic Villages of Northern New Mexico: A Reprint of
　　Volume II of the 1935 Tewa Basin Study, with Supplementary
　　Materials*. Santa Fe: Lightning Tree.
Westphall, Victor
　1965. *The Public Domain in New Mexico, 1854–1891*. Albuquerque:
　　Univ. of New Mexico Press.
　1973. *Thomas Benton Catron and His Era*. Tucson: Univ. of Arizona
　　Press.
　1974. "Fraud and Implications of Fraud in the Land Grants of New

Mexico," *New Mexico Historical Review* 49:189-218.

White, Koch, Kelley and McCarthy, Attorneys at Law and the New Mexico State Planning Office
1971. *Land Title Study*. Santa Fe: State Planning Office.

Wilder, Mitchell A., with Breitenbach, Edgar
1943. *Santos: The Religious Folk Art of New Mexico*. Colorado Springs: Taylor Museum.

Wolf, Eric
1956. "The Virgin of Guadalupe: A Mexican National Symbol," *Journal of American Folklore* 71:34-39.

Writers' Program, Work Projects Administration, State of New Mexico
1940. *New Mexico: A Guide to the Colorful State*. American Guide Series. New York: Hastings House.

Zóbel de Ayala, Fernando
1963. *Philippine Religious Imagery*. Manila: Ateneo de Manila.

Index

Aragón, José Rafael (Córdova image maker): images in Córdova chapel, 26–27, 186; influence on contemporary carvers, 76, 98, 180, 186; mentioned, 11, 98, 224 n.7; polychrome technique, 26–27, 37; photographs of works by: Altar screen and images in Córdova chapel, Plate 9, p. 25, "*Our Lady of Sorrows,*" Plate 10, p. 28, Plate 45, p. 81, *Saint Anthony of Padua, Patron Saint of Córdova* (image attributed to), Plate 17, p. 40

Aragón, María Marcelina (granddaughter of José Rafael Aragón), 224 n.8

Aragón, Miguel. *See* Aragón, José Miguel

Aragón, Rafael. *See* Aragón, José Rafael

Arms, treatment of, in carving, 166, 167

Art: carvings as being, 149, 154, 159; ethnic or tourist, 199–200; Hispano, 46–52, 154, 210; modern Western, 203, 206; religious, 182

Art colonies: Taos and Santa Fe, 44, 51

Artistic expression, 147, 149

Artists: Hispano, 10–12, 49, 64, 86, 140, 145, 149, 154, 210; in America, 86; Indian, 152

Aspen, as carving material, 10, 68, 100, 113, 161, 166, 177

Assembly of God Church, 103, 196

Associations, religious, 15

Attributes, of saints, 166–67, 177, 182–86, 187

Austin, Mary (writer and patron): and José Dolores López, 45–46, 55, 149; manuscript on Hispano art, 44, 225 n.8; mentioned, 3, 152; and "revival," 46–48, 51, 225 n.8

Backwardness, 146

Baptism, 193

Barela, Patrocinio (Taos carver): mentioned, 86, 203; photograph of work by, *El Divino Pastor* ("The Divine Shepherd"), Plate 48, p. 88; shown, Plate 47, p. 87

Base, of carvings, 166, 167, 177

Baskets, 149

Beards, as carving element, 117

Bedell, Eleanor (manager of Native Market), 48

Belts, as carving element, 129, 166

Berg, Margaret (writer), 86

Berninghaus, Oscar (artist), 44

Berried juniper. *See* Juniper, berried

Bible, as carving element: 68, 129, 186, Plate 36, p. 71, Plate 38, p. 73, Plate 74, p. 125, Plate 78, p. 130

Bible Stand, Painted, by José Dolores López: mentioned, 39, 196; shown, Plate 18, p. 41

Birds: as carving element, 166, 177, Plate 23, p. 56, Plate 24, p. 57, Plate 26, p. 59; as carving subject, mentioned, 53, 55,

Birds (cont.)
62, 90, 91, 103, 108, 113, 129, 135, 147, 152, 164, 171; as carving subject, shown, *Rooster and Flying Bird*, by José Dolores López, Plate 25, p. 58, *Pine Tree with Woodpeckers*, by José Dolores López, Plate 27, p. 60, *Birds in the Wheat*, by José Dolores López, Plate 29, p. 62, *Small Bird and Animal Figures*, by Liria López (de García), Plate 49, p. 91, *Small Bird, Animals, and a Tree*, by George and Silvianita López, Plate 85, p. 148

Blessing, of images, 6, 193–94

Blood: as carving element, 164; as cultural construct. *See* Innate behavioral characteristics

Blumenschein, Ernest L. (artist), 44

Borrego Mesa (in Santa Fe National Forest), 161

Boxes: carved, mentioned, 90; carved, shown, *Incised and Stained*, Plate 24, p. 57; as carving element, 90

Boyd, E. (curator and writer): on Córdova chapel, 26, 27, 223–24 n.2; on José Dolores López, 39, 186; mentioned, 100, 117, 177, 179, 187, 225 n.8

Breese, Frances (writer), 177, 187

Breitenbach, Edgar (writer), 29

Brotherhood of Our Father Jesus ("Penitentes"), 15, 16, 31, 39, 44–45, 206

Brown, Cassandra (mother of Lorin W. Brown), 45

Brown, Lorin W. (pseudonym, Lorenzo de Córdova, writer), 26, 45–46, 90, 199, 225 n.5

Bulto, santo de ("carved images in the round"): defined, 10, in Córdova chapel, 26–27; mentioned, 12, 15, 64, 98, 103, 113, 117, 186; Puerto Rican, 7, 187; production of, 160–71

Business principles, 48–50

Bustos, María Teresa (wife of Nasario Guadalupe López), 29

Cahill, Holger (F.A.P. director), 86

Cajetan, Saint: mentioned, 186–87, 206; shown, *a Polychromed Image of, Produced by Alex Ortiz in 1977*, Plate 103, p. 189, *Retablo of*, by José Rafael Aragón, Color Plate 2, facing p. 15, *a Traditional Polychromed Image of*, Plate 102, p. 188

Candelabras, 39, 196

Canjilón, N.M., 11

Capitalism, 200

Carding and spinning, 48

Carpentry, 31, 37, 93, 100, 103, 160. *See also Carpintero*

Carpintero ("carpenter"), 31

Carroll, Charles (writer), 26, 27

Carson National Forest, 161

Cash, 6, 89

Crucifixes: mentioned, 103; shown, by José Dolores López, Plate 20, p. 43, by Nicudemos López, Plate 59, p. 106

Crudeness, 146, 147

Cuevitas ("little caves"), as carving subject: mentioned, 108; shown, by Benita and Ricardo López, Plate 64, p. 112

Cundiyó, N.M., 20

Curios, 147, 149, 154, 159, 206

Curio seekers, 149–52, 159

Curio shops, 140

Curtin, Leonora (patron), 48–50

Customers, carvers': composition of, 145–52, 206; and marketing, 134–59; mentioned, 100, 113, 164, 171, 180, 186; provide prototypes, 186, 187. *See also* Patrons; Tourists

Cuts, in production of carvings, 164–66, 174, 179, 180, 230 n.4, Figure 1, p. 165

Cutting, Senator Bronson (patron), 82

Death: mentioned, 29, 76, 100, 113, 154, 174, 190; shown, *Cart* by Nasario López, Plate 11, p. 30, *Carved Figure of,* by José Dolores López, Plate 41, p. 77, *Skeletal Figure of, Riding in a Cart,* by the López family, Color Plate 3, facing p. 30

Deer, as carving subject, 108

Demonstrations, of Hispano carving, 135, 202

Depression, the Great, 85, 86, 227 n.2

Designs, on carvings and furniture, 53, 76, 100, 117, 167, 171

Devil, as carving element, 64, 68, Plate 33, p. 67

Directions, to carving shops, 142

"Discovery" of Hispano artists, 46, 52

Display, of carvings, 97, 134, 142

Divino Pastor, el ("the Divine Shepherd"), by Patrocinio Barela: mentioned, 86; shown, Plate 48, p. 88

Division of labor, in production of carvings, 103

Dixon, N.M., 159, 203

Domination, American, 36

Domínguez, Fray Francisco Atanasio (describes missions in 1776), 21

Donkeys, as carving element, 90, Plate 42, p. 78, Plate 50, p. 92

Doves, as carving element, 68, Plate 36, p. 71, Plate 38, p. 73

Doweled construction. *See* Joints

Dragon. *See* Michael the Archangel *and the Dragon*

Drawings, 64, 186, 187, 192

Drills, 167, 174, 177

Dunton, Nellie (manager of Spanish Arts Shop), 47

Dyeing, 48

Ears, as carving element, 167

Economic factors: in carving industry, 51–52, 82, 84–98 passim, 100, 103, 124, 129, 144, 158, 193; in Hispano society,

Economic factors (cont.)
51, 200, 227–28 n.2; in "revival," 48–50, 226 n.13; in tourist industry, 141–42

Education, 113, 129, 203

Elizabethtown, N.M., 45

El Llano de los Quemadeños, 31

Ellis, Florence Hawley (writer), 196–97

Ellis, Fremont (artist), 44, 45

El Palacio (journal of the Museum of New Mexico), 47, 64

El Parian Analco (second location of Native Market), 48

Embroidery, 154

Employment, wage labor: and carving, 103, 108, 113, 117, 124, 129, 132, 179; daily, 86–89, 93–98 passim, 103; during depression, 86; importance of, 84–90; and language acquisition, 229 n.2; migratory, 85–86, 93; retirement from, 97, 117; and *ranchero* ideal, 193

Encoding. *See* Abstraction

"Encouragement" of Hispano artists, 46, 52, 86, 152

Encyclopedia, 186

English language, 45, 68, 134, 140, 229 n.2

Ethnic diversity, 44, 51

Española, N.M., 161, 202, 203, 206

Ethnicity. *See* Identity, ethnic

Ethnotheology (Hispano conceptions of religious tenets), 192–97, 201

Eve, Creation from Adam's Rib of, by Rafael Aragón, 76

Exhibitions: of Hispano carvings, 47, 52, 64, 86, 134, 135, 142, 197; museum, 149, 152, 154

Exotic: Hispano and Pueblo cultures as, 44, 51; Hispano villages as, 147; Southwestern ethnic arts as, 149

Experience in carving, 164, 166

Exploitation, 51, 200–201

Expo '67 (visit by George López and Silvianita Trujillo to site of in 1971), 135

Expulsion from Paradise, as carving subject: mentioned, 68, 76, 227 n.17; shown, by José Dolores López, Plate 34, p. 69

External focus, in carving art, 16, 197, 211

Extrapolation, 174

Eyes, as carving element, 167

Eyesight, 103, 174, 179

Facial features, of images, 117, 171, Plate 36, p. 71

Faith, 194

Familialism, 147

Family, 35, 52

Farming: and land rights, 200; mentioned, 36, 51, 82, 84–89, 89–97 passim, 98, 129; and Saint Isidore, 183–84

Feast days, 17, 182–84, Plate 6, p. 18

Federal Art Project (F.A.P.), 86, 228 n.3

Feet, as carving element, 117, 129, 166

Fiesta, of Santa Fe. *See* Santa Fe Fiesta

Filigree designs: in George López's work,

Pigs, as carving subject: mentioned, 90, 108; shown, Plate 49, p. 91
Pine, as carving material, 10, 54, 161
Pine Tree with Woodpeckers, by José Dolores López, Plate 27, p. 60
Plane, hand, 164
Pocketknives: mentioned, 53, 100, 164, 166, 167, 171, 192; sharpening of, 174; shown, Plate 100, p. 176
Polychrome technique: described, 10–11; José Dolores López's departure from, 37, 53, 64, 76, 199; mentioned, 29, 82, 98; recent interest in, 113, 203
Pottery, 152
Poverty, of Hispanos, 85–86
Power tools, in carving production, 160, 161, 164, 192, 197
Prayer, 182, 184, 223 n.9
Preferences, customer, 147, 164, 177, 192, 197. *See also* Market; Patrons
Prices, of carvings: and the connoisseur market, 113, 159; of Córdovan carvings, 90, 134, 158–59, 167; and patrons' perceptions, 149, 152, 154, 206
Priests, 17, 193–94
Primitiveness, 146, 147, 149
Prints, as prototypes, 186–87, 190. *See also* Chromolithographs; Lithographs
Privacy, 142–44, 145
Prizes, 52, 64, 145, 154, 197
Production, rate of, 93, 100, 113, 177–79
Proportions, 129, 177, 187
Protestantism, 53, 89, 146
Prototypes: carvers' theory of role of, 190–92, 230 n.4; of Córdovan carvings, 186–92; of eighteenth- and nineteenth-century images, 10; graphic, 186–87, 190, 191; mentioned, 6, 16, 98, 100, 129, 187, Plate 79, p. 131; plastic, 186, 190, 191; used by George López, 90, 93, 174–77; used by José Dolores López, 64, 76
Publications: on the Córdova carvers, 108, 113, 135, 141, 149, 187, 197; on Hispano images, 203; religious, 187, 190
Public domain, 84
Publicity, 140, 145, 149, 192, 202
Public Works of Art Project, 86, Plate 43, p. 79
Pueblo Quemado, 20–21
Pueblo Indians: arts of, 46, 149, 152; mentioned, 7, 10, 16, 17, 44; use of Catholic images by, 10, 16, 17, 223 n.10
Pueblo (Indian)—Hispano relations, 10, 16, 17, 223 n.10
Puerto Rican image carving, 6, 7, 9, 16, 187

Quaintness, 146
Quality of craftsmanship. *See* Craftsmanship
Quemado. *See* Pueblo Quemado
Questionnaire, use of, 146–52

Rabbits, as carving element, 177
Racism, 50
Rafael the Archangel, as carving subject: mentioned, 100, 159; shown, *Bulto or Carving in the Round of*, by José Rafael Aragón, Color Plate 2, facing p. 15, by George López, Plate 77, p. 128
Railroads, 29, 84, 85
Ranchero ("farmer/rancher"): as a cultural ideal, 84, 200; José Dolores López as, 36, 82; Saint Isidore as patron saint of, 17, 183–84; and wage labor employment, 51, 84–89, 89–97 passim
Ranching, 84–85, 89, 93, 97, 129, 200. *See also* Cattle; Farming; Goat herding; *Ranchero*; Sheep
Rancho ("individual farm/ranch"), 97, 144
Rasp, wood, 164
Rate of production. *See* Production
Recognition, outside: of José Dolores López, 53, 55, 90; markers of, 132, 135, 144, 192, 226–27 n.16; mentioned, 113, 117, 180, 211; and sex roles, 97, 103, 140
Record racks, carved, 52, 53
Reino, Benita (wife of Ricardo López): mentioned, 90, 97, 108–13, 146; photograph of work by, *A Cuevita or Coronita with the Holy Child of Atocha*, Plate 64, p. 112; shown, Plate 90, p. 156, Plate 91, p. 157
Relief, federal, 86, 227–28 n.2
Relojeras ("shelves for clocks"), 31, 53
Repertoire: of Hispano image makers, 52, 184, 203; of specific Córdovan carvers, 31, 53, 90, 100, 108, 124, 129, 187
Resistance, Hispano, 201, 231 n.2
Retablos ("paintings on planar surfaces"): defined, 10–11; mentioned, 12, 15, 27, 29, 76; revival in production of, 129, 152, 154, 206
Retirement, 100, 103
"Revival" of Hispano arts, 46–53, 84, 146
Rinconeras ("corner cupboards"), 31
Rito Quemado, 161
Rito Quemado Valley, 22, 97, 113
Rituals, religious, 12, 15–19, 44–45, 89, 182–83, 184, 186, 198
Roadrunner, as carving subject, 113
Robe, as carving element, 117, 129, 166
Rodríguez, Apolonio (conducts interview in Córdova), 39
Romero, Demetra (second wife of José Dolores López), 89
Romero, Precídez (wife of Rafael López), 97, 103
Rooster and Flying Bird, by José Dolores López, Plate 25, p. 58
Rosaries, carved, 100
Rosary, Our Lady of the. *See* La Conquistadora
Roybal, Max (carver of Albuquerque), 202

Sacristans, 15, 31, 37, 64, 223 n.8

The Wood Carvers of Córdova, New Mexico has been composed on the Variable Input Phototypesetter in ten-point Trump Mediaeval with two points of spacing between the lines. Display type was furnished from the same type font.

The book was designed by Jim Billingsley, composed at Williams, Chattanooga, Tennessee, printed offset by Thomson-Shore, Inc., Dexter, Michigan, and bound by John H. Dekker & Sons, Grand Rapids, Michigan.